McCormack's Guides, issued annually, are written to make life in Santa Clara County easier, happier and understandable. The central theme is useful information, presented in a readable style.

Scholastic Aptitude Test (SAT) scores, the latest academic rankings (STAR test) for public schools, what to look for in private and public schools, college placements by high school, a profile of Catholic schools, a directory of private schools — they are all inside.

The perfect guide for parents or people shopping for homes or apartments or just interested in finding out more about Santa Clara County, its schools and its communities.

"Santa Clara County '99" tells which months have the most rain, which the least, when to expect the fog.

Community profiles. Home prices, rents. Housing trends. New home developments in Santa Clara and nearby counties.

Hospital services and medical care. Directory of hospitals.

Child Care. Directory of infant-care and day-care centers.

Places to visit, things to do. Sports, fun for adults and kids.

Local Colleges and Job Training.

Vital statistics. Population, income and education by town. Republicans and Democrats. Crime, trivia, history. Commuting. Strategies to deal with traffic. And much more.

——————

McCormack's Guides, edited by former newspaper reporters and editors, was established in 1984 and publishes the most popular general-interest guides to California counties. For a list of our other guides and an order form, see the last page.

Publisher and editor Don McCormack formed McCormack's Guides in 1984 to publish annual guides to California counties. A graduate of the University of California-Berkeley, McCormack joined the Contra Costa Times in 1969 and covered police, schools, politics, planning, courts and government. Later with the Richmond Independent and Berkeley Gazette, he worked as a reporter, then editor and columnist. McCormack writes city profile articles for the real estate section of the San Francisco Examiner.

———

Researcher and writer Mary Jennings is a native Californian who holds a Diversified Liberal Arts degree from Saint Mary's College in Moraga. She has worked for many years to improve residential support services for adults with developmental disabilities. Mary now brings her data management and writing experience to publishing.

———

Maps illustrator Louis Liu, a Bay Area resident for 12 years, has a B.A. in Teaching English as a Second Language. He loves art and enjoys drawing and painting. Louis attended Los Medanos College and the Academy of Art College in San Francisco, where he majored in illustration. He is now the art director of Tartan Sports in Hayward, a golf equipment manufacturer and wholesaler. To contact Louis, please call (925) 779-0394 or e-mail: louisliu@jps.net.

This book is dedicated to Vickie, Don, Jack, John, Mary, Paulette, Theresa, Brad, Louis and all the others who help us put out the guides.

DISCLAIMER

Copyright © 1992, 1993, 1994, 1995, 1996, 1997, 1998, 1999 by McCormack's Guides, Inc.

Indexed   ISBN 0-931299-86-1

DON'T PANIC!

Not sure about moving here? Who can you turn to for unbiased information?
> I'll give you honest answers to your questions about living here.
> I believe you need counseling first, before you decide to move.

Your company assigned you to a "relo" agent, but you were not impressed...
> I hear this a lot. Don't be pressured...choose the person best
> suited to help you in the most significant decision left to make.

Wondering exactly where to settle, and how to gather data on each area?
> We'll discuss schools, commutes, and neighborhood factors,
> so you can find a nice home *and* a community that fits your family.

Your head is spinning from all the things to do...it is overwhelming you!
> A great agent provides extra service whenever possible, and keeps
> you on track, so you can focus on the other things you need to do.

You don't know who to call, where to go, what to do, what's fun to see...
> But I do, so consider me a resource for general info, as well as real
> estate expertise. I was born here and I have plenty of tips to share...

Can you call and get some info up front to start you off?
> Yes! I'll help as much as possible by phone, fax, or e-mail and get
> together with you for an orientation later, when you are in town.

What area does Jenny specialize in?
> My service extends throughout Santa Clara and Santa Cruz
> Counties, and I can refer you to wonderful people further away.

What's different about Jenny?...why are her past clients raving fans?
> I am a consultant, not a salesperson. I educate and counsel you, *then*
> facilitate your transaction. I will do what's right for you... period!

JENNIFER MOORE
Consumer Specialist, Broker

(408) 244-3456
jenm@ricochet.net
www.jenmoore.com
RE/MAX Associates

SANTA CLARA
COUNTY '99

Edited by Don McCormack

3211 Elmquist Court, Martinez, CA 94553
Phone: (800) 222-3602 & Fax: (925) 228-7223
bookinfo@mccormacks.com • www.mccormacks.com

Contents

Chapter 1 **Santa Clara County at a Glance** **11**
Population, income, vital statistics. History. Politics.

Chapter 2 **Public School Rankings** **23**
For local schools based on national standard.

Chapter 2b **Latest Test Results** **46**
Rankings based on statewide comparisons.

Chapter 3 **How Public Schools Work** **64**
SAT scores for high schools, college attendance rates,
dropout rates. Ratings for high schools.

Chapter 4 **Private Schools** **86**
What to look for. Directory of private schools. College
attendance rates.

Chapter 5 **Baby Care** **99**
Directory of infant-care centers. Most popular baby
names.

Chapter 6 **Day Care** **104**
How to choose day-care provider. Directory of
day-care providers in Santa Clara County.

Chapter 7 **Hospitals & Health Care** **118**
Overview of local medical care and insurance. Directory
of hospitals.

Chapter 8 **Newcomers Guide** **129**
Where to get a driver's license or a license and shots for
your pet. How to register to vote.

Chapter **9**   **Rental Housing**   **136**
Apartments, hotels, residence hotels, homes, monthly
rents.

Chapter **10**   **City Profiles**   **141**
Home prices. Descriptions of cities and towns.

Chapter **11**   **Fun & Games**   **186**
How teams are chosen, sports & activities organized.
Places to visit. Things to do.

Chapter **12**   **Job Training & Colleges**   **192**
Jobless rate, job training, college directory.

Chapter **13**   **New Housing**   **196**
Developments in Santa Clara, nearby counties.

Chapter **14**   **Commuting**   **207**
Driving miles and costs. Commuting tactics and
strategies. Carpooling, mass transit, alternate routes.

Chapter **15**   **Weather**   **210**
How the weather works. Rainfall. Temperatures.
Tule fog. The influence of the Pacific, coastal ranges,
waterways.

Chapter **16**   **Crime**   **217**
FBI crime ratings for cities in Santa Clara County. A
perspective on crime.

It's the way we offer you choices.

For more information on Hewlett-Packard and the many opportunities available, visit our web site at

www.jobs.hp.com

Or, E-mail your resume indicating Ad# 6968 to: resume@hp.com (Subject Line: Ad# 6968), or send/fax it to Hewlett-Packard Employment Response Center, Attn: Ad# 6968, 3000 Hanover Street, MS20AZ, Palo Alto, CA 94304-1181. FAX: (650) 852-8138. Please be sure to include Ad# 6968 on your resume.

Hewlett-Packard Company is an equal opportunity employer dedicated to affirmative action and workforce diversity.

HEWLETT PACKARD

Expanding Possibilities

www.jobs.hp.com

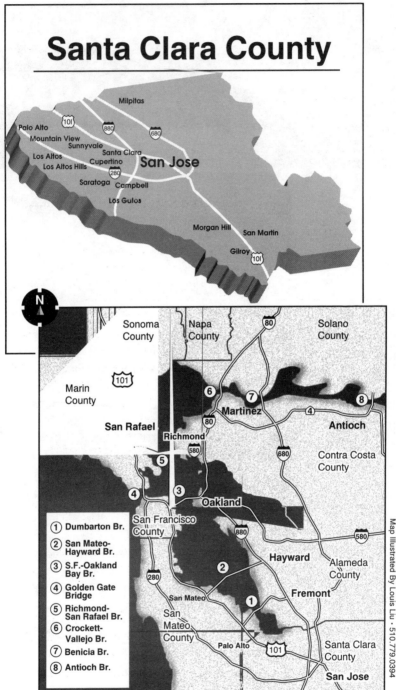

Santa Clara County

Chapter 1

SANTA CLARA COUNTY
at a Glance

LOCATED AT THE SOUTH END OF SAN FRANCISCO BAY, Santa Clara County is a dynamic, fast-changing region and the most populous county in Northern California, 1,689,908 residents.

Its weather is mild, its crime low, its delights many, its rents depressing, its home prices astronomical, its opportunities dazzling and mixed. Almost every month some firm blasts to a new high in the stock market and another firm lays off hundreds. On the "bright" side, thanks to the slowdown in orders from a depressed Asia, rents and home prices show signs of leveling off.

Santa Clara, inspired intellectually by Stanford University, is the birth-place of Silicon Valley, the grouping of cities and industries that over the last 60 years has revolutionized, through computers and technology, how we think and communicate with one another, and how we solve problems.

Rectangular in shape, Santa Clara covers 1,316 square miles, smaller than Delaware, slightly larger than Rhode Island. There are two Santa Claras: one the county, encompassing everything; the second, a city, one of the largest in the county. San Jose, 893,969 residents, is the biggest and most populous city in the county. Monte Sereno, 3,416, has the fewest people.

Palo Alto, which adjoins Stanford, is the brainiest town; Los Altos Hills, the richest; San Jose, increasingly, the most dynamic and becoming recognized as the political leader of the region; Gilroy, in July, the most odoriferous. The town has become famous for its garlic festival.

Most people reside on the flatland of the Santa Clara Valley, which stretches from the Bay down to beyond Gilroy, the southernmost city. If you want a home with a view, generally you have to head for the hills and moun-tains that border the bay and the valley.

In housing and style, Santa Clara favors the suburban tract and the steadiness of the middle class. Crime rates, even in the larger cities, run in ranges on the low side of what's typical for suburban communities.

Single homes outnumber apartments 368,188 to 184,787 or two to one. Santa Clara has its mansions and its estates but the typical home is that old

Santa Clara County Population

City or Area	Male	Female	'90 Total	'98 Total
Campbell	49%	51%	36,048	39,720
Cupertino	50	50	40,263	46,682
Gilroy	49	51	31,487	37,455
Los Altos	48	52	26,303	28,415
Los Altos Hills	50	50	7,514	8,168
Los Gatos	48	52	27,357	30,122
Milpitas	53	47	50,686	62,588
Monte Sereno	49	51	3,287	3,416
Morgan Hill	50	50	23,928	30,786
Mountain View	51	49	67,460	74,730
Palo Alto	49	51	55,900	60,492
San Jose	51	49	782,248	893,969
Santa Clara	51	49	93,613	101,877
Saratoga	49	51	28,061	31,097
Stanford*	58	41	18,097	N.A.
Sunnyvale	50	50	117,229	131,127
Countywide	51	49	1,497,577	1,689,908
California				32,666,550

Source: Census for 1990 figures and Demographic Research Unit of the California Dept. of Finance for 1998 estimates. Stanford is located just outside Palo Alto city limits. **Key**: NA (not available).

American workhorse, the three-bedroom unit (census and state figures).

Rarely does the humidity discomfort or the thermometer drop below freezing. Rain confines itself to the winter and snow to the tops of the local mountains, of which Copernicus, 4,360 feet, is the highest.

On the down side, Santa Clara and much of coastal California straddle active faults. Earthquakes are not a matter of if, but a matter of when. For sound advice on earthquakes, read the first section of the local phone directory.

Sports, Activities, Things to Do

Stanford and two other universities greatly enrich cultural life. Movies, opera, plays, pop and rock, professional and collegiate sports, ballet, symphonies, a children's musical theater, classes of all descriptions, performances by top-notch entertainers — in Santa Clara County you can find them all. Almost every year some new cultural ornament presents itself. In 1998, the big event was the opening of the Tech Museum in downtown San Jose. What you can't find, nearby San Francisco and Oakland usually can provide.

In sports, San Jose is home to the only professional ice hockey team in Northern California, the Sharks. San Jose also fields teams for professional soccer and minor league baseball. Professional football (the Forty Niners and the Raiders) and baseball (the Giants and the Athletics) and basketball (the Warriors) are within a short drive. Just about every town offers the usual smorgasbord of Little League, softball, football, swimming, gymnastics,

Your Contra Costa County Expert
Servicing the East Bay for 18 Years
On-Line Relocation Resources

Charlie Stellini, CRS - CRP

Join me at my website...
www.charliestellini.com

Area Homes For Sale

Finding a home is easy! Now you can search thousands of listings from all over the area.

Homes for Sale in the US & Canada

Take a personal tour of hundreds of thousands of homes for sale.

School Information

Get more information about schools in your new neighborhood.

Community Information

Your guide to information about our communities.

Toll Free: 800 227-7284 • VM: 925 946-2534 • FAX: 925 938-1058

 Executive Brokers SM

Average Household Income

City	1990	1995	*2000
Campbell	$59,746	$61,600	$65,100
Cupertino	89,142	97,200	111,800
Gilroy	57,831	58,300	62,300
Los Altos	122,204	137,600	160,200
Los Altos Hills	215,293	260,400	285,400
Los Gatos	97,453	110,100	128,800
Milpitas	74,096	81,000	93,500
Monte Sereno	164,745	198,000	240,700
Morgan Hill	75,292	77,500	84,800
Mountain View	60,618	64,100	73,700
Palo Alto	83,522	90,000	103,700
San Jose	63,439	65,300	73,100
Santa Clara	60,521	61,700	67,000
Saratoga	137,236	151,600	177,600
Sunnyvale	64,813	66,300	76,600
Remainder	84,721	95,500	110,200
Countywide	70,262	73,800	83,300

Source: Association of Bay Area Governments, *"Projections* 98." Average income per household includes wages and salaries, dividends, interest, rent and transfer payments such as Social Security or public assistance. Based on 1990 Census data and annual increases in the Consumer Price Index. *Projections.

aerobics, tennis and so on. Among children, soccer is turning into the most popular sport. Parks, large and small, are scattered throughout the county. San Francisco Bay is in the county's back yard but rarely is it used for swimming (too cold; current comes from the Arctic.)

Yosemite, Lake Tahoe and the snow country are about six hours to the east. Most residents live within 60 minutes of the fishing boats of Half Moon Bay and the waves of the Pacific.

Because of the mild weather, outdoor sports run almost year round. Many people delight in gardening and hiking and cycling. Indoors, many a night is spent tinkering with this or that machine or computer.

Silicon Valley More a Frame of Mind

Silicon Valley is a term more indicative of a frame of mind than a geographic location but it used to have fairly precise borders, generally Palo Alto to south San Jose. Now high-tech firms (Sun, Oracle) have jumped over the county line into Redwood City and Menlo Park, and on the east side of the Valley and across the Bay, into Milpitas, Newark, Fremont, San Ramon, Livermore and Pleasanton.

To work in Silicon Valley is to profess an interest in, often a passion for, high-tech. Here is where Stephan Wozniak, between raids on his parents' refrigerator, built the first Apple computer. And where his first partner, Steve Jobs, with the IMAC, is turning Apple around.

Here is where Stanford grads David Packard and Bill Hewlett, using the

The South Bay

S A N T A   C L A R A   C O U N T Y

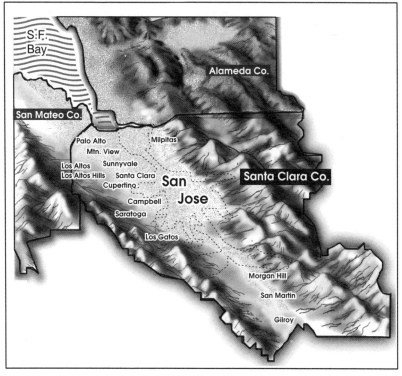

Map Illustrated By Louis Liu · 925.779.0394

latter's master's thesis, built in a Palo Alto garage an audio oscillator. Their first customer, Walt Disney, ordered eight for the soundtrack of "Fantasia." Hewlett-Packard is now one of the biggies in high-tech research, development and manufacturing. Here also is where other firms pursue the golden breakthroughs, the ideas that will transform the ways of multitudes and nations.

Growth Pains

Paradise? Close, but not quite. The freeways are wide and plentiful but inadequate to handle the number of vehicles. Congestion angers many. In the last decade, the county added 202,506 people, a number equivalent then to the population of nine of its 15 cities. Many are the fights over development. If you strip away other fights — schools, traffic, taxes, services, rents, home prices —

Religion in Santa Clara County

Denomination	Churches	Members	Total
African Methodist Episcopal Zion	1	234	309
American Baptist	11	2,353	2,910
Assembly of God	48	7,077	10,532
Baptist General Conference	5	798	987
Baptist Missionary Association	1	44	54
Catholic	52	NA	368,611
Christian & Missionary Alliance	5	1,010	1,383
Church of Christ	13	2,165	2,678
Disciples of Christ	3	406	606
Christian Reformed	4	422	657
Church of Christ, Scientist	12	NR	NR
Church of God (Anderson, Ind.)	3	133	267
Church of God (Cleveland, Tenn.)	7	363	449
Church of God (7th Day)	1	49	69
Church of God (Prophecy)	2	72	89
Church of Jesus Christ, Latter-day Saints	57	NA	23,595
Church of the Nazarene	14	1,742	2,269
Church of Christ	15	1,736	2,267
Congregational Christian	1	52	64
Conservative Baptist	12	NR	NR
Cumberland Presbyterian	2	141	182
Episcopal	19	7,038	9,953
Evangelical Free	4	619	795
Evangelical Lutheran	26	8,717	11,866
Free Methodist	5	202	343
Free Will Baptist	1	87	108
Friends	2	181	271
Mennonite Brethren	6	574	710
Greek Orthodox	2	NR	NR
Independent Fundamental	1	NR	NR
Foursquare Gospel	7	599	741
Lutheran-Missouri Synod	12	3,965	5,184
Mennonite General Conference	1	50	75
North American Baptist	1	64	79
Open Bible Standard	3	NR	NR
Orthodox Church in America	1	NR	NR
Pentecostal Church of God	7	214	566
Pentecostal Holiness	5	1,677	2,074
Christian Brethren	2	290	425
Presbyterian (USA)	26	9,078	11,228
Presbyterian Church in America	5	162	251
Primitive Baptists	1	8	10
Reformed Church in America	1	337	422
Romanian Orthodox Episcopate	1	NR	NR
Salvation Army	4	320	340
Seventh-day Adventist	18	4,754	5,880
Southern Baptist	45	17,103	21,153
Syrian Antioch	1	NA	400
Unitarian-Universalist	4	865	1,154

Religion in Santa Clara County

Denomination	Churches	Members	Total
United Church of Christ	12	3,393	4,197
United Methodist	32	13,463	16,651
Wisconsin Evangelical Lutheran	3	816	1,161
Jewish*	13	NA	32,000
Independent, Charismatic*	5	NA	9,760
Independent, Non-Charismatic*	7	NA	9,550
Santa Clara County totals	552	105,394	579,833

Source: Glenmary Research Center, Atlanta, Ga. **Key**: Churches and temples (Number in the county); Members (Communicant, confirmed, full members); Total (All adherents); NA (Not applicable); NR (Not reported). *Estimates. Our apologies to Muslims and members of other religions, we have not been able to obtain numbers on these groups.

you will find underneath a county that is running hard to keep up with a rapidly growing population.

Many schools score high but a good number do not. In recent years, voters in most local school districts have approved construction bonds or funds to improve instruction. After years of beggaring its schools, the state of California, thanks to the thriving economy, is putting up billions to lower class sizes and make other improvements. But the results may take a while to show themselves. The prudent parent will take an active interest in a child's school.

Crime is low, not nonexistent. You should always take precautions. In 1997, homicides in Santa Clara County totaled 62. By contrast, San Francisco, with less than half the population, recorded 59 homicides. Preliminary figures for 1998 show that homicides in California, like the rest of the nation, continue to drop.

The Loma Prieta quake in 1989 scared holy hell out of thousands, killed several and caused damage in the millions. But few residents quit Santa Clara County and the population keeps growing. In sum, the good, the promising, the delightful, far outweigh the bad and the ominous.

A Changing Ethnic Mix

The county is changing from predominantly Caucasian — or in the local lingo: Anglo — to minority-majority. The sum of all minorities outnumbers or will soon outnumber Caucasians. This is often stated in a way that implies that minorities form a bloc that votes, thinks and acts in concert. They don't. A man from the highlands of Vietnam may have little in common with a man descended from people who roamed the highlands of Scotland. But he also may have little in common with a fellow recently arrived from the Mexican desert.

Women and Minorities in Seats of Power

Women have discovered what men always knew: It is fun to give orders, command attention and respect, and pull down high salaries. The majority of students at most, if not all, of the county's colleges and universities are women, and women routinely win seats on school boards, city councils and the board of supervisors. In 1998, Santa Clara County elected its first woman sheriff, Laurie Smith.

Minorities are also showing up more on city councils and government bodies. In 1998 Ron Gonzales was elected mayor of San Jose.

A Little History

Spanish expeditions arrived in 1769 and 1776, intrepid and brave but late. Having ignored California since claiming it in the 1500s, Spain was dismayed to find other countries interested in her province.

The Spanish explorers and those who followed were supposed to plant the flag, subdue and convert the Indians and colonize the land. The flag was planted, great ranches carved out, but the colonists were few and the Indians, through disease, hostility and misguided benevolence, were almost exterminated. On the other side of the continent, the United States secured its independence, bought the Midwest and heard the siren call of California. Over the mountains the Americans came, first for land, then gold. They kicked over the flag (Mexico's, Spain having been ousted) and by purchase, violence, swindles and squatting drove the rancheros into obscurity.

Left behind were city names and a fondness for romanticized Spanish architecture that has influenced the design of banks, churches, colleges and hamburger stands. Also remaining: a mild sense of guilt about seizing the land from the Mexicans, who in the perverse ways of history re-established themselves in Santa Clara County through later immigration.

Era of Rustic Happiness

The new Californians built roads, cities and railroads, cultivated the county into fabled abundance and — in the great American tradition of boosterism and speculation — spent much time and ink trying to lure others to Santa Clara County. Thousands did come but never enough to turn Santa Clara into a metropolis. Well into the 20th century, the county tended the pear, prune and tomato — an era of rustic happiness, fondly recalled in local histories.

On 13 March, 1884, Leland Stanford Jr., age 16, died of typhoid fever. His saddened mom and dad (grocer, railroad tycoon, governor) founded and endowed Stanford University in memory of their only child. Santa Clara County owes much of its prosperity to Stanford U.

The War Boom

On Dec. 7, 1941, the Japanese bombed Pearl Harbor, a blunder that inadvertently did more for real estate in Santa Clara County than 90 years of booster hoopla. War industries blossomed and thousands of servicemen, recalling that pleasant sunshine, returned to the county after the war. The war also made America a superpower, which entailed the support of a military

Santa Clara County Ethnic Makeup

City	Cauc.	Af.Am.	Hisp.	Asn./Pl	N. Am.
Campbell	28,029	677	3,839	3,281	196
Cupertino	28,621	344	1,986	9,193	99
Gilroy	15,029	315	14,885	1,060	115
Los Altos	22,728	107	795	2,621	40
Los Altos Hills	6,107	57	202	1,143	4
Los Gatos	24,344	187	1,367	1,350	90
Milpitas	21,257	2,805	9,434	16,756	338
Monte Sereno	2,816	9	139	314	6
Morgan Hill	16,616	364	5,594	1,188	120
Mountain View	43,543	3,194	10,821	9,539	290
Palo Alto	45,640	1,548	2,792	5,715	128
San Jose	387,747	34,254	208,388	146,568	3,831
Santa Clara	59,754	2,281	14,260	16,802	372
Saratoga	22,761	118	940	4,185	48
Stanford	11,808	936	1,436	3,787	102
Sunnyvale	75,440	3,790	15,444	21,945	446
Countywide	869,874	52,583	314,564	251,496	6,694

Source: 1990 Census. Key: Causc. (Caucasian); Af.Am. (African-American); Hisp. (Hispanic); Asn./Pl (Asian/Pacific Islander); N. Am. (Native American including American Indian, Eskimo and Aleut). Not included, a small number identified by Census as "other race."

establishment. For decades, defense dollars drove much of the county's economy. Down went the orchards, up went the housing tracts, slowly at first, with some wringing of hands, then rapidly as people poured in. The population, 290,000 people in 1950, doubled, then doubled again.

In 1951, prompted by Fred Terman, vice president of Stanford, the university opened 700 acres for development. Electronics companies, attracted by the proximity of big brains, snapped up parcels. The result: Silicon Valley.

Tinkerers, Entrepreneurs

Actually, it wasn't quite that easy. Santa Clara County has a soft spot for the tinkerers, the Main Street whiz kids who get an idea into their heads, then spend days and weeks in their garages working it into something practical.

Hewlett and Packard, Jobs and Wozniak (Apple) epitomize the romance of the garage. They took their ideas and built industries. Of course, they drew on the work of others. The Apple could not have been built without the micropro-cessor, a 1971 Silicon Valley invention. The whole technological revolution would have stalled in its tracks without the transistor, developed in Bell Labs, New Jersey, but the co-inventor was William Shockley, Palo Alto native.

Modern Santa Clara County

Modern Santa Clara County: flourishing, growing, continually arguing over development. San Jose is still building but the days of the fast zonings and marching subdivisions are gone. The city has spent the last two decades putting

How Residents Earn Their Money

City	EX	PF	TC	SA	CL	SV	AG	MF
Campbell	17%	17%	6%	13%	17%	10%	1%	19%
Cupertino	25	27	7	13	12	5	1	10
Gilroy	10	12	4	11	14	12	6	30
Los Altos	29	31	5	13	11	5	1	7
Los Altos Hills	33	32	3	12	9	4	10	6
Los Gatos	23	26	5	16	12	7	1	11
Milpitas	14	16	7	10	17	9	1	27
Monte Sereno	31	31	3	15	9	5	1	6
Morgan Hill	16	16	6	14	15	9	3	21
Mountain View	18	23	8	9	14	10	2	15
Palo Alto	23	36	8	10	10	6	1	6
San Jose	14	15	6	11	17	12	1	25
Santa Clara	16	19	7	10	18	9	1	20
Saratoga	32	26	5	13	12	5	1	7
Stanford	10	41	9	5	21	11	*0	4
Sunnyvale	18	23	8	19	15	8	1	18
Santa Clara County	16	19	6	11	16	10	1	21

Source: 1990 Census. Figures are percent of population, rounded to the nearest whole number. Key: EX (executive and managerial); PF (professional specialty); TC (technicians); SA (sales); CL (clerical and administrative support); SV (service occupations, including household, protective and other services); AG (agricultural, including farming, fishing, forestry); MF (manufacturing, including precision production, craft, repair; also machine operators, assemblers, inspectors, equipment cleaners and handlers, helpers and laborers). *Less than 0.5 percent.

muscle on its downtown, trying to make it the great center that many believe it should be.

With the collapse of the Soviet Union and the end of the Cold War, defense spending was sharply curtailed and this forced painful cutbacks in local industries. The Navy in 1994 quit Moffett Field, its airbase near Mountain View. But so far Santa Clara County seems to be able to shrug off bad news. If one door closes, another opens and people are always searching for the new device or software or killer application that will propel the "game" into another dimension. In 1998, venture capitalists invested over $3 billion in local startups.

How Government Works

To Sacramento and Washington is where the money goes first these days and that's where much of the power resides. If you want more or less spent on roads, welfare, warfare, schools or pensions, write your congressman, senator or state legislator. Although weakened, local governments are far from penniless and enjoy considerable powers. Major agencies include:

Board of Supervisors

Five members are elected countywide, but by districts. (Gilroy, south end of the county, votes for its supervisor, Milpitas, northeast, for its supervisor and so on.) Supervisors are regional and municipal governors. They control

Education Level of Population Age 18 & Older

City or Town	HS	SC	AA	BA	Grad
Campbell	22%	27%	10%	21%	8%
Cupertino	12	24	9	28	20
Gilroy	22	23	8	10	4
Los Altos	12	20	6	32	26
Los Altos Hills	7	20	4	30	35
Los Gatos	15	26	8	29	16
Milpitas	22	25	9	16	7
Monte Sereno	7	20	8	31	30
Morgan Hill	22	25	10	17	8
Mountain View	16	23	8	24	15
Palo Alto	10	17	5	31	31
San Jose	21	24	8	16	7
Santa Clara	22	26	8	20	9
Saratoga	12	21	7	31	24
Stanford	16	35	1	22	26
Sunnyvale	19	24	8	23	11
Santa Clara County	20	24	8	19	11

Source: 1990 Census. Figures are percent of population age 18 and older, rounded to the nearest whole number. Not shown are adults with less than a 9th grade education or with some high school education but no diploma or GED. **Key:** HS (adults with high school diploma or GED only, no college); SC (adults with some college education); AA (adults with an associate degree); BA (adults with a bachelor's degree only); Grad (adults with a master's or higher degree).

spending for courts, animal services, many libraries, social services, public health. In their municipal hats, they build roads, decide zonings and, through the sheriff's department, provide police protection for unincorporated areas and some cities under contractual arrangements. If you live outside the limits of any city, you will be governed from San Jose, seat of county government. This sometimes gets confusing. In some areas, the county governs one side of a street and a city the other side. Sheriff's deputies patrol on one side, city police the other.

City Councils

Generally five members (San Jose has 10 plus an elected mayor, the tie breaker), one council for each of the county's 15 cities.

Councils are responsible for repairing roads, keeping neighborhoods safe, maintaining parks, providing recreation and other municipal chores. Much of their time goes to planning and development.

Special Service Districts

California grew so fast and chaotically that some regional needs, such as sewer and water, were met on an emergency basis by forming taxing districts with their own elected directors. Although rarely in the public's eye, these agencies perform vital functions.

Santa Clara County Voter Registration

City	Demo	Repub	Clinton	Dole
Campbell	9,875	7,183	7,574	4,332
Cupertino	9,291	9,495	9,123	6,182
Gilroy	8,567	4,521	5,374	3,131
Los Altos	7,431	9,411	7,806	6,654
Los Altos Hills	1,794	2,966	1,760	2,178
Los Gatos	7,849	8,690	7,017	5,563
Milpitas	10,743	7,879	8,658	4,756
Monte Sereno	838	1,291	776	935
Morgan Hill	6,649	6,310	5,094	4,436
Mountain View	18,017	10,211	15,470	6,359
Palo Alto	21,032	10,891	19,223	6,664
San Jose	193,435	121,255	139,040	74,019
Santa Clara	25,482	15,785	19,372	9,479
Saratoga	6,465	10,454	6,250	7,413
Sunnyvale	29,529	21,977	25,107	13,797
Unincorporated	28,372	18,826	19,965	12,393

Source: County registrar of voters, November, 1996. Key: Demo (Democrat), Repub (Republican). Voter registration drops sharply after a presidential election. Although dated, this chart, from the 1996 presidential election, probably gives a more accurate picture of party affiliation than off-year registration counts.

Presidential Voting in Santa Clara County

Year	Democrat	D-Votes	Republican	R-Votes
1948	Truman*	41,905	Dewey	52,982
1952	Stevenson	59,350	Eisenhower*	87,554
1956	Stevenson	72,528	Eisenhower*	105,657
1960	Kennedy*	117,667	Nixon	131,735
1964	Johnson*	161,422	Goldwater	93,448
1968	Humphrey	175,511	Nixon*	163,446
1972	McGovern	208,505	Nixon*	237,329
1976	Carter*	208,023	Ford	219,188
1980	Carter	166,955	Reagan*	229,048
1984	Mondale	229,865	Reagan*	288,638
1988	Dukakis	277,810	Bush*	254,442
1992	Clinton*	276,391	Bush	155,984
1996	Clinton*	297,639	Dole	168,291

Source: California Secretary of State's office. * Election winner nationally.

School Boards

Generally composed of five persons. There are 33 school districts in Santa Clara County, each with an elected school board. A real hodgepodge. Members hire or fire principals and superintendents, negotiate teacher salaries, decide how much should be spent on computers and shop and whether the children should wear uniforms, and more.

Santa Clara has four community college districts: Foothill-DeAnza, Gavilan, San Jose-Evergreen, and West Valley-Mission. They are governed by locally elected boards.

Chapter 2

SANTA CLARA COUNTY
School Rankings

After an interruption of about five years, the California Dept. of Education in 1998 administered a state-wide test, called STAR, to the great majority of public school students. Here are the county results, broken out by individual school and school district.

STAR is based on a national norm. The test was developed by giving it to a representative sample of United States students. The highest score is 99, the lowest is 1. A score of 50 is considered average. A school scoring 75 means that it has done better than about 75 percent of other schools in the nation.

Small school districts, one or two schools, sometimes posted the same "district" scores as individual school scores. For example, in a district with one elementary school and one intermediate school, the scores for both schools would be duplicated in the district scores. In these cases, we deleted the district scores and retained the school scores. Some schools with small enrollments reported few scores. In a few instances, we deleted these schools.

The STAR test became embroiled in arguments over the inclusion of students who spoke little or no English or spoke it with difficulty. These students were placed in a category called "limited English speaking." What constitutes "limited English" may differ from school to school.

These scores include all students, full English and limited-English-speaking. For data on how limited-English-speaking scored as a separate group, contact the individual schools or district. STAR results are also available for individual students (but this info is released only to parents).

As STAR was new for many districts, it should not be considered the final word on achievement. Several years of testing will give a more accurate picture. The California Dept. of Education is developing its own standards and test, to be presented possibly in a few years.

For decades, the California Dept. of Education broke out score percentiles that allowed easy comparisons between California schools. The department no longer does this but for ease of comparison, McCormack's Guides continues the practice in Chapter 2B.

Scores range from 1-99, with 50 the average. A school scoring 75 has done better than 75 percent of other public schools in the U.S.
Key: Rd (read) Ma (math) Lg (Language), Sp (spelling), Sci (science) and SS (social science).

Santa Clara County

Grade	Rd	Ma	Lg	Sp	Sci	SS
2	53	55	53	51		
3	49	55	53	50		
4	54	53	56	52		
5	53	56	58	51		
6	54	61	58	53		
7	53	60	61	55		
8	53	58	57	46		
9	43	62	56		50	50
10	38	53	44		50	45
11	42	55	50		49	61

Alum Rock Union Elem.

Grade	Rd	Ma	Lg	Sp
2	26	31	24	26
3	19	25	22	24
4	22	25	29	22
5	25	28	30	27
6	25	30	31	24
7	27	33	35	30
8	30	33	34	30

Arbuckle Elem.

Grade	Rd	Ma	Lg	Sp
2	28	26	17	30
3	12	15	10	23
4	20	22	24	17
5	16	20	24	22

Cassell Elem.

Grade	Rd	Ma	Lg	Sp
2	39	48	31	41
3	26	30	29	37
4	28	41	37	33
5	26	34	31	34

Chavez Elem.

Grade	Rd	Ma	Lg	Sp
2	15	15	11	17
3	14	24	18	17
4	13	21	21	11
5	16	19	28	21

Cureton Elem.

Grade	Rd	Ma	Lg	Sp
2	35	48	40	33
3	32	19	33	25
4	25	20	31	28
5	29	30	32	31

Dorsa Elem.

Grade	Rd	Ma	Lg	Sp
2	20	24	16	18
3	14	18	15	17
4	19	16	24	17
5	22	18	28	26

Fischer Middle

Grade	Rd	Ma	Lg	Sp
6	21	26	27	20
7	25	28	32	22
8	29	30	32	28

George Middle

Grade	Rd	Ma	Lg	Sp
6	36	44	37	35
7	37	43	42	42
8	37	38	42	39

Goss Elem.

Grade	Rd	Ma	Lg	Sp
2	15	22	17	19
3	15	20	18	20
4	14	14	25	16
5	16	12	15	14

Hubbard Elem.

Grade	Rd	Ma	Lg	Sp
2	11	17	11	17
3	14	18	15	17
4	14	13	18	10
5	18	25	22	18

Linda Vista Elem.

Grade	Rd	Ma	Lg	Sp
2	38	45	36	34
3	34	30	38	30
4	46	41	42	39
5	37	35	39	34

Lyndale Elem.

Grade	Rd	Ma	Lg	Sp
2	33	38	36	32
3	24	30	25	26
4	25	27	28	21
5	23	28	25	28

Mathson Middle

Grade	Rd	Ma	Lg	Sp
6	16	19	22	14
7	17	24	25	20
8	21	29	26	19

McCollam Elem.

Grade	Rd	Ma	Lg	Sp
2	33	47	38	32
3	27	39	30	36
4	30	31	37	30
5	41	42	42	45

Meyer Elem.

Grade	Rd	Ma	Lg	Sp
2	22	23	19	21
3	15	19	18	19
4	24	23	30	23
5	24	23	29	24

Miller Elem.

Grade	Rd	Ma	Lg	Sp
2	18	23	19	21
3	11	21	16	16
4	20	26	23	24
5	18	23	24	20

Ocala Middle

Grade	Rd	Ma	Lg	Sp
6	26	36	36	25
7	30	37	39	34
8	30	37	36	33

Painter Elem.

Grade	Rd	Ma	Lg	Sp
2	35	46	41	42
3	25	36	25	33
4	18	25	24	23
5	21	30	24	31

Pala Middle

Grade	Rd	Ma	Lg	Sp
6	26	27	32	24
7	28	32	39	33
8	27	30	33	27

Rogers Elem.

Grade	Rd	Ma	Lg	Sp
2	32	45	31	39
3	29	37	30	44
4	36	43	45	46
5	36	45	49	50

Ryan Elem.

Grade	Rd	Ma	Lg	Sp
2	17	27	18	19
3	14	23	17	20
4	14	16	22	13
5	21	24	29	21

San Antonio Elem.

Grade	Rd	Ma	Lg	Sp
2	16	17	13	16
3	12	21	19	19
4	12	19	24	15
5	33	50	41	30

Sheppard Elem.

Grade	Rd	Ma	Lg	Sp
6	30	34	36	36
7	31	39	38	38
8	36	35	40	38

WE'VE GOT THE SPOT
:• FOR YOU!

- Relocation Specialist
- Complimentary Area Orientation Tours
- General Contractor's License
- Income Property & 1031 Exchanges
- San Francisco Bay Area Native
- Board Member, SF Apartment Association

 *Expert in San Francisco and San Mateo*

We make the process fun and easy!
:• *Jim Laufenberg*
415-621-4114 or 888-565-4114 Toll Free
A 24 Hour Service

Scores range from 1-99, with 50 the average. A school scoring 75 has done better than 75 percent of other public schools in the U.S.
Key: Rd (read) Ma (math) Lg (Language), Sp (spelling), Sci (science) and SS (social science).

Grade	Rd	Ma	Lg	Sp	Sci	SS
ALUM ROCK (Continued)						
Shields Elem.						
2	28	34	28	27		
3	18	27	23	23		
4	23	20	26	17		
5	21	20	21	21		
Slonaker Elem.						
2	18	19	15	25		
3	19	33	23	22		
4	24	35	32	32		
5	29	37	35	26		
Berryessa Elem. School Dist.						
2	52	56	53	56		
3	45	54	52	57		
4	50	51	54	55		
5	50	54	56	54		
6	51	60	54	54		
7	52	60	58	58		
8	51	57	54	47		
Brooktree Elem.						
2	65	56	60	50		
3	46	51	54	55		
4	44	44	53	47		
5	41	45	55	47		
Cherrywood Elem.						
2	37	46	40	46		
3	44	60	51	59		
4	44	52	53	50		
5	47	54	54	50		
Laneview Elem.						
2	54	65	52	57		
3	42	54	42	54		
4	46	50	47	53		
5	45	41	46	56		
Majestic Way Elem.						
2	51	59	49	59		
3	44	53	47	54		
4	50	51	53	54		
5	47	57	58	57		
Morrill Middle						
6	45	55	52	52		
7	46	56	53	57		
8	48	59	52	48		
Noble Elem.						
2	57	56	59	60		
3	41	50	49	51		
4	51	47	56	47		
5	47	42	51	45		
6	40	*	*	*		
7	55	28	44	48		
Northwood Elem.						
2	54	65	54	54		
3	62	72	69	74		
4	59	56	55	60		
5	63	70	67	64		
Piedmont Middle						
6	54	63	54	53		
7	50	59	57	53		
8	52	55	53	45		

Grade	Rd	Ma	Lg	Sp	Sci	SS
Ruskin Elem.						
2	67	71	72	71		
3	52	64	65	68		
4	68	67	69	71		
5	71	77	73	70		
Sierramont Middle						
6	57	64	58	57		
7	60	69	66	65		
8	54	59	60	49		
Summerdale Elem.						
2	37	37	37	43		
3	39	49	43	55		
4	40	38	45	47		
5	48	49	47	48		
Toyon Elem.						
2	54	55	57	59		
3	42	50	48	46		
4	54	46	54	53		
5	48	51	49	54		
Vinci Park Elem.						
2	43	47	46	57		
3	41	47	49	56		
4	46	59	57	63		
5	48	57	62	55		
Cambrian Elem. School Dist.						
2	67	73	74	66		
3	65	69	69	61		
4	66	67	72	69		
5	71	74	77	62		
6	70	71	71	61		
7	72	70	79	67		
8	69	66	68	53		
Bagby Elem.						
2	71	78	74	70		
3	71	73	74	60		
4	65	65	71	74		
5	71	76	79	64		
Fammatre Elem.						
2	66	69	76	62		
3	67	72	71	64		
4	71	72	75	68		
5	72	82	77	66		
Farnham Elem.						
2	60	69	73	63		
3	63	67	66	63		
4	63	70	69	69		
5	84	87	86	69		
Ida Price Middle						
6	70	71	71	61		
7	72	70	79	67		
8	69	66	68	53		
Sartorette Elem						
2	67	72	71	69		
3	57	62	63	52		
4	64	59	76	61		
5	54	43	59	47		

Scores range from 1-99, with 50 the average. A school scoring 75 has done better than 75 percent of other public schools in the U.S.
Key: Rd (read) Ma (math) Lg (Language), Sp (spelling), Sci (science) and SS (social science).

Grade	Rd	Ma	Lg	Sp	Sci	SS
Campbell Elem. School Dist.						
2	48	53	52	42		
3	50	57	55	46		
4	55	54	57	48		
5	55	55	60	50		
6	49	58	59	47		
7	49	50	63	50		
8	49	52	57	40		
Blackford Elem.						
2	36	36	35	33		
3	52	60	56	47		
4	55	53	62	50		
5	53	50	50	47		
Campbell Middle						
5	39	40	49	41		
6	38	43	45	34		
7	43	42	55	44		
8	44	43	53	34		
Capri Elem.						
2	52	57	61	47		
3	60	73	70	54		
4	57	60	61	49		
5	58	48	62	50		
Castlemont Elem.						
2	50	57	54	41		
3	59	72	64	51		
4	60	60	61	57		
5	67	61	61	54		
Forest Hill Elem.						
2	55	65	68	53		
3	61	71	62	53		
4	73	75	70	68		
5	62	79	66	62		
Hazelwood Elem.						
2	58	68	64	52		
3	53	63	60	53		
4	55	59	57	46		
Lynhaven Elem.						
2	56	52	64	50		
3	37	39	42	37		
4	49	50	54	48		
5	46	40	53	45		
Marshall Lane Elem.						
2	76	75	73	68		
3	68	67	72	64		
4	74	72	72	68		
5	80	82	81	67		
Monroe Middle						
5	49	45	51	46		
6	52	58	60	48		
7	44	48	56	45		
8	50	52	54	40		
Rolling Hills Middle						
5	58	61	71	55		
6	55	67	67	53		
7	57	58	74	57		
8	53	62	65	47		
Rosemary Elem.						
2	24	36	27	24		
3	28	38	34	27		
4	28	26	32	21		

Grade	Rd	Ma	Lg	Sp	Sci	SS
Sherman Oaks Elem.						
2	21	30	24	17		
3	22	20	23	27		
4	26	25	34	22		
Campbell High School Dist.						
9	44	61	56		50	51
10	39	50	44		49	47
11	42	52	50		50	63
Blackford High-Cont.						
10	17	21	17		21	23
11	21	20	23		25	29
Del Mar High						
9	37	49	48		39	41
10	32	45	39		40	40
11	35	46	45		42	56
Leigh High						
9	53	66	63		56	59
10	48	57	52		56	55
11	52	59	58		59	71
Prospect High						
9	41	61	51		48	46
10	32	42	34		41	38
11	44	54	51		49	64
Westmont High						
9	45	66	58		55	54
10	43	56	51		59	54
11	43	56	49		53	66
Cupertino Elem. School Dist						
2	76	79	79	77		
3	74	80	79	75		
4	78	82	79	80		
5	75	82	80	73		
6	79	88	80	78		
7	77	86	82	78		
8	73	83	79	68		
Blue Hills Elem.						
2	83	85	86	82		
3	81	86	85	85		
4	85	89	86	89		
5	82	86	85	81		
6	84	94	85	90		
Collins Elem.						
2	81	88	84	84		
3	74	81	78	79		
4	84	86	83	88		
5	83	87	85	81		
6	82	91	80	84		
Cupertino Int.						
6	95	98	95	96		
7	80	84	82	77		
8	74	78	77	67		
De Vargas Elem.						
2	47	44	48	55		
3	48	66	54	60		
4	43	59	57	50		
5	41	58	52	46		
6	67	75	70	61		

Scores range from 1-99, with 50 the average. A school scoring 75 has done better than 75 percent of other public schools in the U.S.
Key: Rd (read) Ma (math) Lg (Language), Sp (spelling), Sci (science) and SS (social science).

CUPERTINO ELEM. (Continued)

Dilworth Elem.

Grade	Rd	Ma	Lg	Sp	Sci	SS
2	75	80	79	80		
3	74	87	83	83		
4	77	81	81	80		
5	74	82	76	73		
6	83	91	84	83		

Eisenhower Elem.

Grade	Rd	Ma	Lg	Sp	Sci	SS
2	70	69	77	71		
3	71	74	70	68		
4	69	64	66	66		
5	73	70	79	72		
6	78	79	79	81		

Faria Elem.

Grade	Rd	Ma	Lg	Sp	Sci	SS
2	86	92	86	94		
3	86	93	92	91		
4	91	94	92	95		
5	85	94	90	90		
6	89	94	90	93		

Garden Gate Elem.

Grade	Rd	Ma	Lg	Sp	Sci	SS
2	68	78	78	78		
3	70	83	78	73		
4	76	78	80	75		
5	75	80	83	78		
6	77	83	72	76		

Hyde Int.

Grade	Rd	Ma	Lg	Sp	Sci	SS
6	61	90	72	67		
7	63	76	76	65		
8	57	73	68	49		

Kennedy Int.

Grade	Rd	Ma	Lg	Sp	Sci	SS
7	80	89	84	83		
8	79	85	83	76		

Lincoln Elem.

Grade	Rd	Ma	Lg	Sp	Sci	SS
2	77	76	75	82		
3	76	75	80	76		
4	84	85	83	88		
5	77	85	85	76		
6	79	87	84	80		

McAuliffe Elem.

Grade	Rd	Ma	Lg	Sp	Sci	SS
2	78	73	72	69		
3	87	79	84	68		
4	77	71	69	63		
5	85	81	80	71		
6	86	87	80	72		

Meyerholz Elem.

Grade	Rd	Ma	Lg	Sp	Sci	SS
2	76	81	73	77		
3	69	69	65	61		
4	73	80	73	72		
5	65	65	67	63		
6	74	81	77	72		

Miller Int.

Grade	Rd	Ma	Lg	Sp	Sci	SS
6	96	98	96	97		
7	83	92	87	83		
8	80	90	84	77		

Montclaire Elem.

Grade	Rd	Ma	Lg	Sp	Sci	SS
2	86	86	86	83		
3	86	83	88	81		
4	89	92	88	89		
5	84	82	88	81		
6	85	91	83	82		

Muir Elem.

Grade	Rd	Ma	Lg	Sp	Sci	SS
2	61	80	70	65		
3	71	82	75	72		
4	73	83	72	72		
5	60	77	67	65		
6	64	83	67	58		

Nimitz Elem.

Grade	Rd	Ma	Lg	Sp	Sci	SS
2	48	66	66	46		
3	37	47	45	42		
4	53	66	64	54		
5	43	63	58	37		
6	49	68	54	41		

Portal (Louis) Elem.

Grade	Rd	Ma	Lg	Sp	Sci	SS
2	83	87	85	89		
3	84	89	89	90		
4	88	87	83	88		
5	86	95	90	88		
6	86	90	85	83		

Regnart Elem.

Grade	Rd	Ma	Lg	Sp	Sci	SS
2	79	85	89	86		
3	81	85	88	83		
4	89	92	90	92		
5	85	92	87	81		
6	86	94	90	90		

Sedgwick Elem.

Grade	Rd	Ma	Lg	Sp	Sci	SS
2	72	71	71	68		
3	68	66	69	63		
4	68	66	71	70		
5	69	63	73	65		
6	72	76	69	67		

Stevens Creek Elem.

Grade	Rd	Ma	Lg	Sp	Sci	SS
2	81	78	83	78		
3	80	85	85	81		
4	82	79	79	76		
5	77	84	83	73		
6	81	85	80	77		

Stocklmeir Elem.

Grade	Rd	Ma	Lg	Sp	Sci	SS
2	74	78	78	71		
3	77	77	83	69		
4	76	79	78	80		
5	79	84	81	73		
6	70	78	72	61		

West Valley Elem.

Grade	Rd	Ma	Lg	Sp	Sci	SS
2	77	75	79	71		
3	82	85	84	74		
4	82	88	84	85		
5	82	85	82	76		
6	81	90	82	78		

East Side High School Dist.

Grade	Rd	Ma	Lg	Sp	Sci	SS
9	32	52	46		41	38
10	26	41	32		39	33
11	30	42	39		36	47

Apollo High (Cont.)

Grade	Rd	Ma	Lg	Sp	Sci	SS
11	20	20	23		20	27

Foothill High (Cont.)

Grade	Rd	Ma	Lg	Sp	Sci	SS
9	14	24	29		21	25
10	11	17	12		21	17
11	16	17	21		16	27

WHEN IN NEED OF A
REAL ESTATE PROFESSIONAL

ASK FOR GEORGENE

SERVING SANTA CLARA COUNTY

GEORGENE LAUB — Broker-Owner, GRI
REALTY MART ASSOCIATES, INC.
1010 W. FREMONT AVE. SUITE 300
SUNNYVALE, CA 94087

Bus: (408) 738-0208   Fax: (408) 738-0209
e-mail: laub@glaub.com   http://www.glaub.com

Scores range from 1-99, with 50 the average. A school scoring 75 has done better than 75 percent of other public schools in the U.S.
Key: Rd (read) Ma (math) Lg (Language), Sp (spelling), Sci (science) and SS (social science).

EAST SIDE UNION (Continued)

Genesis High (Cont.)

Grade	Rd	Ma	Lg	Sp	Sci	SS
11	19	15	23		23	28

Hill High

Grade	Rd	Ma	Lg	Sp	Sci	SS
9	23	42	37		30	29
10	18	35	23		28	23
11	23	37	32		29	39

Independence High

Grade	Rd	Ma	Lg	Sp	Sci	SS
9	31	54	45		42	36
10	26	42	31		37	33
11	32	47	41		39	50

Lick High

Grade	Rd	Ma	Lg	Sp	Sci	SS
9	22	40	36		36	27
10	18	32	23		31	25
11	24	31	35		34	43

Mt. Pleasant High

Grade	Rd	Ma	Lg	Sp	Sci	SS
9	37	54	49		42	42
10	27	40	28		39	31
11	30	40	34		34	46

Oak Grove High

Grade	Rd	Ma	Lg	Sp	Sci	SS
9	39	56	51		53	46
10	32	45	37		52	44
11	37	48	46		48	59

Overfelt High

Grade	Rd	Ma	Lg	Sp	Sci	SS
9	21	42	35		30	29
10	17	34	22		27	23
11	21	36	29		25	36

Pegasus High (Cont.)

Grade	Rd	Ma	Lg	Sp	Sci	SS
11	25	21	28		22	32

Phoenix High (Cont.)

Grade	Rd	Ma	Lg	Sp	Sci	SS
11	5	18	10		15	31

Piedmont Hills High

Grade	Rd	Ma	Lg	Sp	Sci	SS
9	46	67	58		53	45
10	40	60	45		56	45
11	41	56	50		49	58

Santa Teresa High

Grade	Rd	Ma	Lg	Sp	Sci	SS
9	42	59	60		53	50
10	37	46	49		53	46
11	39	47	53		49	54

Silver Creek High

Grade	Rd	Ma	Lg	Sp	Sci	SS
9	37	57	50		42	43
10	30	47	37		39	39
11	33	47	41		36	54

Yerba Buena High

Grade	Rd	Ma	Lg	Sp	Sci	SS
9	19	39	32		30	25
10	17	36	21		27	20
11	23	41	30		28	33

Evergreen Elem. School Dist.

Grade	Rd	Ma	Lg	Sp
2	59	67	61	59
3	51	69	61	62
4	53	61	60	61
5	51	59	59	54
6	55	66	65	61
7	50	60	63	59
8	51	59	58	52

Cadwallader Elem.

Grade	Rd	Ma	Lg	Sp
2	45	55	53	52
3	36	49	47	56
4	47	55	57	44
5	48	56	62	54
6	61	65	73	60

Cedar Grove Elem.

Grade	Rd	Ma	Lg	Sp
2	54	56	55	50
3	52	75	67	62
4	54	68	62	61
5	40	45	45	49
6	52	65	64	58

Chaboya Middle

Grade	Rd	Ma	Lg	Sp
6	50	63	56	55
7	49	60	61	57
8	54	61	62	54

Dove Hill Elem.

Grade	Rd	Ma	Lg	Sp
2	52	63	47	50
3	37	64	53	47
4	36	49	45	44
5	43	49	47	44
6	54	66	64	54

Evergreen Elem.

Grade	Rd	Ma	Lg	Sp
2	79	79	77	76
3	64	76	72	70
4	60	73	67	70
5	63	77	65	69

Holly Oak Elem.

Grade	Rd	Ma	Lg	Sp
2	64	69	67	59
3	50	73	61	62
4	51	67	61	57
5	44	56	56	47
6	59	74	75	72

Laurelwood Elem.

Grade	Rd	Ma	Lg	Sp
2	70	68	71	60
3	65	70	66	60
4	67	61	67	61
5	62	60	67	55
6	57	63	64	58

LeyVa Int.

Grade	Rd	Ma	Lg	Sp
6	44	57	53	55
7	47	57	60	55
8	45	53	51	47

Millbrook Elem.

Grade	Rd	Ma	Lg	Sp
2	62	74	64	64
3	47	67	52	56
4	57	58	62	70
5	56	70	65	60
6	62	78	75	73

Montgomery Elem.

Grade	Rd	Ma	Lg	Sp
2	58	66	67	55
3	60	76	69	67
4	46	47	50	51
5	54	57	57	50
6	43	49	50	47

Norwood Creek Elem.

Grade	Rd	Ma	Lg	Sp
2	64	69	71	71
3	61	81	70	73
4	67	79	73	77
5	65	73	70	67

Scores range from 1-99, with 50 the average. A school scoring 75 has done better than 75 percent of other public schools in the U.S.
Key: Rd (read) Ma (math) Lg (Language), Sp (spelling), Sci (science) and SS (social science).

EVERGREEN ELEM. DISTRICT (Continued)

Quimby Oak Int.

Grade	Rd	Ma	Lg	Sp	Sci	SS
6	64	74	71	67		
7	53	63	68	63		
8	55	62	60	56		

Silver Oak Elem.

Grade	Rd	Ma	Lg	Sp	Sci	SS
2	71	80	69	70		
3	70	80	79	75		
4	77	79	78	81		
5	71	75	75	69		
6	75	79	85	80		

Smith Elem.

Grade	Rd	Ma	Lg	Sp	Sci	SS
2	38	49	40	47		
3	34	61	46	55		
4	33	44	45	43		
5	30	44	47	39		

Whaley Elem.

Grade	Rd	Ma	Lg	Sp	Sci	SS
2	52	64	48	52		
3	36	48	48	55		
4	34	45	47	50		
5	34	47	48	43		

Franklin-McKinley Elem. Dist.

Grade	Rd	Ma	Lg	Sp	Sci	SS
2	24	34	26	27		
3	20	30	27	32		
4	21	24	33	24		
5	22	28	34	30		
6	24	32	31	27		
7	24	35	33	28		
8	27	38	34	27		

Fair Jr. High

Grade	Rd	Ma	Lg	Sp	Sci	SS
7	20	33	29	22		
8	26	37	33	26		

Franklin Elem.

Grade	Rd	Ma	Lg	Sp	Sci	SS
2	25	41	30	31		
3	20	33	30	35		
4	16	22	28	17		
5	21	21	30	28		
6	28	33	36	29		

Hellyer Elem.

Grade	Rd	Ma	Lg	Sp	Sci	SS
2	35	54	46	41		
3	24	33	34	43		
4	30	34	40	37		
5	26	36	41	37		

Hillsdale Elem.

Grade	Rd	Ma	Lg	Sp	Sci	SS
2	15	20	16	17		
3	20	37	31	30		
4	20	23	30	22		
5	26	26	38	38		

Kennedy Elem.

Grade	Rd	Ma	Lg	Sp	Sci	SS
2	30	33	35	35		
3	25	41	33	41		
4	22	30	35	26		
5	27	36	36	34		
6	26	35	35	33		

Los Arboles Elem.

Grade	Rd	Ma	Lg	Sp	Sci	SS
2	19	35	24	22		
3	19	22	21	30		
4	25	32	39	26		
5	26	29	33	29		
6	19	27	25	23		

McKinley Elem.

Grade	Rd	Ma	Lg	Sp	Sci	SS
2	17	21	12	15		
3	9	12	12	13		
4	10	15	17	12		
5	13	17	24	15		

Meadows Elem.

Grade	Rd	Ma	Lg	Sp	Sci	SS
2	23	33	21	26		
3	22	32	27	36		
4	26	28	42	31		
5	21	26	40	30		
6	34	40	43	44		

Santee Elem.

Grade	Rd	Ma	Lg	Sp	Sci	SS
2	13	22	12	13		
3	17	26	21	23		
4	11	16	22	16		
5	9	15	17	15		
6	13	24	18	12		

Seven Trees Elem.

Grade	Rd	Ma	Lg	Sp	Sci	SS
2	18	25	22	23		
3	16	31	24	23		
4	18	20	27	20		
5	19	28	29	26		
6	23	30	29	21		

Stonegate Elem.

Grade	Rd	Ma	Lg	Sp	Sci	SS
2	43	47	41	45		
3	29	29	37	48		
4	33	29	44	38		
5	45	47	54	53		
6	32	40	45	35		
7	51	70	65	55		
8	42	47	53	44		

Sylvandale Jr. High

Grade	Rd	Ma	Lg	Sp	Sci	SS
6	27	34	30	30		
7	24	34	32	31		
8	26	39	32	26		

Windmill Springs Elem.

Grade	Rd	Ma	Lg	Sp	Sci	SS
2	36	57	37	41		
3	19	36	30	40		
4	25	30	42	35		
5	21	30	32	34		
6	17	28	24	18		
7	29	41	39	34		
8	32	48	46	33		

Fremont Union HighSchool Dist.

Grade	Rd	Ma	Lg	Sp	Sci	SS
9	58	79	71		65	63
10	56	76	64		68	63
11	57	76	66		66	73

Alternative Program

Grade	Rd	Ma	Lg	Sp	Sci	SS
10	30	27	22		33	35
11	37	39	44		46	55

Cupertino High

Grade	Rd	Ma	Lg	Sp	Sci	SS
9	51	68	63		59	55
10	50	72	59		65	57
11	53	71	60		62	69

Fremont High

Grade	Rd	Ma	Lg	Sp	Sci	SS
9	40	60	54		49	44
10	34	47	37		43	37
11	40	48	48		42	54

Scores range from 1-99, with 50 the average. A school scoring 75 has done better than 75 percent of other public schools in the U.S.
Key: Rd (read) Ma (math) Lg (Language), Sp (spelling), Sci (science) and SS (social science).

Grade	Rd	Ma	Lg	Sp	Sci	SS
FREMONT HIGH DIST. (Continued)						
Homestead High						
9	55	72	67		57	59
10	55	72	63		64	59
11	55	72	63		61	67
Lynbrook High						
9	69	89	80		74	75
10	67	88	75		80	77
11	68	89	76		79	85
Monta Vista High						
9	66	89	80		74	73
10	66	88	78		81	78
11	69	90	79		78	84
Gilroy Unified School Dist.						
2	46	36	42	41		
3	35	34	37	33		
4	39	34	41	34		
5	40	37	43	35		
6	48	51	51	42		
7	39	38	43	37		
8	42	37	42	35		9
34	52	48		43	46	
10	31	41	36		44	36
11	35	43	42		44	54
Aprea Fundamental School						
2	71	77	72	70		
3	65	65	67	70		
4	70	74	70	71		
5	68	65	65	61		
6	62	72	66	64		
Brownell Academy						
7	41	39	46	39		
8	42	39	45	35		
El Roble Elem.						
2	57	54	47	50		
3	40	29	33	23		
4	31	29	37	26		
5	34	28	34	28		
6	48	48	49	39		
Eliot Elem.						
2	44	26	46	38		
3	41	39	50	42		
4	38	30	37	29		
5	31	17	33	24		
6	32	44	38	24		
Gilroy High						
9	34	52	48		43	46
10	32	43	38		46	37
11	40	48	47		48	59
Glen View Elem.						
2	35	23	26	40		
3	17	21	17	24		
4	24	25	36	27		
5	28	40	37	26		
6	34	39	44	29		
Jordan Elem.						
2	35	31	35	32		
3	17	14	20	17		
4	24	19	29	16		
5	32	24	29	26		
6	63	54	56	47		

Grade	Rd	Ma	Lg	Sp	Sci	SS
Kelley Elem.						
2	38	34	45	33		
3	32	39	34	27		
4	41	37	41	34		
5	38	35	44	34		
6	53	56	48	43		
Las Animas Elem.						
2	36	23	30	31		
3	28	29	42	30		
4	26	21	25	21		
5	34	30	35	35		
6	30	34	36	28		
Mt. Madonna High (Cont.)						
10	13	19	16		19	22
11	12	14	16		19	26
Rucker Elem.						
2	37	26	32	29		
3	49	35	51	38		
4	59	39	49	51		
5	51	43	55	38		
6	63	54	69	53		
San Ysidro Elem.						
2	34	23	26	35		
3	22	27	28	25		
4	19	18	31	21		
5	37	35	40	28		
6	45	50	58	46		
So. Valley School Of						
7	37	36	39	35		
8	41	35	40	34		
Lakeside Joint Elem. School Dist.						
Lakeside Elem.						
2	65	73	79	54		
3	71	76	71	69		
4	82	79	77	64		
5	76	75	75	61		
6	75	73	75	71		
Loma Prieta Elem. School Dist.						
2	72	66	74	61		
3	74	76	75	65		
4	83	79	75	73		
5	73	75	66	61		
6	72	77	77	72		
7	72	66	75	69		
8	73	74	77	61		
English Middle						
6	72	77	77	72		
7	72	66	75	69		
8	73	74	77	61		
Loma Prieta Elem.						
2	72	66	74	61		
3	74	76	75	65		
4	83	79	75	73		
5	73	75	66	61		

Scores range from 1-99, with 50 the average. A school scoring 75 has done better than 75 percent of other public schools in the U.S.
Key: Rd (read) Ma (math) Lg (Language), Sp (spelling), Sci (science) and SS (social science).

Los Altos Elem. School Dist.

Grade	Rd	Ma	Lg	Sp	Sci	SS
2	84	86	87	81		
3	86	89	88	80		
4	88	87	83	88		
5	87	91	87	83		
6	87	92	88	87		
7	84	92	90	81		
8	84	89	89	75		

Almond Elem.

Grade	Rd	Ma	Lg	Sp
2	85	85	88	84
3	85	91	90	77
4	88	87	84	90
5	90	95	91	85
6	84	92	85	83

Blach Int.

Grade	Rd	Ma	Lg	Sp
7	85	93	91	85
8	88	92	91	81

Bullis-Purissima Elem.

Grade	Rd	Ma	Lg	Sp
2	84	89	88	80
3	85	89	84	81
4	87	90	82	87
5	86	94	85	84
6	88	95	88	89

Egan Int.

Grade	Rd	Ma	Lg	Sp
7	83	91	89	78
8	80	85	87	70

Loyola Elem.

Grade	Rd	Ma	Lg	Sp
2	77	80	86	83
3	86	87	85	73
4	90	91	83	90
5	89	90	86	82
6	88	93	90	87

Oak Avenue Elem.

Grade	Rd	Ma	Lg	Sp
2	87	88	88	79
3	88	88	90	82
4	88	88	85	89
5	89	91	88	87
6	89	94	91	87

Santa Rita Elem.

Grade	Rd	Ma	Lg	Sp
2	87	91	89	82
3	87	90	88	83
4	89	85	85	86
5	84	87	84	78
6	85	88	84	86

Springer Elem.

Grade	Rd	Ma	Lg	Sp
2	81	84	85	78
3	86	89	88	84
4	83	83	81	82
5	88	89	88	82
6	88	93	89	88

Los Gatos Elem. School Dist.

Grade	Rd	Ma	Lg	Sp
2	74	76	80	66
3	79	82	81	69
4	81	77	78	77
5	76	77	74	65
6	81	84	81	74
7	77	79	80	69
8	80	83	82	63

Blossom Hill Elem.

Grade	Rd	Ma	Lg	Sp
2	72	72	80	69
3	80	81	82	74
4	81	80	76	78
5	82	84	82	78

Daves Avenue Elem.

Grade	Rd	Ma	Lg	Sp
2	77	82	82	68
3	83	81	84	69
4	83	81	84	81
5	76	75	75	63

Fisher Middle

Grade	Rd	Ma	Lg	Sp
6	81	84	81	74
7	77	79	80	69
8	80	83	82	63

Lexington Elem.

Grade	Rd	Ma	Lg	Sp
2	65	72	72	51
3	69	81	73	60
4	79	67	72	73
5	67	69	65	43

Louise Van Meter Elem.

Grade	Rd	Ma	Lg	Sp
2	74	73	82	65
3	77	84	80	66
4	78	74	75	71
5	72	75	69	60

Los Gatos-Saratoga H.S. Dist.

Grade	Rd	Ma	Lg	Sp	Sci	SS
9	75	85	81		76	80
10	74	82	75		81	77
11	76	84	82		80	88

Los Gatos High

Grade	Rd	Ma	Lg	Sp	Sci	SS
9	73	84	77		74	77
10	74	79	74		82	75
11	75	81	77		80	87

Saratoga High

Grade	Rd	Ma	Lg	Sp	Sci	SS
9	78	86	85		78	83
10	73	85	77		81	80
11	78	87	88		80	89

Luther Burbank Elem. Dist.
Luther Burbank Elem.

Grade	Rd	Ma	Lg	Sp
2	33	34	21	29
3	26	19	25	26
4	28	20	37	24
5	33	31	32	36
6	28	28	27	26
7	46	44	42	37
8	30	28	33	29

Milpitas Unified School Dist.

Grade	Rd	Ma	Lg	Sp	Sci	SS
2	54	58	48	58		
3	47	56	49	53		
4	53	55	56	56		
5	54	60	59	58		
6	60	66	64	65		
7	60	68	67	65		
8	55	57	54	49		
9	38	59	52		48	46
10	35	51	42		47	42
11	36	54	46		45	59

Scores range from 1-99, with 50 the average. A school scoring 75 has done better than 75 percent of other public schools in the U.S.
Key: Rd (read) Ma (math) Lg (Language), Sp (spelling), Sci (science) and SS (social science).

MILPITAS DIST. (Continued)

Burnett Elem.

Grade	Rd	Ma	Lg	Sp	Sci	SS
2	49	51	40	55		
3	44	51	43	50		
4	43	49	49	54		
5	37	44	52	49		
6	49	55	64	62		

Calaveras Hills High (Cont.)

Grade	Rd	Ma	Lg	Sp	Sci	SS
9	25	32	32		38	30
10	18	19	18		37	34
11	16	16	15		14	31

Curtner Elem.

Grade	Rd	Ma	Lg	Sp	Sci	SS
2	64	63	58	66		
3	62	75	62	72		
4	62	66	63	71		
5	71	79	71	71		
6	69	80	71	78		

Milpitas High

Grade	Rd	Ma	Lg	Sp	Sci	SS
9	38	60	53		49	47
10	36	53	44		48	43
11	37	56	47		46	60

Pomeroy Elem.

Grade	Rd	Ma	Lg	Sp	Sci	SS
2	63	69	61	65		
3	50	57	58	57		
4	69	75	70	69		
5	62	67	68	57		
6	73	81	77	74		

Randall Elem.

Grade	Rd	Ma	Lg	Sp	Sci	SS
2	53	62	40	50		
3	37	58	40	50		
4	46	57	38	49		
5	37	56	53	45		
6	53	57	63	65		

Rancho Milpitas Jr. High

Grade	Rd	Ma	Lg	Sp	Sci	SS
7	53	64	61	56		
8	53	53	52	44		

Rose Elem.

Grade	Rd	Ma	Lg	Sp	Sci	SS
2	52	54	39	55		
3	42	48	42	44		
4	46	39	50	44		
5	39	40	41	51		
6	49	48	52	48		

Russell Jr. High

Grade	Rd	Ma	Lg	Sp	Sci	SS
7	67	72	72	73		
8	58	61	56	53		

Sinnott Elem.

Grade	Rd	Ma	Lg	Sp	Sci	SS
2	65	76	63	65		
3	60	66	60	61		
4	61	67	60	60		
5	69	79	72	68		
6	71	80	71	74		

Spangler Elem.

Grade	Rd	Ma	Lg	Sp	Sci	SS
2	38	41	32	46		
3	35	36	39	40		
4	44	43	48	51		
5	38	36	39	47		
6	60	53	59	58		

Weller Elem

Grade	Rd	Ma	Lg	Sp	Sci	SS
2	44	43	35	47		
3	43	48	46	46		
4	49	43	49	50		
5	53	49	55	58		
6	52	58	54	62		

Zanker Elem.

Grade	Rd	Ma	Lg	Sp	Sci	SS
2	60	57	53	66		
3	53	60	49	56		
4	52	55	61	47		
5	64	73	68	70		
6	55	63	62	58		

Moreland Elem. District

Grade	Rd	Ma	Lg	Sp	Sci	SS
2	70	70	70	63		
3	59	64	64	58		
4	61	54	60	57		
5	61	66	65	56		
6	62	73	67	59		
7	59	72	70	61		
8	60	61	68	50		

Anderson Elem.

Grade	Rd	Ma	Lg	Sp	Sci	SS
2	41	37	41	45		
3	29	36	35	30		
4	35	36	37	32		
5	38	49	44	39		

Baker Elem.

Grade	Rd	Ma	Lg	Sp	Sci	SS
2	64	63	67	60		
3	55	55	57	55		
4	58	45	53	55		
5	59	66	64	57		

Castro Middle

Grade	Rd	Ma	Lg	Sp	Sci	SS
6	67	76	68	63		
7	64	73	70	65		
8	62	61	68	51		

Country Lane Elem.

Grade	Rd	Ma	Lg	Sp	Sci	SS
2	79	82	78	75		
3	73	72	77	69		
4	77	71	74	74		
5	77	75	78	67		

Easterbrook Elem.

Grade	Rd	Ma	Lg	Sp	Sci	SS
2	68	66	64	56		
3	65	62	70	66		
4	56	50	60	50		
5	64	61	68	60		

Latimer Elem.

Grade	Rd	Ma	Lg	Sp	Sci	SS
2	72	67	71	63		
3	58	68	65	59		
4	62	55	62	58		
5	59	71	60	49		

Moreland Discovery

Grade	Rd	Ma	Lg	Sp	Sci	SS
2	73	79	76	54		
3	83	80	83	64		

Payne Elem.

Grade	Rd	Ma	Lg	Sp	Sci	SS
2	75	86	81	72		
3	59	72	65	64		
4	62	56	64	63		
5	71	74	76	66		

Rogers Middle

Grade	Rd	Ma	Lg	Sp	Sci	SS
6	57	70	66	55		
7	55	71	71	58		
8	59	61	67	50		

Scores range from 1-99, with 50 the average. A school scoring 75 has done better than 75 percent of other public schools in the U.S.
Key: Rd (read) Ma (math) Lg (Language), Sp (spelling), Sci (science) and SS (social science).

Grade	Rd	Ma	Lg	Sp	Sci	SS
Morgan Hill Unified School Dist.						
2	54	51	53	51		
3	51	54	52	49		
4	56	50	55	47		
5	50	48	51	42		
6	57	59	55	48		
7	55	56	57	50		
8	58	57	58	41		
9	50	68	57		57	56
10	38	52	40		52	50
11	47	58	50		57	67
Britton Middle School						
7	54	53	55	48		
8	58	55	59	40		
9	47	66	55		55	54
Burnett Elem.						
2	53	44	53	48		
3	31	28	35	32		
4	47	36	51	35		
5	39	32	34	28		
6	49	49	52	42		
Central High-Cont.						
10	9	18	7		20	19
11	32	25	31		28	36
El Toro Elem.						
2	56	56	63	57		
3	55	55	56	49		
4	65	46	55	40		
5	47	43	47	38		
6	50	54	48	38		
Encinal Elem.						
4	68	68	70	67		
5	53	49	51	40		
6	58	60	56	55		
Jackson Elem.						
2	42	34	36	36		
3	46	61	47	39		
4	54	50	48	51		
5	51	56	48	41		
6	61	70	57	45		
Live Oak High						
10	41	54	43		54	52
11	48	59	50		58	68
Los Paseos Elem.						
2	60	61	55	53		
3	59	74	62	56		
Murphy Middle School						
7	56	59	59	52		
8	57	58	57	42		
9	54	70	59		60	59
Nordstrom Elem.						
2	70	69	76	67		
3	59	56	58	58		
4	54	53	60	53		
5	67	63	67	57		
6	67	80	66	63		

Scores range from 1-99, with 50 the average. A school scoring 75 has done better than 75 percent of other public schools in the U.S.
Key: Rd (read) Ma (math) Lg (Language), Sp (spelling), Sci (science) and SS (social science).

Grade	Rd	Ma	Lg	Sp	Sci	SS
MORGAN HILL DIST. (Continued)						
Paradise Valley Elem.						
2	58	61	57	50		
3	65	66	61	52		
4	57	53	56	53		
5	68	63	71	58		
6	66	68	67	59		
San Martin/Gwinn Elem.						
2	43	38	39	43		
3	41	41	42	51		
4	50	50	50	41		
5	33	35	42	36		
6	47	41	42	41		
Walsh Elem.						
2	40	30	33	46		
3	40	40	41	45		
4	47	39	45	35		
5	40	45	45	34		
6	48	43	44	35		
Mountain View Elem.School Dist.						
2	58	61	60	51		
3	55	56	53	50		
4	56	52	56	50		
5	53	50	55	49		
6	54	56	51	47		
7	53	57	57	50		
8	51	56	55	43		
Bubb Elem.						
2	75	75	84	71		
3	80	77	80	73		
4	78	75	74	71		
5	72	69	71	67		
Castro Elem.						
2	26	35	21	26		
3	15	22	15	16		
4	26	26	30	18		
5	26	26	29	27		
Graham Middle						
6	54	56	51	47		
7	53	57	57	50		
8	51	56	55	43		
Landels Elem.						
2	68	72	81	65		
3	61	62	58	60		
4	64	56	64	64		
5	61	53	61	56		
Slater Elem.						
2	60	58	48	44		
3	61	65	56	56		
4	40	43	44	41		
5	45	47	52	39		
Mt. Pleasant Elem. School Dist.						
2	37	39	37	40		
3	33	39	35	42		
4	47	51	54	45		
5	33	35	48	40		
6	38	43	47	47		
7	38	40	47	47		
8	45	41	50	41		

Grade	Rd	Ma	Lg	Sp	Sci	SS
Boeger Junior High						
7	38	40	46	47		
8	46	41	50	42		
Foothill Intermdiate						
4	55	62	60	59		
5	33	35	48	40		
6	38	43	47	47		
Mt. Pleasant Elem.						
2	27	26	27	28		
3	24	29	24	27		
4	46	41	51	34		
Sanders Elem.						
2	34	39	31	40		
3	30	37	29	40		
4	33	41	40	30		
Valle Vista Elem.						
2	45	50	50	50		
3	47	48	52	57		
4	56	61	74	60		
Mt View-Los Altos						
9	56	75	66		62	66
10	52	65	60		63	57
11	55	68	61		62	71
Alta Vista High (Cont.)						
10	30	29	26		26	24
11	23	19	26		22	35
Los Altos High						
9	54	74	66		59	65
10	50	65	60		65	57
11	59	74	64		66	73
Moffett High (Alt.)						
10	44	34	37		39	49
11	44	24	45		30	47
Mountain View High						
9	58	77	66		65	67
10	57	68	64		65	60
11	62	76	67		71	79
Oak Grove Elem. School Dist.						
2	50	54	50	46		
3	45	52	46	43		
4	52	55	55	47		
5	50	57	54	48		
6	54	66	57	52		
7	55	61	60	54		
8	54	64	56	43		
Anderson Elem.						
2	35	30	34	34		
3	57	66	50	41		
4	61	63	57	47		
5	62	67	68	63		
6	60	71	60	62		
Baldwin Elem.						
2	61	73	57	58		
3	46	55	47	44		
4	57	56	69	57		
5	49	59	48	54		
6	55	70	54	50		
Bernal Int.						
7	62	72	70	62		
8	62	77	66	50		

Scores range from 1-99, with 50 the average. A school scoring 75 has done better than 75 percent of other public schools in the U.S.
Key: Rd (read) Ma (math) Lg (Language), Sp (spelling), Sci (science) and SS (social science).

Blossom Valley Elem.

Grade	Rd	Ma	Lg	Sp	Sci	SS
2	73	72	75	66		
3	56	66	57	59		
4	59	60	60	57		
5	51	59	61	59		
6	66	87	71	71		

Christopher Elem.

Grade	Rd	Ma	Lg	Sp	Sci	SS
2	20	17	19	22		
3	18	20	26	26		
4	30	38	37	24		
5	31	33	29	26		
6	37	43	38	32		

Davis Elem.

Grade	Rd	Ma	Lg	Sp	Sci	SS
7	48	52	50	48		
8	44	48	45	37		

Del Roble Elem.

Grade	Rd	Ma	Lg	Sp	Sci	SS
2	40	41	48	40		
3	47	59	54	44		
4	61	69	65	61		
5	36	47	41	43		
6	60	69	63	60		

Edenvale Elem.

Grade	Rd	Ma	Lg	Sp	Sci	SS
2	40	44	39	32		
3	30	51	30	33		
4	38	60	46	35		
5	30	44	37	31		
6	28	47	34	24		

Frost Elem.

Grade	Rd	Ma	Lg	Sp	Sci	SS
2	54	60	68	49		
3	50	58	52	49		
4	37	55	44	41		
5	49	55	54	42		
6	70	82	72	69		

Glider Elem.

Grade	Rd	Ma	Lg	Sp	Sci	SS
2	57	54	56	53		
3	56	56	56	61		
4	65	74	69	61		
5	57	67	67	58		
6	60	70	69	60		

Hayes Elem.

Grade	Rd	Ma	Lg	Sp	Sci	SS
2	65	62	65	61		
3	45	52	49	49		
4	72	73	67	60		
5	55	68	57	57		
6	68	65	66	66		

Herman Int.

Grade	Rd	Ma	Lg	Sp	Sci	SS
7	55	57	61	53		
8	56	67	57	44		

Miner Elem.

Grade	Rd	Ma	Lg	Sp	Sci	SS
2	30	42	27	24		
3	27	34	33	26		
4	31	30	40	34		
5	37	46	40	31		
6	42	43	46	34		

Oak Ridge Elem.

Grade	Rd	Ma	Lg	Sp	Sci	SS
2	57	58	60	47		
3	56	54	53	45		
4	50	43	51	46		
5	61	68	67	55		
6	62	76	62	56		

Parkview Elem.

Grade	Rd	Ma	Lg	Sp	Sci	SS
2	65	68	58	62		
3	51	66	48	50		
4	53	62	59	63		
5	56	59	61	58		
6	51	68	56	53		

Sakamoto Elem.

Grade	Rd	Ma	Lg	Sp	Sci	SS
2	59	59	59	56		
3	57	59	57	48		
4	71	65	74	65		
5	61	60	59	53		
6	62	74	61	55		

San Anselmo Elem.

Grade	Rd	Ma	Lg	Sp	Sci	SS
2	52	66	61	50		
3	39	32	42	46		
4	54	45	54	46		
5	58	58	58	46		
6	57	71	60	58		

Santa Teresa Elem.

Grade	Rd	Ma	Lg	Sp	Sci	SS
2	56	75	56	50		
3	47	62	47	47		
4	48	66	55	47		
5	63	71	66	60		
6	56	66	57	52		

Stipe Elem.

Grade	Rd	Ma	Lg	Sp	Sci	SS
2	27	37	25	27		
3	27	37	30	28		
4	29	30	32	22		
5	40	45	46	37		
6	39	56	44	42		

Taylor Elem.

Grade	Rd	Ma	Lg	Sp	Sci	SS
2	67	73	67	59		
3	57	60	47	58		
4	65	63	67	59		
5	55	57	57	54		
6	61	73	69	58		

Orchard Elem. School Dist.
Orchard Elem.

Grade	Rd	Ma	Lg	Sp	Sci	SS
2	29	25	26	31		
3	20	29	24	29		
4	29	26	34	26		
5	25	24	30	27		
6	33	39	32	29		
7	34	29	29	28		
8	32	31	26	30		

Palo Alto Unified School Dist.

Grade	Rd	Ma	Lg	Sp	Sci	SS
2	80	84	82	77		
3	82	82	82	74		
4	86	82	80	81		
5	86	88	85	79		
6	85	89	81	81		
7	81	87	85	80		
8	80	87	85	71		
9	77	90	81		79	83
10	74	86	76		81	80
11	79	89	82		83	90

Scores range from 1-99, with 50 the average. A school scoring 75 has done better than 75 percent of other public schools in the U.S.
Key: Rd (read) Ma (math) Lg (Language), Sp (spelling), Sci (science) and SS (social science).

Grade	Rd	Ma	Lg	Sp	Sci	SS
PALO ALTO DIST. (Continued)						
Addison Elem.						
2	74	75	72	63		
3	87	89	86	77		
4	84	73	77	76		
5	89	84	84	76		
Briones Elem.						
2	67	84	75	64		
3	73	69	72	66		
4	81	77	75	74		
5	74	74	71	67		
Duveneck Elem.						
2	83	86	86	83		
3	84	81	83	75		
4	88	82	79	78		
5	90	91	91	86		
El Carmelo Elem.						
2	78	77	76	69		
3	81	81	78	69		
4	81	76	71	71		
5	85	90	86	80		
Escondido Elem.						
2	76	84	80	72		
3	81	83	79	73		
4	85	80	83	85		
5	75	74	76	64		
Fairmeadow Elem.						
2	79	88	88	82		
3	76	79	76	67		
4	79	80	75	73		
5	85	92	82	78		
Gunn High						
9	77	92	81		82	84
10	72	86	74		79	77
11	79	89	80		86	89
Hays Elem.						
2	88	90	91	83		
3	92	94	92	88		
4	91	90	88	89		
5	90	93	90	85		
Hoover Elem.						
2	85	89	86	89		
3	82	89	86	87		
4	94	91	89	94		
5	94	95	90	88		
Jordan Middle						
6	85	88	82	81		
7	81	86	86	78		
8	82	85	84	72		
Nixon Elem.						
2	76	84	79	71		
3	83	78	82	71		
4	88	88	80	81		
5	82	89	88	79		
Ohlone Elem.						
2	78	76	77	69		
3	79	70	76	63		
4	84	70	79	74		
5	85	85	84	73		

Grade	Rd	Ma	Lg	Sp	Sci	SS
Palo Alto High						
9	76	88	81		74	82
10	76	86	78		82	82
11	79	88	83		81	91
Palo Verde Elem.						
2	86	88	90	86		
3	80	86	83	71		
4	87	80	79	85		
5	86	88	86	78		
Stanford Middle						
6	85	90	81	80		
7	81	88	84	81		
8	78	89	85	69		
San Jose Unified School Dist.						
2	40	39	38	36		
3	41	41	42	37		
4	44	39	46	37		
5	45	43	49	41		
6	45	46	44	41		
7	44	46	49	45		
8	47	48	47	40		
9	38	56	51		46	50
10	36	47	42		46	44
11	44	52	50		49	65
Allen Elem.						
2	52	48	38	51		
3	30	30	28	32		
4	45	41	40	45		
5	50	58	55	54		
Almaden Elem.						
2	50	65	51	40		
3	35	41	41	37		
4	22	24	30	15		
5	37	34	46	26		
Bachrodt Elem.						
2	19	26	23	25		
3	21	29	28	28		
4	19	22	26	15		
5	21	18	23	22		
Booksin Elem.						
2	64	68	70	60		
3	65	61	62	57		
4	60	62	65	60		
5	71	64	74	61		
Broadway High-Cont.						
9	15	17	26		19	20
10	10	13	12		18	14
11	18	15	26		15	31
Burnett Middle						
6	19	19	22	18		
7	20	20	25	22		
8	21	22	21	21		
Carson Elem.						
2	52	32	53	41		
3	48	51	48	42		
4	39	41	44	37		
5	47	47	54	39		
Castillero Middle						
6	55	53	50	50		
7	57	54	62	54		
8	61	58	61	47		

Scores range from 1-99, with 50 the average. A school scoring 75 has done better than 75 percent of other public schools in the U.S.
Key: Rd (read) Ma (math) Lg (Language), Sp (spelling), Sci (science) and SS (social science).

Grade	Rd	Ma	Lg	Sp	Sci	SS
Cory Elem.						
2	36	34	33	28		
Darling Elem.						
2	17	26	14	18		
3	20	29	26	22		
4	20	21	25	25		
5	23	26	30	20		
Empire Gardens Elem.						
2	18	16	21	23		
3	15	17	18	17		
4	30	25	28	26		
5	22	23	23	26		
Erikson Elem.						
2	38	25	36	36		
3	28	19	36	24		
4	29	26	33	21		
5	32	34	41	37		
Gardner Elem.						
2	16	17	14	17		
3	27	40	34	28		
4	18	16	24	17		
5	34	25	34	35		
Grant Elem.						
2	28	25	23	27		
3	22	23	24	20		
4	24	29	33	18		
5	19	20	28	21		
Graystone Elem.						
2	68	65	67	65		
3	78	77	74	74		
4	85	84	79	85		
5	80	85	76	74		
Gunderson High						
9	28	48	45		37	44
10	25	39	37		37	35
11	31	44	41		39	53
Gunderson Plus-Cont.						
11	21	*	17		23	34
Hacienda Sci/Environ						
2	50	40	51	38		
3	59	47	51	48		
4	58	41	54	48		
5	63	43	51	51		
Hammer Montessori Elem.						
2	41	26	29	34		
Harte Middle						
6	74	80	71	70		
7	72	79	77	68		
8	73	79	74	65		
Hester Elem.						
2	28	24	24	25		
3	23	28	22	24		
4	32	25	33	23		
5	26	23	30	37		
Hoover Middle						
6	30	29	31	29		
7	29	31	33	34		
8	33	33	34	31		
Leland High						
9	61	80	70		68	67
10	63	75	69		71	69
11	66	79	71		72	85
Leland Plus-Cont.						
11	30	29	30		32	41
Liberty High						
7	26	*	17	17		
8	38	21	26	22		
9	24	27	28		33	26
10	22	23	21		36	23
11	26	24	29		37	43
Lincoln High						
9	44	57	55		46	55
10	45	48	51		52	55
11	50	52	56		51	71
Los Alamitos Elem.						
2	68	65	69	61		
3	71	63	64	64		
4	69	66	63	61		
5	68	64	72	68		
Lowell Elem.						
2	12	18	13	22		
3	15	26	22	22		
4	21	19	24	20		
5	20	24	27	22		
Mann Elem.						
2	17	18	12	22		
3	14	14	16	17		
4	19	16	*	17		
5	37	38	38	33		
Muir Mid						
6	39	41	41	39		
7	35	37	39	34		
8	37	39	39	34		
Olinder Elem.						
2	19	21	17	17		
3	16	14	17	17		
4	13	8	18	11		
5	22	20	27	17		
Pioneer High						
9	45	69	56		57	59
10	34	52	37		47	41
11	42	50	47		48	61
Randol Elem.						
2	*	41	30	30		
3	51	60	53	46		
4	57	63	56	50		
5	56	56	57	55		
Reed Elem.						
2	62	57	66	56		
3	58	56	62	50		
4	66	66	70	57		
5	54	54	60	54		
River Glen Elem.						
2	32	43	37	20		
3	47	49	53	34		
4	41	45	47	24		
5	38	38	54	31		
6	48	57	50	36		
7	46	42	55	39		

Scores range from 1-99, with 50 the average. A school scoring 75 has done better than 75 percent of other public schools in the U.S.
Key: Rd (read) Ma (math) Lg (Language), Sp (spelling), Sci (science) and SS (social science).

Grade	Rd	Ma	Lg	Sp	Sci	SS

SAN JOSE UNIFIED DIST. (Continued)

San Jose High Academy

Grade	Rd	Ma	Lg	Sp	Sci	SS
9	25	41	39		33	36
10	23	32	29		34	31
11	31	39	41		36	52

Schallenberger Elem.

Grade	Rd	Ma	Lg	Sp
2	44	41	39	37
3	53	49	49	39
4	58	35	54	42
5	64	55	72	52

Simonds Elem.

Grade	Rd	Ma	Lg	Sp
2	64	70	71	57
3	64	67	60	55
4	64	52	63	61
5	60	50	60	54

Steinbeck Middle

Grade	Rd	Ma	Lg	Sp
6	32	33	32	29
7	34	41	35	37
8	35	39	35	28

Tamien Elem.

Grade	Rd	Ma	Lg	Sp
2	15	16	6	12

Terrell Elem.

Grade	Rd	Ma	Lg	Sp
2	37	41	43	34
3	46	40	45	45
4	56	39	52	35
5	50	51	59	45

Trace Elem.

Grade	Rd	Ma	Lg	Sp
3	37	41	37	31
4	34	40	48	35
5	43	40	44	32

Washington Elem.

Grade	Rd	Ma	Lg	Sp
2	14	18	13	11
3	9	14	14	12
4	17	14	26	12
5	18	19	27	14

Williams Elem.

Grade	Rd	Ma	Lg	Sp
2	77	85	80	75
3	81	86	84	80
4	83	81	82	81
5	80	83	80	76

Willow Glen Elem.

Grade	Rd	Ma	Lg	Sp
2	46	44	46	35
3	43	35	43	30
4	50	37	52	35
5	37	34	39	34

Willow Glen High

Grade	Rd	Ma	Lg	Sp	Sci	SS
9	31	44	44		38	43
10	29	40	34		39	39
11	35	40	41		42	55

Willow Glen Middle

Grade	Rd	Ma	Lg	Sp
6	42	40	45	41
7	41	39	46	47
8	45	40	46	40

Willow Glen Plus-Cont.

Grade	Rd	Ma	Lg	Sp	Sci	SS
11	35	26	35		26	52

Santa Clara Unified School Dist.

Grade	Rd	Ma	Lg	Sp	Sci	SS
2	49	51	53	50		
3	51	49	50	50		
4	51	46	55	50		
5	51	49	56	49		
6	49	50	51	48		
7	51	54	56	53		
8	49	52	48	42		
9	36	53	56		45	45
10	33	49	41		46	42
11	36	49	46		43	57

Bowers Elem.

Grade	Rd	Ma	Lg	Sp
2	47	49	49	43
3	44	54	40	47
4	54	47	61	56
5	44	54	59	45

Bracher Elem.

Grade	Rd	Ma	Lg	Sp
2	63	75	70	63
3	43	47	45	50
4	41	36	44	41
5	49	42	52	55

Braly Elem.

Grade	Rd	Ma	Lg	Sp
2	41	44	34	45
3	55	53	56	57
4	57	54	59	50
5	54	57	51	49

Briarwood Elem.

Grade	Rd	Ma	Lg	Sp
2	50	39	52	50
3	45	37	42	50
4	45	40	51	44
5	50	49	55	57

Buchser Middle

Grade	Rd	Ma	Lg	Sp
6	48	47		46
7	48	54		50
8	48	47		41

Cabrillo Middle

Grade	Rd	Ma	Lg	Sp
6	40	40	44	46
7	43	39	47	50
8	42	46	41	40

Haman Elem.

Grade	Rd	Ma	Lg	Sp
2	37	36	39	42
3	38	22	31	35
4	49	39	44	45
5	40	26	35	43

Hughes Elem.

Grade	Rd	Ma	Lg	Sp
2	40	41	44	46
3	54	63	63	57
4	51	47	63	58
5	39	37	52	48

Laurelwood Elem.

Grade	Rd	Ma	Lg	Sp
2	64	66	68	63
3	67	60	67	62
4	67	71	75	71
5	66	67	70	53

Mayne Elem.

Grade	Rd	Ma	Lg	Sp
2	22	23	17	26
3	19	12	19	20
4	25	25	27	20
5	33	33	36	26

Scores range from 1-99, with 50 the average. A school scoring 75 has done better than 75 percent of other public schools in the U.S.
Key: Rd (read) Ma (math) Lg (Language), Sp (spelling), Sci (science) and SS (social science).

Grade	Rd	Ma	Lg	Sp	Sci	SS
Millikin Elem.						
2	83	91	91	83		
3	77	90	88	77		
4	78	79	80	76		
5	74	80	82	71		
Montague Elem.						
2	52	60	70	63		
3	44	51	51	62		
4	47	53	58	56		
5	41	42	51	46		
New Valley High (Cont.)						
10	10	19	9		16	15
11	18	22	20		28	31
Peterson Middle						
6	57	59	56	51		
7	58	64	61	58		
8	55	62	55	45		
Pomeroy Elem.						
2	65	65	69	66		
3	56	42	48	54		
4	48	41	54	44		
5	48	51	55	47		
Ponderosa Elem.						
2	51	53	52	56		
3	57	62	59	54		
4	62	55	70	67		
5	65	58	66	61		
Santa Clara High						
9	37	54	56		47	46
10	35	56	41		51	46
11	38	52	47		47	61
Scott Lane Elem.						
2	28	21	27	31		
3	35	30	30	30		
4	25	29	30	29		
5	25	29	33	33		
Sutter Elem.						
2	47	56	59	52		
3	58	65	59	49		
4	58	42	58	54		
5	53	39	54	42		
Washington Elem.						
2	54	56	47	37		
3	57	49	52	45		
4	65	56	58	48		
5	80	61	77	64		
Westwood Elem.						
2	42	40	47	40		
3	45	35	44	39		
4	56	39	60	49		
5	55	51	64	46		
Wilcox High						
9	37	55	58		45	46
10	32	50	46		46	42
11	37	53	50		44	59
Wilson Altern.						
7	*	38	35	48		
8	41	34	30	29		
9	32	32	40		34	32
10	38	34	34		39	34
11	36	33	39		36	46

Grade	Rd	Ma	Lg	Sp	Sci	SS
Saratoga Elem. School Dist.						
2	83	88	86	82		
3	86	91	88	84		
4	85	86	84	87		
5	86	91	90	84		
6	84	91	86	88		
7	85	93	90	86		
8	83	90	87	77		
Argonaut Elem.						
2	88	90	88	89		
3	84	90	88	88		
4	88	90	87	92		
5	87	91	91	88		
Foothill Elem.						
2	77	88	83	76		
3	88	88	88	81		
4	81	82	80	84		
5	83	88	84	78		
Redwood Middle						
6	84	91	86	88		
7	85	93	90	86		
8	83	90	87	77		
Saratoga Elem.						
2	81	85	89	78		
3	84	94	87	81		
4	85	83	83	82		
5	90	94	93	83		
Sunnyvale Elem. School Dist.						
2	56	63	59	56		
3	50	61	57	56		
4	53	62	61	55		
5	59	66	66	57		
6	55	65	61	57		
7	52	54	61	55		
8	54	56	54	46		
Bishop Elem.						
2	50	50	51	49		
3	49	67	60	56		
4	44	57	57	46		
5	56	67	68	53		
Cherry Chase Elem.						
2	75	75	80	69		
3	60	63	59	54		
4	45	53	48	39		
5	51	50	41	44		
Columbia Middle						
6	47	53	52	51		
7	45	44	53	47		
8	44	43	43	39		
Cumberland Elem.						
2	53	67	56	51		
3	64	70	65	58		
4	77	76	77	79		
5	79	84	84	75		
Ellis Elem.						
2	62	73	73	63		
3	50	76	60	63		
4	46	66	54	48		

Scores range from 1-99, with 50 the average. A school scoring 75 has done better than 75 percent of other public schools in the U.S.
Key: Rd (read) Ma (math) Lg (Language), Sp (spelling), Sci (science) and SS (social science).

SUNNYVALE ELEM. DIST. (Continued)

Grade	Rd	Ma	Lg	Sp	Sci	SS
5	53	71	60	50		

Fairwood Elem.

Grade	Rd	Ma	Lg	Sp	Sci	SS
2	50	45	36	53		
3	25	39	34	46		
4	48	51	54	50		
5	53	55	68	54		

Lakewood Elem.

Grade	Rd	Ma	Lg	Sp	Sci	SS
2	43	55	47	49		
3	43	49	50	58		
4	54	63	56	59		
5	61	63	61	61		

San Miguel Elem.

Grade	Rd	Ma	Lg	Sp	Sci	SS
2	61	63	68	65		
3	53	68	67	62		
4	61	75	76	68		
5	53	67	67	59		

Sunnyvale Middle

Grade	Rd	Ma	Lg	Sp	Sci	SS
6	63	77	70	64		
7	61	65	71	63		
8	64	69	65	52		

Vargas Elem.

Grade	Rd	Ma	Lg	Sp	Sci	SS
2	59	67	58	57		
3	44	44	47	48		
4	45	44	55	50		
5	63	58	67	58		

Union Elem. School Dist.

Grade	Rd	Ma	Lg	Sp	Sci	SS
2	68	69	73	65		
3	74	73	75	65		
4	68	65	69	63		
5	70	68	73	65		
6	66	70	67	60		
7	69	70	70	60		
8	66	68	68	55		

Alta Vista Elem.

Grade	Rd	Ma	Lg	Sp	Sci	SS
2	72	71	77	71		
3	80	81	83	69		
4	79	71	82	77		
5	80	82	81	72		

Athenour Elem.

Grade	Rd	Ma	Lg	Sp	Sci	SS
2	63	61	75	63		
3	65	55	68	53		
4	57	56	60	54		
5	66	54	65	60		

Carlton Elem.

Grade	Rd	Ma	Lg	Sp	Sci	SS
2	66	70	71	57		
3	78	84	82	66		
4	65	63	67	59		
5	74	72	74	63		

Dartmouth Middle

Grade	Rd	Ma	Lg	Sp	Sci	SS
6	62	67	70	60		
7	68	64	71	59		
8	66	62	69	55		

Guadalupe Elem.

Grade	Rd	Ma	Lg	Sp	Sci	SS
2	71	77	78	72		
3	80	77	78	70		
4	73	70	68	67		
5	77	82	86	78		

Lietz Elem.

Grade	Rd	Ma	Lg	Sp	Sci	SS
2	62	57	62	59		
3	65	67	67	65		
4	66	63	63	59		
5	59	56	67	56		

Lone Hill Elem.

Grade	Rd	Ma	Lg	Sp	Sci	SS
2	73	79	75	67		
3	77	70	77	67		
4	68	62	70	58		
5	66	60	66	61		

Noddin Elem.

Grade	Rd	Ma	Lg	Sp	Sci	SS
2	71	81	78	70		
3	79	85	81	74		
4	71	75	74	70		
5	73	74	71	66		

Oster Elem.

Grade	Rd	Ma	Lg	Sp	Sci	SS
2	64	56	66	57		
3	65	58	63	56		
4	65	49	63	54		
5	63	65	74	65		

Union Middle

Grade	Rd	Ma	Lg	Sp	Sci	SS
6	70	72	65	59		
7	71	76	70	60		
8	66	75	67	55		

Whisman Elem. School Dist.

Grade	Rd	Ma	Lg	Sp	Sci	SS
2	50	50	55	52		
3	50	49	51	53		
4	58	39	57	51		
5	49	40	48	47		
6	54	55	52	50		
7	53	49	58	54		
8	56	47	58	46		

Crittenden Middle

Grade	Rd	Ma	Lg	Sp	Sci	SS
5	49	40	48	47		
6	54	55	52	50		
7	53	49	58	54		
8	56	47	58	46		

Monta Loma Elem.

Grade	Rd	Ma	Lg	Sp	Sci	SS
2	50	53	54	49		
3	49	45	47	47		
4	52	33	57	52		

Theuerkauf Elem.

Grade	Rd	Ma	Lg	Sp	Sci	SS
2	45	44	51	51		
3	49	48	57	56		
4	61	40	54	49		

Whisman Elem.

Grade	Rd	Ma	Lg	Sp	Sci	SS
2	57	53	58	56		
3	50	56	48	54		
4	58	46	63	54		

Chapter 2b

SANTA CLARA COUNTY
Latest Test Results

- **What do these numbers mean?**

These percentile rankings, drawn from the scores on the 1998 STAR test, compare California schools and grades, one against the other.

If a school scores in the 91st percentile, it has done better than 91 percent of the other public schools in the state. If it scores in the 51st percentile, it has done better than 51 percent of the others; the 40th rank, better than 40 percent of the others. If a school scores in the first percentile, 99 percent of the other schools have scored higher.

- **How do these numbers differ from the rankings in Chapter 2.**

The results broken out in Chapter 2 are based on a comparison against a national norm or standard where the national average is 50.

Although the results in Chapter 2B are based on the same data as the results in the Chapter 2, the Chapter 2B approach presents the results in a different way. Chapter 2B isolates California schools and simply ranks them one against the other, without regard to a national standard. These scores have no "average." Readers should interpret the Chapter 2B scores as a rough measure of how California schools compare against one another.

Note: Chapter 2 ranks school districts and schools. Chapter 2B is limited just to schools.

- **Do the numbers in this chapter tell whether California education is improving?**

No. Ranking systems don't recognize overall gains or losses. If every school in California raised raw scores 20 percent, some schools would still be ranked at the bottom, a few at the top. The same if every raw score dropped. A ranking system shows how one school did against all other schools.

- **Are scores an accurate reflection of school and instructional quality?**

No. Scores are strongly influenced by family background and other social forces. See Chapter 3 on How Public Schools Work.

Scores range from 1-99. A school scoring 75 has done better than 75 percent of other public schools in California.
Key: Rd (read) Ma (math) Lg (Language), Sp (spelling), Sci (science) and SS (social science).

Grade	Rd	Ma	Lg	Sp	Sci	SS
Alum Rock Union Elem. School Dist.						
Arbuckle Elem.						
2	45	30	24	45		
3	17	8	3	31		
4	36	32	27	31		
5	27	25	30	35		
Cassell Elem.						
2	62	68	50	65		
3	51	42	48	59		
4	50	65	53	58		
5	47	54	44	57		
Chavez Elem.						
2	17	7	8	17		
3	23	28	24	16		
4	17	29	19	13		
5	27	23	38	33		
Cureton Elem.						
2	57	68	62	51		
3	59	16	55	36		
4	45	26	43	51		
5	51	47	46	52		
Dorsa Elem.						
2	29	25	21	19		
3	23	14	15	16		
4	34	15	27	31		
5	40	19	38	43		
Fischer Middle School						
6	28	24	28	28		
7	45	38	44	34		
8	46	41	47	52		
George Middle School						
6	53	55	47	54		
7	61	63	58	66		
8	57	56	61	72		
Goss Elem.						
2	17	20	24	22		
3	26	19	24	24		
4	21	9	30	28		
5	27	5	8	14		
Hubbard Elem.						
2	7	10	8	17		
3	23	14	15	16		
4	21	7	11	10		
5	32	37	25	25		
Linda Vista Elem.						
2	61	64	57	53		
3	62	42	62	46		
4	71	65	60	65		
5	61	56	57	57		
Lyndale Elem.						
2	53	53	57	49		
3	47	42	41	38		
4	45	44	37	39		
5	42	43	32	46		
Mathson Middle						
6	16	11	18	13		
7	31	30	31	30		
8	32	39	36	33		
McCollam Elem.						
2	53	67	59	49		
3	52	58	50	57		
4	53	51	53	54		
5	65	64	60	72		
Meyer Elem.						
2	34	22	28	26		
3	26	16	24	21		
4	44	34	41	43		
5	44	32	40	39		
Miller Elem.						
2	25	22	28	26		
3	14	21	18	14		
4	36	42	24	45		
5	32	32	30	30		
Ocala Middle						
6	38	42	45	37		
7	52	54	54	54		
8	48	54	52	61		
Painter Elem.						
2	57	65	63	66		
3	49	53	41	52		
4	32	39	27	43		
5	38	47	30	52		
Pala Middle						
6	37	26	38	35		
7	49	45	54	52		
8	43	42	48	50		
Rogers Elem.						
2	52	64	50	61		
3	55	55	50	70		
4	60	68	64	73		
5	60	68	69	78		
Ryan Elem.						
2	22	32	26	22		
3	23	26	21	24		
4	21	15	22	19		
5	38	35	40	33		
San Antonio Elem.						
2	19	10	13	14		
3	17	21	27	21		
4	14	23	27	25		
5	56	74	59	50		
Sheppard Middle School						
6	44	39	45	55		
7	53	57	52	60		
8	55	51	58	70		

Scores range from 1-99. A school scoring 75 has done better than 75 percent of other public schools in California.
Key: Rd (read) Ma (math) Lg (Language), Sp (spelling), Sci (science) and SS (social science).

Grade	Rd	Ma	Lg	Sp	Sci	SS	Grade	Rd	Ma	Lg	Sp	Sci	SS
Shields Elem.							**Ruskin Elem.**						
2	45	46	45	39			2	92	91	92	96		
3	35	36	37	31			3	80	86	89	95		
4	42	26	32	31			4	90	90	91	94		
5	38	25	23	33			5	92	94	93	95		
Slonaker Elem.							**Sierramont Middle**						
2	25	14	18	35			6	78	80	77	83		
3	37	48	37	28			7	85	90	85	93		
4	44	57	45	57			8	78	83	83	86		
5	51	59	51	43			10		22				
Berryessa Union Elem. School Dist.							**Summerdale Elem.**						
Brooktree Elem.							2	60	52	58	67		
2	90	77	82	77			3	68	71	68	84		
3	75	73	80	84			4	64	61	64	74		
4	68	69	74	74			5	72	73	67	76		
5	65	68	76	75			**Toyon Elem.**						
Cherrywood Elem.							2	79	76	79	86		
2	60	65	62	71			3	71	72	74	73		
3	73	82	77	88			4	78	72	76	80		
4	68	78	74	78			5	72	75	69	83		
5	71	78	75	78			**Vinci Park Elem.**						
Laneview Elem.							2	67	67	68	84		
2	79	86	75	84			3	70	68	75	85		
3	71	76	67	82			4	71	84	79	89		
4	71	76	67	80			5	72	80	83	84		
5	69	63	65	85			**Cambrian Elem. School Dist.**						
Majestic Way Elem.							**Bagby Elem.**						
2	76	80	72	86			2	95	95	93	95		
3	73	75	73	83			3	94	93	95	89		
4	75	77	74	82			4	88	89	93	96		
5	71	80	79	86			5	93	94	96	92		
Morrill Middle							**Fammatre Elem.**						
6	64	70	69	77			2	91	89	94	89		
7	70	79	71	85			3	92	92	93	93		
8	71	83	73	85			4	92	94	96	92		
Noble Elem.							5	93	97	95	93		
2	83	77	81	88			**Farnham Elem.**						
3	70	72	75	79			2	85	89	92	90		
4	76	73	78	74			3	90	88	90	92		
5	71	64	71	72			4	86	92	91	93		
6	57						5	99	99	99	95		
7	80	38	60	75			**Ida Price Middle**						
Northwood Elem.							6	91	86	90	87		
2	79	86	77	81			7	95	91	96	94		
3	89	92	92	98			8	93	89	89	90		
4	83	82	77	87			**Sartorette Elem.**						
5	87	90	87	92			2	92	91	91	95		
Piedmont Middle							3	85	84	88	80		
6	75	78	71	78			4	87	84	96	88		
7	75	82	76	81			5	78	66	80	75		
8	75	79	74	81									

Scores range from 1-99. A school scoring 75 has done better than 75 percent of other public schools in California.
Key: Rd (read) Ma (math) Lg (Language), Sp (spelling), Sci (science) and SS (social science).

Campbell Union Elem. School Dist.

Grade	Rd	Ma	Lg	Sp	Sci	SS
Blackford Elem.						
2	58	50	56	51		
3	80	82	82	74		
4	79	79	85	78		
5	77	74	70	75		
Campbell Middle						
5	63	62	69	67		
6	55	53	59	53		
7	67	61	73	68		
8	66	63	74	63		
Capri Elem.						
2	77	78	83	73		
3	87	93	93	83		
4	81	85	84	77		
5	82	71	83	78		
Castlemont Elem.						
2	75	78	77	65		
3	86	92	89	79		
4	84	85	84	84		
5	90	84	82	83		
Forest Hill Elem.						
2	80	86	88	80		
3	88	91	87	81		
4	93	95	92	92		
5	86	96	87	90		
Hazelwood Elem.						
2	84	88	85	79		
3	81	85	86	81		
4	79	84	79	73		
Lynhaven Elem.						
2	82	73	85	77		
3	65	58	67	59		
4	74	76	76	76		
5	70	62	73	72		
Marshall Lane Elem.						
2	97	94	92	94		
3	93	88	94	93		
4	94	94	93	93		
5	97	97	97	94		
Monroe Middle						
5	73	68	71	73		
6	72	74	79	72		
7	68	70	74	70		
8	74	75	76	74		
Rolling Hills Middle						
5	82	84	91	84		
6	76	82	87	78		
7	82	81	92	86		
8	76	85	87	84		
Rosemary Elem.						

Grade	Rd	Ma	Lg	Sp	Sci	SS
2	38	50	44	33		
3	54	56	57	41		
4	50	42	45	39		
Sherman Oaks Elem.						
2	32	38	38	17		
3	44	19	37	41		
4	47	39	48	41		

Campbell Union High School Dist.

Grade	Rd	Ma	Lg	Sp	Sci	SS
Blackford High (Cont.)						
10	51	48	43		26	50
11	49	26	40		44	33
Del Mar High						
9	74	79	73		66	71
10	74	81	77		69	77
11	71	72	74		72	76
Leigh High						
9	90	91	91		89	91
10	90	91	89		87	91
11	90	86	90		89	92
Prospect High						
9	80	88	77		80	78
10	74	79	71		70	75
11	81	82	83		80	85
Westmont High						
9	84	91	85		88	87
10	86	90	88		90	90
11	80	84	80		85	87

Cupertino Union Elem. School Dist.

Grade	Rd	Ma	Lg	Sp	Sci	SS
Blue Hills Elem.						
2	99	98	99	99		
3	98	99	99	99		
4	99	99	99	99		
5	98	98	99	99		
6	98	99	99	99		
Collins Elem.						
2	99	99	98	99		
3	96	97	97	99		
4	98	99	99	99		
5	98	99	98	99		
6	98	99	97	99		
Cupertino Int.						
6	99	99	99	99		
7	98	97	97	98		
8	96	96	96	98		
De Vargas Elem.						
2	72	63	71	82		
3	77	88	80	89		
4	67	84	79	78		
5	65	81	72	73		
6	88	90	89	87		

Scores range from 1-99. A school scoring 75 has done better than 75 percent of other public schools in California.
Key: Rd (read) Ma (math) Lg (Language), Sp (spelling), Sci (science) and SS (social science).

Grade	Rd	Ma	Lg	Sp	Sci	SS	Grade	Rd	Ma	Lg	Sp	Sci	SS
Dilworth Elem.							**Montclaire Elem.**						
2	97	96	96	98			2	99	99	99	99		
3	96	99	98	99			3	99	98	99	99		
4	96	98	98	98			4	99	99	99	99		
5	94	97	95	97			5	99	97	99	99		
6	98	99	98	99			6	99	99	98	98		
Eisenhower Elem.							**Muir Elem.**						
2	94	89	95	96			2	86	96	90	92		
3	94	93	93	95			3	94	98	95	97		
4	91	88	88	91			4	93	98	94	95		
5	94	90	96	97			5	84	94	87	92		
6	96	93	96	98			6	85	96	87	84		
Faria Elem.							**Nimitz Elem.**						
2	99	99	99	100			2	73	87	87	71		
3	99	99	99	99			3	65	68	71	67		
4	99	99	99	99			4	77	90	87	82		
5	99	99	99	99			5	67	85	79	61		
6	99	99	99	99			6	69	83	72	63		
Garden Gate Elem.							**Portal Elem.**						
2	93	95	95	98			2	99	99	99	99		
3	94	98	97	98			3	99	99	99	99		
4	95	97	98	96			4	99	99	99	99		
5	95	96	98	98			5	99	99	99	99		
6	96	95	91	97			6	99	98	99	99		
Hyde Int.							**Regnart Elem.**						
6	83	98	91	92			2	98	98	99	99		
7	88	94	94	93			3	98	98	99	99		
8	81	93	89	86			4	99	99	99	99		
Kennedy Int.							5	99	99	99	99		
7	98	99	98	99			6	99	99	99	99		
8	98	98	98	99			**Sedgwick Elem.**						
Lincoln Elem.							2	95	91	91	94		
2	98	94	93	99			3	93	88	92	92		
3	97	94	97	98			4	90	90	93	94		
4	98	99	99	99			5	91	85	93	92		
5	96	98	98	98			6	92	91	88	92		
6	97	97	98	98			**Stevens Creek Elem.**						
McAuliffe							2	99	96	98	98		
2	98	92	92	95			3	98	98	99	99		
3	99	96	99	95			4	98	97	98	97		
4	96	93	91	89			5	96	98	98	97		
5	99	97	97	96			6	97	97	97	97		
6	99	97	97	95			**Stocklmeir Elem.**						
Meyerholz Elem.							2	96	95	95	96		
2	97	97	92	98			3	97	95	98	96		
3	93	90	89	90			4	95	97	97	98		
4	93	97	94	95			5	97	98	97	97		
5	88	87	87	91			6	91	92	91	87		
6	94	94	95	95			**West Valley Elem.**						
Miller Int.							2	98	94	96	96		
6	100	99	100	100			3	99	98	99	98		
7	99	99	99	99			4	98	99	99	99		
8	98	99	98	99			5	98	98	98	98		
							6	97	98	98	97		

Scores range from 1-99. A school scoring 75 has done better than 75 percent of other public schools in California.
Key: Rd (read) Ma (math) Lg (Language), Sp (spelling), Sci (science) and SS (social science).

East Side Union High School Dist.

Grade	Rd	Ma	Lg	Sp	Sci	SS
Apollo High (Cont.)						
11	47	26	40		29	28
Foothill High (Cont.)						
9	33	46	41		19	35
10	34	37	27		26	30
11	38	16	37		16	28
Genesis High (Cont.)						
11	46	9	40		38	30
Hill High						
9	55	72	57		48	47
10	53	72	56		47	50
11	53	60	57		52	52
Independence High						
9	67	83	69		71	62
10	66	79	67		65	67
11	65	74	69		69	69
Lick High						
9	53	69	55		61	42
10	53	68	56		54	54
11	55	52	61		62	58
Mt. Pleasant High						
9	75	83	74		71	72
10	67	77	64		68	64
11	63	65	59		62	63
Oak Grove High						
9	77	84	77		86	78
10	74	81	74		84	82
11	73	75	76		79	79
Overfelt High						
9	51	72	54		48	47
10	51	70	54		45	50
11	49	59	52		44	47
Pegasus High (Cont.)						
11	56	30	50		35	40
Phoenix High (Cont.)						
11	4	20	5		12	37
Piedmont Hills High						
9	85	92	85		86	76
10	83	92	83		87	83
11	78	84	82		80	78
Santa Teresa High						
9	81	87	88		86	83
10	80	82	87		85	84
11	76	74	85		80	74
Silver Creek High						
9	75	86	76		71	74
10	72	83	74		68	76
11	68	74	69		64	74
Yerba Buena High						
9	46	69	48		48	35
10	51	73	52		45	41
11	53	66	54		50	42

Evergreen Elem. School Dist.

Grade	Rd	Ma	Lg	Sp	Sci	SS
Cadwallader Elem.						
2	70	76	75	79		
3	64	71	73	85		
4	72	81	79	71		
5	72	79	83	83		
6	83	80	92	86		
Cedar Grove Elem.						
2	79	77	78	77		
3	80	94	91	91		
4	78	91	85	88		
5	64	68	64	77		
6	72	80	84	84		
Chaboya Middle						
6	70	78	74	80		
7	74	82	80	86		
8	78	85	84	91		
Dove Hill Elem.						
2	77	84	69	77		
3	65	86	79	74		
4	60	75	64	71		
5	67	73	67	71		
6	75	81	84	79		
Evergreen Elem.						
2	98	96	95	98		
3	90	94	94	96		
4	84	94	89	94		
5	87	94	86	95		
Holly Oak Elem.						
2	89	89	88	86		
3	78	93	86	91		
4	76	90	84	84		
5	68	79	77	75		
6	81	89	94	95		
Laurelwood Elem.						
2	94	88	91	88		
3	91	90	90	89		
4	89	86	89	88		
5	86	83	87	84		
6	78	78	84	84		
LeyVa Int.						
6	62	73	70	80		
7	71	80	79	83		
8	67	76	72	84		
Millbrook Elem.						
2	87	93	85	91		
3	76	88	78	85		
4	81	83	85	94		
5	80	90	86	89		
6	84	92	94	96		

Scores range from 1-99. A school scoring 75 has done better than 75 percent of other public schools in California.
Key: Rd (read) Ma (math) Lg (Language), Sp (spelling), Sci (science) and SS (social science).

Montgomery

Grade	Rd	Ma	Lg	Sp	Sci	SS
2	84	87	88	82		
3	87	94	92	95		
4	71	73	71	79		
5	78	80	78	78		
6	61	62	66	71		

Norwood Creek Elem.

Grade	Rd	Ma	Lg	Sp	Sci	SS
2	89	89	91	96		
3	88	97	93	98		
4	89	97	94	97		
5	88	92	90	94		

Quimby Oak Int.

Grade	Rd	Ma	Lg	Sp	Sci	SS
6	85	89	90	92		
7	78	85	87	91		
8	79	86	83	92		

Silver Oak Elem.

Grade	Rd	Ma	Lg	Sp	Sci	SS
2	95	96	89	95		
3	94	96	97	98		
4	96	97	97	98		
5	93	93	94	95		
6	94	93	99	98		

Smith Elem.

Grade	Rd	Ma	Lg	Sp	Sci	SS
2	61	69	62	73		
3	62	84	72	84		
4	57	69	64	70		
5	60	67	67	64		

Whaley Elem.

Grade	Rd	Ma	Lg	Sp	Sci	SS
2	77	85	71	79		
3	64	69	74	84		
4	58	70	67	78		
5	57	70	68	69		

Franklin-McKinley Elem. School Dist.

Fair Jr. High

Grade	Rd	Ma	Lg	Sp	Sci	SS
7	37	47	39	34		
8	42	54	48	48		

Franklin Elem.

Grade	Rd	Ma	Lg	Sp	Sci	SS
2	40	58	49	47		
3	39	48	50	56		
4	27	32	37	31		
5	38	28	42	46		
6	41	37	45	44		

Hellyer Elem.

Grade	Rd	Ma	Lg	Sp	Sci	SS
2	57	75	68	65		
3	47	48	57	69		
4	53	55	57	63		
5	47	57	59	62		

Hillsdale Elem.

Grade	Rd	Ma	Lg	Sp	Sci	SS
2	17	16	21	17		
3	39	55	52	46		
4	36	34	41	41		
5	47	39	55	63		

Kennedy Elem.

Grade	Rd	Ma	Lg	Sp	Sci	SS
2	49	44	56	54		
3	49	61	55	65		
4	40	49	50	48		
5	49	57	53	57		
6	38	40	43	51		

Los Arboles Elem.

Grade	Rd	Ma	Lg	Sp	Sci	SS
2	27	49	39	29		
3	37	24	32	46		
4	45	52	56	48		
5	47	45	48	48		
6	24	26	24	33		

McKinley Elem.

Grade	Rd	Ma	Lg	Sp	Sci	SS
2	22	18	10	12		
3	7	4	7	7		
4	8	12	8	17		
5	17	17	30	16		

Meadows Elem.

Grade	Rd	Ma	Lg	Sp	Sci	SS
2	36	44	33	38		
3	44	46	45	57		
4	47	45	60	56		
5	38	39	58	50		
6	50	49	56	67		

Santee Elem.

Grade	Rd	Ma	Lg	Sp	Sci	SS
2	11	20	10	7		
3	32	33	32	31		
4	11	15	22	28		
5	5	12	13	16		
6	9	20	9	9		

Seven Trees Elem.

Grade	Rd	Ma	Lg	Sp	Sci	SS
2	25	27	35	31		
3	29	44	39	31		
4	32	26	35	37		
5	34	43	40	43		
6	32	32	32	30		

Stonegate Elem.

Grade	Rd	Ma	Lg	Sp	Sci	SS
2	67	67	63	70		
3	55	40	61	75		
4	57	47	63	64		
5	69	70	75	82		
6	47	49	59	54		
7	76	91	84	83		
8	63	69	74	80		

Sylvandale Jr. High

Grade	Rd	Ma	Lg	Sp	Sci	SS
6	39	39	34	46		
7	43	49	44	50		
8	42	57	47	48		

Scores range from 1-99. A school scoring 75 has done better than 75 percent of other public schools in California.
Key: Rd (read) Ma (math) Lg (Language), Sp (spelling), Sci (science) and SS (social science).

Grade	Rd	Ma	Lg	Sp	Sci	SS
Windmill Springs Elem.						
2	58	78	58	65		
3	37	53	50	63		
4	45	49	60	61		
5	38	47	46	57		
6	18	28	22	23		
7	51	60	54	54		
8	50	70	66	61		

Fremont Union High School Dist.

Grade	Rd	Ma	Lg	Sp	Sci	SS
Alt. Program						
9		24				
10	72	60	54		58	71
11	73	63	73		76	75
Cupertino High						
9	89	92	91		92	88
10	91	97	93		94	92
11	90	94	91		92	90
Fremont High						
9	78	88	80		81	75
10	77	83	75		73	74
11	77	75	79		72	74
Homestead High						
9	92	95	93		90	91
10	94	97	95		93	93
11	91	94	93		91	88
Lynbrook High						
9	98	99	98		99	98
10	98	99	98		99	99
11	98	99	98		98	98
Monta Vista High						
9	97	99	99		99	98
10	98	99	99		99	99
11	98	99	99		98	98

Gilroy Unified School Dist.

Grade	Rd	Ma	Lg	Sp	Sci	SS
Aprea Fundamental						
2	95	95	92	95		
3	91	87	91	96		
4	91	95	92	94		
5	90	87	86	89		
6	84	87	86	90		
Brownell Academy of Humanities and Fine Arts						
7	65	57	63	61		
8	63	57	64	65		
El Roble Elem.						
2	83	75	69	77		
3	69	40	55	31		
4	54	47	53	48		
5	57	43	49	47		
6	68	61	64	60		

Grade	Rd	Ma	Lg	Sp	Sci	SS
Eliot Elem.						
2	69	30	68	59		
3	70	58	76	67		
4	62	49	53	53		
5	54	17	48	40		
6	47	55	48	35		
Gilroy High						
9	71	81	73		73	78
10	74	80	76		77	74
11	77	75	78		79	80
Glen View Elem.						
2	57	23	42	63		
3	32	21	21	34		
4	44	39	52	50		
5	50	62	54	43		
6	50	47	57	44		
Jordan Elem.						
2	57	40	56	49		
3	32	7	29	17		
4	44	23	39	28		
5	55	35	40	43		
6	85	69	74	71		
Kelley Elem.						
2	61	46	67	51		
3	59	58	57	41		
4	66	60	59	60		
5	62	56	63	57		
6	74	71	63	66		
Las Animas Elem.						
2	58	23	49	47		
3	54	40	67	46		
4	47	29	30	39		
5	58	47	51	59		
6	44	39	45	42		
Mt. Madonna High (Cont.)						
9		24				
10	41	43	42		19	47
11	29	6	22		26	25
Rucker Elem.						
2	60	30	51	43		
3	78	52	77	60		
4	83	62	70	79		
5	75	66	76	63		
6	85	69	88	78		
San Ysidro Elem.						
2	55	23	42	54		
3	44	36	47	36		
4	34	20	43	39		
5	61	56	58	47		
6	64	64	77	70		
So. Valley School of Science and Global Studies						
7	61	52	54	56		
8	61	51	58	63		

Scores range from 1-99. A school scoring 75 has done better than 75 percent of other public schools in California.
Key: Rd (read) Ma (math) Lg (Language), Sp (spelling), Sci (science) and SS (social science).

Lakeside Joint Elem. School Dist.
Lakeside Elem.

Grade	Rd	Ma	Lg	Sp	Sci	SS
2	90	92	96	81		
3	94	95	93	96		
4	98	97	97	90		
5	95	93	94	89		
6	94	88	94	94		

Loma Prieta Union Elem. School Dist.
English Middle

Grade	Rd	Ma	Lg	Sp	Sci	SS
6	92	91	95	95		
7	95	88	93	95		
8	95	94	96	95		

Loma Prieta Elem.

Grade	Rd	Ma	Lg	Sp	Sci	SS
2	95	87	93	89		
3	96	95	95	93		
4	98	97	96	95		
5	94	93	87	89		

Los Altos Elem. School Dist.
Almond Elem.

Grade	Rd	Ma	Lg	Sp	Sci	SS
2	99	98	99	99		
3	99	99	99	99		
4	99	99	99	99		
5	99	99	99	99		
6	98	99	99	99		

Blach Int.

Grade	Rd	Ma	Lg	Sp	Sci	SS
7	99	99	99	99		
8	99	99	99	99		

Bullis-Purissima Elem.

Grade	Rd	Ma	Lg	Sp	Sci	SS
2	99	99	99	99		
3	99	99	99	99		
4	99	99	98	99		
5	99	99	99	99		
6	99	99	99	99		

Egan Int.

Grade	Rd	Ma	Lg	Sp	Sci	SS
7	99	99	99	98		
8	98	98	99	98		

Loyola Elem.

Grade	Rd	Ma	Lg	Sp	Sci	SS
2	98	96	99	99		
3	99	99	99	98		
4	99	99	99	99		
5	99	99	99	99		
6	99	99	99	99		

Oak Ave. Elem.

Grade	Rd	Ma	Lg	Sp	Sci	SS
2	99	99	99	98		
3	99	99	99	99		
4	99	99	99	99		
5	99	99	99	99		
6	99	99	99	99		

Santa Rita Elem.

Grade	Rd	Ma	Lg	Sp	Sci	SS
2	99	99	99	99		
3	99	99	99	99		
4	99	99	99	99		
5	99	99	98	98		
6	99	98	98	99		

Springer Elem.

Grade	Rd	Ma	Lg	Sp	Sci	SS
2	99	98	99	98		
3	99	99	99	99		
4	98	98	98	98		
5	99	99	99	99		
6	99	99	99	99		

Los Gatos Union Elem. School Dist.
Blossom Hill Elem.

Grade	Rd	Ma	Lg	Sp	Sci	SS
2	95	92	96	95		
3	98	97	98	98		
4	97	97	96	97		
5	98	98	98	98		

Daves Ave. Elem.

Grade	Rd	Ma	Lg	Sp	Sci	SS
2	98	97	97	94		
3	99	97	99	96		
4	98	98	99	98		
5	95	93	94	91		

Fisher Middle

Grade	Rd	Ma	Lg	Sp	Sci	SS
6	98	96	97	96		
7	97	96	96	95		
8	99	98	98	96		

Lexington Elem.

Grade	Rd	Ma	Lg	Sp	Sci	SS
2	90	92	92	78		
3	93	97	94	89		
4	97	90	94	95		
5	90	90	86	69		

Louise Van Meter Elem.

Grade	Rd	Ma	Lg	Sp	Sci	SS
2	96	92	97	92		
3	97	98	97	94		
4	96	95	96	94		
5	93	93	89	89		

Los Gatos-Saratoga High School Dist.
Los Gatos High

Grade	Rd	Ma	Lg	Sp	Sci	SS
9	99	98	98		99	99
10	99	98	98		99	99
11	99	97	98		99	99

Saratoga High

Grade	Rd	Ma	Lg	Sp	Sci	SS
9	99	99	99		99	99
10	99	99	99		99	99
11	99	99	99		99	99

Scores range from 1-99. A school scoring 75 has done better than 75 percent of other public schools in California.
Key: Rd (read) Ma (math) Lg (Language), Sp (spelling), Sci (science) and SS (social science).

Grade	Rd	Ma	Lg	Sp	Sci	SS
Luther Burbank Elem. School Dist.						
Luther Burbank Elem.						
2	53	46	33	43		
3	51	16	41	38		
4	50	26	53	45		
5	56	49	46	60		
6	41	29	28	39		
7	70	65	58	58		
8	48	37	48	54		
Milpitas Unified School Dist.						
Burnett Elem.						
2	74	72	62	82		
3	73	73	68	78		
4	67	75	70	82		
5	61	67	72	77		
6	69	70	84	88		
Calaveras Hills High (Cont.)						
9	59	60	48		64	50
10	53	43	46		65	69
11	38	13	18		8	38
Curtner Elem.						
2	89	84	80	93		
3	89	94	87	97		
4	86	90	86	94		
5	93	96	91	96		
6	90	94	91	97		
Milpitas High						
9	76	88	79		81	79
10	79	89	82		79	81
11	73	84	78		77	81
Pomeroy Elem.						
2	88	89	83	92		
3	79	79	84	86		
4	91	95	92	93		
5	86	89	88	86		
6	93	94	95	96		
Rancho Milpitas Jr. High						
7	78	86	80	84		
8	77	76	74	80		
Randall Elem.						
2	78	83	62	77		
3	65	80	65	78		
4	71	83	55	77		
5	61	79	73	72		
6	74	73	83	90		
Rose Elem.						
2	77	75	61	82		
3	71	70	67	70		
4	71	63	71	71		
5	63	62	59	80		
6	69	61	69	72		

Grade	Rd	Ma	Lg	Sp	Sci	SS
Russell Jr. High						
7	91	92	91	97		
8	82	85	78	90		
Sinnott Elem.						
2	90	94	84	92		
3	87	88	86	90		
4	85	90	83	87		
5	91	96	92	94		
6	92	94	91	96		
Spangler Elem.						
2	61	58	51	71		
3	63	53	63	63		
4	69	68	68	79		
5	62	57	57	75		
6	82	68	78	84		
Weller Elem.						
2	69	61	56	73		
3	72	70	72	73		
4	74	68	70	78		
5	77	73	76	87		
6	72	74	72	88		
Zanker Elem.						
2	85	78	76	93		
3	81	83	75	85		
4	76	81	84	75		
5	88	92	88	95		
6	76	78	81	84		
Moreland Elem. School Dist.						
Anderson Elem.						
2	65	52	63	70		
3	55	53	58	46		
4	59	58	53	57		
5	62	73	63	64		
Baker Elem.						
2	89	84	88	88		
3	83	78	83	84		
4	82	70	74	82		
5	83	88	85	86		
Castro Middle						
6	88	91	87	89		
7	89	93	89	93		
8	86	85	89	88		
Country Lane Elem.						
2	98	97	95	97		
3	96	92	96	96		
4	96	93	95	96		
5	96	93	96	94		
Easterbrook Elem.						
2	93	87	85	83		
3	91	84	93	94		
4	80	76	82	78		
5	88	84	88	89		

Scores range from 1-99. A school scoring 75 has done better than 75 percent of other public schools in California.
Key: Rd (read) Ma (math) Lg (Language), Sp (spelling), Sci (science) and SS (social science).

Latimer Elem.

Grade	Rd	Ma	Lg	Sp	Sci	SS
2	95	88	91	90		
3	86	89	89	88		
4	86	81	85	85		
5	83	91	81	77		

Moreland Discovery

Grade	Rd	Ma	Lg	Sp	Sci	SS
2	96	96	94	81		
3	99	96	99	93		

Payne Elem.

Grade	Rd	Ma	Lg	Sp	Sci	SS
2	97	99	97	96		
3	86	92	89	93		
4	86	82	87	89		
5	93	93	95	93		

Rogers Middle

Grade	Rd	Ma	Lg	Sp	Sci	SS
6	79	85	86	81		
7	80	91	90	86		
8	83	85	88	87		

Morgan Hill Unified School Dist.

Britton Middle School

Grade	Rd	Ma	Lg	Sp	Sci	SS
7	79	76	73	75		
8	82	79	82	74		
9	86	91	82		88	87

Burnett Elem.

Grade	Rd	Ma	Lg	Sp	Sci	SS
2	78	63	76	74		
3	58	38	58	50		
4	72	58	72	61		
5	63	50	49	47		
6	69	62	69	64		

Central High (Cont.)

Grade	Rd	Ma	Lg	Sp	Sci	SS
10	26	40	5		23	38
11	66	40	55		50	47

El Toro Elem.

Grade	Rd	Ma	Lg	Sp	Sci	SS
2	82	77	84	84		
3	83	78	82	77		
4	88	72	77	66		
5	71	66	67	63		
6	70	69	63	58		

Encinal Elem.

Grade	Rd	Ma	Lg	Sp	Sci	SS
4	90	91	92	92		
5	77	73	71	65		
6	80	76	74	81		

Jackson Elem.

Grade	Rd	Ma	Lg	Sp	Sci	SS
2	66	46	57	56		
3	75	84	73	62		
4	78	76	68	79		
5	75	79	68	67		
6	83	85	76	68		

Live Oak High

Grade	Rd	Ma	Lg	Sp	Sci	SS
10	84	89	81		86	89
11	86	86	82		89	89

Los Paseos Elem.

Grade	Rd	Ma	Lg	Sp	Sci	SS
2	85	82	78	80		
3	86	93	87	85		

Murphy Middle School

Grade	Rd	Ma	Lg	Sp	Sci	SS
7	81	82	78	79		
8	81	82	79	77		
9	91	94	87		93	91

Nordstrom Elem.

Grade	Rd	Ma	Lg	Sp	Sci	SS
2	94	89	94	93		
3	86	78	84	87		
4	78	79	82	80		
5	90	85	87	86		
6	88	94	86	89		

Paradise Valley/Machado Elem.

Grade	Rd	Ma	Lg	Sp	Sci	SS
2	84	82	79	77		
3	91	88	86	80		
4	81	79	78	80		
5	90	85	91	87		
6	87	83	87	85		

San Martin/Gwinn Elem.

Grade	Rd	Ma	Lg	Sp	Sci	SS
2	67	53	61	67		
3	70	61	67	79		
4	75	76	71	68		
5	56	56	60	60		
6	66	51	54	63		

Walsh Elem.

Grade	Rd	Ma	Lg	Sp	Sci	SS
2	64	38	53	71		
3	69	59	66	71		
4	72	62	64	61		
5	64	68	64	57		
6	68	53	57	54		

Mountain View-Los Altos Union High School Dist.

Alta Vista High (Cont.)

Grade	Rd	Ma	Lg	Sp	Sci	SS
9	24					
10	72	64	61		43	52
11	53	24	46		35	46

Los Altos High

Grade	Rd	Ma	Lg	Sp	Sci	SS
9	91	95	93		92	95
10	91	95	94		94	92
11	94	95	94		94	93

Moffett High (Alt.)

Grade	Rd	Ma	Lg	Sp	Sci	SS
9	24					
10	87	70	75		68	86
11	81	38	74		55	65

Mountain View High

Grade	Rd	Ma	Lg	Sp	Sci	SS
9	94	97	93		96	96
10	95	96	95		94	94
11	95	96	95		97	97

Mountain View Elem. School Dist.

Bubb Elem.

Grade	Rd	Ma	Lg	Sp	Sci	SS
2	97	94	98	96		
3	98	95	98	98		
4	96	95	95	94		
5	93	90	91	94		

Scores range from 1-99. A school scoring 75 has done better than 75 percent of other public schools in California.
Key: Rd (read) Ma (math) Lg (Language), Sp (spelling), Sci (science) and SS (social science).

Castro Elem.

Grade	Rd	Ma	Lg	Sp	Sci	SS
2	42	49	33	38		
3	27	24	15	14		
4	47	42	41	33		
5	47	39	40	45		

Graham Middle School

Grade	Rd	Ma	Lg	Sp	Sci	SS
6	75	71	67	71		
7	78	80	76	77		
8	74	80	77	79		

Landels Elem.

Grade	Rd	Ma	Lg	Sp	Sci	SS
2	93	92	97	92		
3	88	84	84	89		
4	87	82	87	90		
5	85	76	82	85		

Slater Elem.

Grade	Rd	Ma	Lg	Sp	Sci	SS
2	85	79	71	69		
3	88	87	82	85		
4	64	68	63	68		
5	69	70	72	64		

Mt. Pleasant Elem. School Dist.

Boeger Jr. High

Grade	Rd	Ma	Lg	Sp	Sci	SS
7	61	59	63	73		
8	69	61	71	77		

Foothill Int.

Grade	Rd	Ma	Lg	Sp	Sci	SS
4	79	87	83	86		
5	56	56	68	65		
6	55	53	62	71		

Mt. Pleasant Elem.

Grade	Rd	Ma	Lg	Sp	Sci	SS
2	44	30	44	41		
3	47	40	39	41		
4	71	65	72	60		

Sanders Elem.

Grade	Rd	Ma	Lg	Sp	Sci	SS
2	55	55	50	63		
3	57	55	48	63		
4	57	65	57	54		

Valle Vista Elem.

Grade	Rd	Ma	Lg	Sp	Sci	SS
2	70	71	73	77		
3	76	69	78	86		
4	80	86	95	87		

Oak Grove Elem. School Dist.

Anderson Elem.

Grade	Rd	Ma	Lg	Sp	Sci	SS
2	57	38	54	53		
3	85	88	76	65		
4	85	87	79	74		
5	86	88	88	91		
6	81	86	79	88		

Baldwin Elem.

Grade	Rd	Ma	Lg	Sp	Sci	SS
2	86	92	79	85		
3	75	78	73	70		
4	81	82	91	84		
5	73	82	68	83		
6	76	85	72	75		

Bernal Int.

Grade	Rd	Ma	Lg	Sp	Sci	SS
7	87	92	89	90		
8	86	95	88	87		

Blossom Valley Elem.

Grade	Rd	Ma	Lg	Sp	Sci	SS
2	96	92	93	93		
3	84	88	83	88		
4	83	85	83	84		
5	75	82	82	88		
6	87	97	90	94		

Christopher Elem.

Grade	Rd	Ma	Lg	Sp	Sci	SS
2	29	10	28	29		
3	35	19	43	38		
4	53	61	53	45		
5	54	52	40	43		
6	54	53	48	49		

Davis Elem.

Grade	Rd	Ma	Lg	Sp	Sci	SS
7	73	74	68	75		
8	66	70	64	68		

Del Roble Elem.

Grade	Rd	Ma	Lg	Sp	Sci	SS
2	64	58	71	63		
3	76	82	80	70		
4	85	91	87	88		
5	60	70	59	69		
6	81	84	83	86		

Edenvale Elem.

Grade	Rd	Ma	Lg	Sp	Sci	SS
2	64	63	61	49		
3	57	73	50	52		
4	62	85	66	61		
5	53	67	54	52		
6	41	60	41	35		

Frost Elem.

Grade	Rd	Ma	Lg	Sp	Sci	SS
2	80	81	88	75		
3	78	80	78	77		
4	62	81	63	68		
5	73	78	75	68		
6	91	95	91	93		

Glider Elem.

Grade	Rd	Ma	Lg	Sp	Sci	SS
2	83	75	78	80		
3	84	78	82	90		
4	88	95	91	88		
5	81	88	88	87		
6	81	85	88	86		

Hayes Elem.

Grade	Rd	Ma	Lg	Sp	Sci	SS
2	90	83	86	89		
3	74	74	75	77		
4	93	94	89	87		
5	79	89	78	86		
6	89	80	86	91		

Herman Int.

Grade	Rd	Ma	Lg	Sp	Sci	SS
7	80	80	80	81		
8	80	89	79	80		

Scores range from 1-99. A school scoring 75 has done better than 75 percent of other public schools in California.
Key: Rd (read) Ma (math) Lg (Language), Sp (spelling), Sci (science) and SS (social science).

Miner Elem.

Grade	Rd	Ma	Lg	Sp	Sci	SS
2	49	60	44	33		
3	52	50	55	38		
4	54	49	58	60		
5	61	69	58	52		
6	60	53	60	53		

Oak Ridge Elem.

Grade	Rd	Ma	Lg	Sp	Sci	SS
2	83	79	82	73		
3	84	77	79	71		
4	75	68	72	73		
5	85	89	88	84		
6	84	91	81	82		

Parkview Elem.

Grade	Rd	Ma	Lg	Sp	Sci	SS
2	90	88	80	89		
3	79	88	74	78		
4	77	87	81	89		
5	80	82	82	87		
6	71	83	74	78		

Sakamoto Elem.

Grade	Rd	Ma	Lg	Sp	Sci	SS
2	85	80	81	83		
3	85	82	83	76		
4	92	89	95	91		
5	85	83	80	82		
6	84	89	81	81		

San Anselmo Elem.

Grade	Rd	Ma	Lg	Sp	Sci	SS
2	77	87	83	77		
3	68	46	67	73		
4	78	71	76	73		
5	82	81	79	73		
6	79	86	79	84		

Santa Teresa Elem.

Grade	Rd	Ma	Lg	Sp	Sci	SS
2	82	94	78	77		
3	76	84	73	74		
4	73	90	77	74		
5	87	91	87	89		
6	77	81	76	77		

Stipe Elem.

Grade	Rd	Ma	Lg	Sp	Sci	SS
2	44	52	40	39		
3	52	55	50	43		
4	52	49	45	41		
5	64	68	65	62		
6	56	71	57	64		

Taylor Elem.

Grade	Rd	Ma	Lg	Sp	Sci	SS
2	92	92	88	87		
3	85	82	73	87		
4	88	88	89	86		
5	79	80	78	83		
6	83	88	88	84		

Orchard Elem. School Dist.

Orchard Elem.

Grade	Rd	Ma	Lg	Sp	Sci	SS
2	47	27	42	47		
3	39	40	39	45		
4	52	42	48	48		
5	45	35	42	45		
6	48	47	38	44		
7	57	40	39	44		
8	50	43	36	56		

Palo Alto Unified School Dist.

Addison Elem.

Grade	Rd	Ma	Lg	Sp	Sci	SS
2	96	94	92	90		
3	99	99	99	99		
4	98	94	97	97		
5	99	98	98	98		

Briones Elem.

Grade	Rd	Ma	Lg	Sp	Sci	SS
2	92	98	93	91		
3	96	90	94	94		
4	97	96	96	96		
5	94	93	91	94		

Duveneck Elem.

Grade	Rd	Ma	Lg	Sp	Sci	SS
2	99	99	99	99		
3	99	97	99	98		
4	99	98	98	97		
5	99	99	99	99		

El Carmelo Elem.

Grade	Rd	Ma	Lg	Sp	Sci	SS
2	98	95	94	95		
3	99	97	97	96		
4	97	96	93	94		
5	99	99	99	99		

Escondido Elem.

Grade	Rd	Ma	Lg	Sp	Sci	SS
2	97	98	96	96		
3	99	98	97	98		
4	99	97	99	99		
5	95	93	95	92		

Fairmeadow Elem.

Grade	Rd	Ma	Lg	Sp	Sci	SS
2	98	99	99	99		
3	97	96	96	95		
4	97	97	96	95		
5	99	99	98	98		

Gunn High

Grade	Rd	Ma	Lg	Sp	Sci	SS
9	99	99	99		99	99
10	99	99	98		99	99
11	99	99	99		99	99

Hays Elem.

Grade	Rd	Ma	Lg	Sp	Sci	SS
2	99	99	99	99		
3	99	99	99	99		
4	99	99	99	99		
5	99	99	99	99		

Scores range from 1-99. A school scoring 75 has done better than 75 percent of other public schools in California.
Key: Rd (read) Ma (math) Lg (Language), Sp (spelling), Sci (science) and SS (social science).

Grade	Rd	Ma	Lg	Sp	Sci	SS	Grade	Rd	Ma	Lg	Sp	Sci	SS
Hoover Elem.							**Broadway High (Cont.)**						
2	99	99	99	99			9	36	33	35		12	15
3	99	99	99	99			10	30	29	27		14	17
4	99	99	99	99			11	43	9	46		12	38
5	99	99	99	99			**Burnett Middle**						
Jordan Middle School							6	24	11	18	23		
6	99	98	98	98			7	37	19	31	34		
7	98	98	98	98			8	32	24	25	38		
8	99	98	98	99			**Carson Elem.**						
Nixon Elem.							2	77	42	76	65		
2	97	98	96	96			3	77	73	74	67		
3	99	95	98	97			4	64	65	63	63		
4	99	99	98	98			5	71	70	75	64		
5	98	99	99	99			**Castillero Middle**						
Ohlone Elem.							6	76	68	66	75		
2	98	94	95	95			7	82	77	81	82		
3	98	91	96	92			8	85	82	84	84		
4	98	92	98	96			**Cory Elem.**						
5	99	98	98	97			2	58	46	53	41		
Palo Alto High							**Darling Elem.**						
9	99	99	99		99	99	2	22	30	15	19		
10	99	99	99		99	99	3	39	40	43	29		
11	99	99	99		99	99	4	36	29	30	46		
Palo Verde Elem.							5	42	39	42	30		
2	99	99	99	99			**Empire Gardens Elem.**						
3	98	99	99	97			2	25	8	33	31		
4	99	97	98	99			3	27	12	24	17		
5	99	99	99	98			4	53	39	37	48		
Stanford Middle							5	40	32	28	43		
6	99	98	97	98			**Erikson Elem.**						
7	98	98	98	99			2	61	27	57	56		
8	98	99	99	98			3	54	16	59	34		
							4	52	42	46	39		
San Jose Unified School Dist.							5	55	54	59	62		
Allen Elem.							**Gardner Elem.**						
2	77	68	59	78			2	19	10	15	17		
3	57	42	47	50			3	52	59	57	43		
4	70	65	58	72			4	32	15	27	31		
5	74	81	76	83			5	58	37	49	59		
Almaden Elem.							**Grant Elem.**						
2	75	86	74	63			2	46	27	36	39		
3	63	61	66	59			3	44	26	39	24		
4	40	37	41	25			4	44	47	46	33		
5	61	54	66	43			5	34	25	38	33		
Bachrodt Elem.							**Graystone Elem.**						
2	27	30	36	35			2	93	86	88	92		
3	42	40	47	43			3	98	95	95	98		
4	34	32	32	25			4	99	99	98	99		
5	38	20	28	35			5	97	98	95	97		
Booksin Elem.							**Gunderson High**						
2	89	88	90	88			9	63	78	69		62	75
3	91	84	87	86			10	64	76	75		65	71
4	84	87	88	87			11	64	71	69		69	73
5	93	86	93	89									

Scores range from 1-99. A school scoring 75 has done better than 75 percent of other public schools in California.
Key: Rd (read) Ma (math) Lg (Language), Sp (spelling), Sci (science) and SS (social science).

Grade	Rd	Ma	Lg	Sp	Sci	SS
Gunderson Plus Cont. High						
10		23				
11	49		25		39	44
Hacienda Sci./Enivronmental Magnet						
2	75	56	74	60		
3	86	68	77	76		
4	82	65	76	76		
5	87	66	71	80		
Hammer Elem.						
2	65	30	47	53		
Harte Middle School						
6	94	94	90	93		
7	95	96	95	95		
8	95	96	94	97		
Hester Elem.						
2	46	25	39	35		
3	45	38	34	34		
4	56	39	46	43		
5	47	33	43	62		
Hoover Middle						
6	44	30	36	44		
7	51	43	46	54		
8	51	47	49	57		
Leland High						
9	96	97	95		97	96
10	97	97	97		97	98
11	97	97	97		97	98
Leland Plus High (Cont.)						
11	63	49	54		58	55
Liberty High						
7	46		15	24		
8	58	21	36	40		
9	58	51	40		54	39
10	60	53	52		63	50
11	58	38	52		66	58
Lincoln High						
9	83	86	82		76	88
10	88	84	88		84	91
11	88	80	88		83	92
Los Alamitos Elem.						
2	93	86	89	89		
3	94	85	89	93		
4	91	90	86	88		
5	90	86	92	94		
Lowell Elem.						
2	9	12	13	29		
3	27	33	34	29		
4	39	23	27	37		
5	36	35	36	35		
Mann Elem.						
2	22	12	10	29		
3	23	7	18	17		
4	34	15		31		
5	61	60	55	55		

Grade	Rd	Ma	Lg	Sp	Sci	SS
Muir Middle						
6	56	51	52	60		
7	58	54	54	54		
8	57	57	56	63		
Olinder Elem.						
2	27	18	24	17		
3	29	7	21	17		
4	17	1	11	13		
5	40	25	36	22		
Pioneer High						
9	84	93	83		90	91
10	77	88	75		79	79
11	79	77	78		79	82
Randol Elem.						
2	*	58	49	46		
3	80	83	79	73		
4	81	88	78	78		
5	80	79	78	84		
Reed Elem.						
2	87	78	87	83		
3	86	78	87	78		
4	89	90	92	84		
5	78	78	81	83		
River Glen Elem.						
2	52	61	58	24		
3	76	71	79	54		
4	66	71	67	45		
5	62	60	75	52		
6	68	73	66	55		
7	70	61	73	61		
San Jose High Acad.						
9	59	71	60		54	62
10	61	68	65		61	64
11	64	63	69		64	72
Schallenberger Elem.						
2	69	58	61	58		
3	81	71	75	62		
4	82	57	76	69		
5	88	79	92	81		
Simonds Elem.						
2	89	90	91	84		
3	90	88	86	84		
4	87	78	86	88		
5	84	74	81	83		
Steinbeck Middle						
6	47	37	38	44		
7	57	60	48	58		
8	54	57	51	52		
Tamien Elem.						
2	17	8	1	5		

Scores range from 1-99. A school scoring 75 has done better than 75 percent of other public schools in California.
Key: Rd (read) Ma (math) Lg (Language), Sp (spelling), Sci (science) and SS (social science).

Terrell Elem.

Grade	Rd	Ma	Lg	Sp	Sci	SS
2	60	58	65	53		
3	75	59	71	71		
4	80	62	73	61		
5	74	75	80	72		

Trace Elem.

Grade	Rd	Ma	Lg	Sp	Sci	SS
3	65	61	61	48		
4	58	64	68	61		
5	67	62	63	54		

Washington Elem.

Grade	Rd	Ma	Lg	Sp	Sci	SS
2	14	12	13	3		
3	8	7	12	5		
4	29	9	32	17		
5	32	23	36	14		

Williams Elem.

Grade	Rd	Ma	Lg	Sp	Sci	SS
2	98	98	97	97		
3	99	99	99	99		
4	98	98	98	98		
5	97	97	97	98		

Willow Glen Elem.

Grade	Rd	Ma	Lg	Sp	Sci	SS
2	71	63	68	54		
3	72	52	68	46		
4	75	60	73	61		
5	61	54	57	57		

Willow Glen High

Grade	Rd	Ma	Lg	Sp	Sci	SS
9	68	74	67		64	74
10	70	77	71		68	76
11	71	65	69		72	75

Willow Glen Middle

Grade	Rd	Ma	Lg	Sp	Sci	SS
6	60	49	59	63		
7	65	57	63	73		
8	67	59	66	74		

Willow Glen Plus High(Cont.)

Grade	Rd	Ma	Lg	Sp	Sci	SS
10		23				
11	71	43	61		47	72

Juvenile Hall/Comm.

Grade	Rd	Ma	Lg	Sp	Sci	SS
7	28	6	6	29		
8	28	10	11	30		
9	33	36	17		22	26
10	41	40	27		30	17
11	38	24	25		35	21

Santa Clara Unified School Dist.

Bowers Elem.

Grade	Rd	Ma	Lg	Sp	Sci	SS
2	72	69	72	67		
3	73	77	64	74		
4	78	73	84	83		
5	68	78	80	72		

Bracher Elem.

Grade	Rd	Ma	Lg	Sp	Sci	SS
2	88	94	90	90		
3	72	68	71	78		
4	66	58	63	68		
5	73	64	72	84		

Braly Elem.

Grade	Rd	Ma	Lg	Sp	Sci	SS
2	65	63	54	70		
3	83	75	82	86		
4	81	80	81	78		
5	78	81	71	77		

Briarwood Elem.

Grade	Rd	Ma	Lg	Sp	Sci	SS
2	75	55	75	77		
3	74	55	67	78		
4	70	64	72	71		
5	74	73	76	86		

Buchser Middle

Grade	Rd	Ma	Lg	Sp	Sci	SS
6	68	60		70		
7	73	77		77		
8	71	69		76		

Cabrillo Middle School

Grade	Rd	Ma	Lg	Sp	Sci	SS
6	57	49	57	70		
7	67	57	64	77		
8	63	68	60	74		

Haman Elem.

Grade	Rd	Ma	Lg	Sp	Sci	SS
2	60	50	61	66		
3	67	24	52	56		
4	74	63	63	72		
5	64	39	51	69		

Hughes Elem.

Grade	Rd	Ma	Lg	Sp	Sci	SS
2	64	58	66	71		
3	82	85	88	86		
4	76	73	86	85		
5	63	59	72	76		

Laurelwood Elem.

Grade	Rd	Ma	Lg	Sp	Sci	SS
2	89	87	88	90		
3	92	83	91	91		
4	89	93	96	94		
5	89	89	90	82		

Mayne Elem.

Grade	Rd	Ma	Lg	Sp	Sci	SS
2	34	23	24	38		
3	37	4	27	24		
4	46	39	35	37		
5	56	52	53	43		

Millikin Elem.

Grade	Rd	Ma	Lg	Sp	Sci	SS
2	99	99	99	99		
3	97	99	99	99		
4	96	97	98	97		
5	94	96	98	96		

Montague Elem.

Grade	Rd	Ma	Lg	Sp	Sci	SS
2	77	81	90	90		
3	73	73	78	91		
4	72	79	80	83		
5	65	64	71	73		

New Valley (Cont.)

Grade	Rd	Ma	Lg	Sp	Sci	SS
9		25				
10	30	43	13		9	22
11	43	33	33		51	38

Scores range from 1-99. A school scoring 75 has done better than 75 percent of other public schools in California.
Key: Rd (read) Ma (math) Lg (Language), Sp (spelling), Sci (science) and SS (social science).

Grade	Rd	Ma	Lg	Sp	Sci	SS
Peterson Middle						
6	79	75	74	76		
7	83	86	80	86		
8	79	86	77	81		
Pomeroy Elem.						
2	90	86	89	93		
3	84	62	74	83		
4	73	65	76	71		
5	72	75	76	75		
Ponderosa Elem.						
2	76	74	75	83		
3	85	84	85	83		
4	86	81	92	92		
5	88	81	87	89		
Santa Clara High						
9	75	83	83		78	78
10	78	90	79		82	84
11	74	80	78		78	82
Scott Lane Elem.						
2	46	18	44	47		
3	63	42	50	47		
4	46	47	41	53		
5	45	45	48	55		
Sutter Elem.						
2	72	77	81	79		
3	86	87	85	77		
4	82	67	80	82		
5	77	61	75	68		
Washington Elem.						
2	80	77	69	58		
3	85	71	78	72		
4	88	82	80	76		
5	97	84	95	92		
Westwood Elem.						
2	66	56	69	63		
3	74	52	69	62		
4	80	63	83	77		
5	79	75	85	73		
Wilcox High						
9	75	83	85		75	78
10	75	86	84		77	80
11	73	81	82		75	80
Wilson Alt.						
7		56	48	75		
8	61	49	44	54		
9	69	59	61		57	55
10	81	71	71		68	69
11	72	55	67		64	63

Grade	Rd	Ma	Lg	Sp	Sci	SS
Saratoga Union Elem. School Dist.						
Argonaut Elem.						
2	99	99	99	99		
3	99	99	99	99		
4	99	99	99	99		
5	99	99	99	99		
Foothill Elem.						
2	98	99	98	98		
3	99	99	99	99		
4	97	98	98	99		
5	98	99	98	98		
Redwood Middle						
6	98	99	99	99		
7	99	99	99	99		
8	99	99	99	99		
Saratoga Elem.						
2	99	98	99	98		
3	99	99	99	99		
4	99	98	99	98		
5	99	99	100	99		
Sunnyvale Elem. School Dist.						
Bishop Elem.						
2	75	71	74	75		
3	78	88	86	85		
4	68	83	79	73		
5	80	89	88	82		
Cherry Chase Elem.						
2	97	94	97	95		
3	87	85	85	83		
4	70	79	68	65		
5	75	74	59	71		
Columbia Middle						
6	67	68	69	76		
7	69	65	71	73		
8	66	64	62	72		
Cumberland Elem.						
2	78	88	78	78		
3	90	91	89	87		
4	96	96	97	98		
5	97	98	98	98		
Ellis Elem.						
2	87	92	92	90		
3	79	95	86	92		
4	71	90	76	76		
5	77	91	81	78		
Fairwood Elem.						
2	75	64	57	80		
3	49	58	57	73		
4	73	77	76	78		
5	77	79	88	83		

Scores range from 1-99. A school scoring 75 has done better than 75 percent of other public schools in California.
Key: Rd (read) Ma (math) Lg (Language), Sp (spelling), Sci (science) and SS (social science).

Grade	Rd	Ma	Lg	Sp	Sci	SS
Lakewood Elem.						
2	67	76	69	75		
3	72	71	76	87		
4	78	88	78	86		
5	85	85	82	89		
San Miguel Elem.						
2	86	84	88	92		
3	81	89	91	91		
4	85	95	96	93		
5	77	89	88	88		
Sunnyvale Middle						
6	85	91	89	90		
7	85	87	90	91		
8	88	91	87	89		
Vargas Elem.						
2	85	88	80	84		
3	73	65	73	76		
4	70	69	77	78		
5	87	81	88	87		

Union Elem. School Dist.
Alta Vista Elem.

Grade	Rd	Ma	Lg	Sp	Sci	SS
2	95	91	95	96		
3	98	97	99	96		
4	97	93	98	97		
5	97	97	97	97		
Athenour Elem.						
2	88	82	93	90		
3	91	78	91	81		
4	81	82	83	82		
5	89	78	86	89		
Carlton Elem.						
2	91	90	91	84		
3	98	98	98	94		
4	88	88	89	86		
5	94	91	93	91		
Dartmouth Middle						
6	84	82	89	86		
7	92	86	90	88		
8	90	86	90	91		
Guadalupe Elem.						
2	95	95	95	96		
3	98	95	97	96		
4	93	92	90	92		
5	96	97	99	98		
Lietz Elem.						
2	87	78	83	87		
3	91	89	91	93		
4	89	88	86	86		
5	83	79	88	85		

Grade	Rd	Ma	Lg	Sp	Sci	SS
Lone Hill Elem.						
2	96	96	94	93		
3	97	91	96	95		
4	90	87	92	85		
5	89	83	87	89		
Noddin Elem.						
2	95	97	95	95		
3	98	99	98	98		
4	92	95	95	94		
5	94	93	91	93		
Oster Elem.						
2	89	77	87	84		
3	91	80	88	85		
4	88	75	86	82		
5	87	87	93	92		
Union Middle						
6	91	87	85	85		
7	94	94	89	88		
8	90	94	88	91		

Whisman Elem. School Dist.
Crittenden Middle

Grade	Rd	Ma	Lg	Sp	Sci	SS
5	73	62	68	75		
6	75	70	69	75		
7	78	71	77	82		
8	80	69	80	82		
Monta Loma Elem.						
2	76	74	77	75		
3	78	66	73	74		
4	76	54	79	80		
Theuerkauf Elem.						
2	70	63	74	78		
3	78	69	83	85		
4	85	64	76	77		
Whisman Elem.						
2	83	74	80	83		
3	79	79	74	83		
4	82	72	86	82		

Chapter **3**

SANTA CLARA COUNTY

How Public Schools Work

SCORES MEASURE ACADEMIC success but they have their shortcomings. Some students know the material but are not adept at taking tests and some tests are so poorly designed that they fail to assess what has been taught. The rankings in the previous chapter do not break out students as individuals. A basic exam tests the least the children should know, not the most. Scores cannot assess goodness, kindness or wisdom or predict how helpful students will be to society.

There are other legitimate criticisms of probably every test given to California school children. Nonetheless, the tests have their value and except for a few cases probably give an accurate picture of how the schools are doing academically. Students who do well in elementary school generally do well in high school and score high on the SAT and go on to succeed in college. With rare exceptions, the scores correlate with teacher assessments, and so on. The exceptions cannot be ignored. A student who does poorly in one educational arrangement may thrive in another.

When your children attend a school with high test scores, they are not assured of success. These schools have their failures. Neither can you be certain that your children will get the best teachers or the right programs. Other schools with lower scores might do better on these points. What you can be certain of is that your children are entering a setting that has proven successful for many students.

The main problem with making sense out of scores concerns what is called socioeconomics, a theory educators love, hate and widely believe.

Socioeconomics

In its crudest form, socioeconomics means rich kids score high, middle-class kids score about the middle and poor kids score low. Not all the time, not predictably by individual. Many children from poor and middle-class homes succeed in school and attend the best colleges. But as a general rule socioeconomics enjoys much statistical support.

Compare the rankings in the preceding chapter with income by cities. Los Altos Hills and Los Gatos, rich or well-to-do, high scores; Alum Rock Elemen-

Scholastic Aptitude Test (SAT) Scores

High School	*Enrollment	No. Tested	Verbal	Math
Cupertino	301	144	519	583
Del Mar	280	84	503	513
Fremont	438	132	476	522
Gilroy	427	125	489	500
Gunderson	237	64	492	521
Gunn	333	313	598	641
Hill	424	159	434	472
Homestead	422	265	534	588
Independence	870	371	449	480
Leigh	383	149	540	559
Leland	412	296	551	591
Lick	264	65	450	470
Lincoln	309	120	530	514
Live Oak	601	235	521	543
Los Altos	322	206	557	588
Los Gatos	345	240	563	580
Lynbrook	332	248	577	636
Milpitas	549	263	484	523
Monta Vista	449	346	576	652
Mt. Pleasant	430	142	466	492
Mountain View	262	191	554	597
Oak Grove	532	185	485	522
Overfelt	381	112	443	481
Palo Alto	305	269	593	629
Piedmont Hills	401	177	482	518
Pioneer	264	100	496	526
Prospect	340	140	528	552
San Jose	178	77	498	506
Santa Clara	348	141	467	510
Santa Teresa	500	202	516	532
Saratoga	268	231	590	636
Silver Creek	481	190	454	503
Westmont	312	125	543	564
Wilcox	405	185	469	530
Willow Glen	206	42	488	494
Yerba Buena	407	109	433	505
County	15,069	6,457	**519	**557

Source: California Dept. of Education, 1997-98 tests. SAT scores are greatly influenced by who and how many take the test. The state education department has been pushing schools to have more students take the SAT. A school that has more marginal students taking the test will, by one line of reasoning, be doing a good job, but the scores are likely to be lower. *Senior class. **County Average

tary School District (East San Jose), low income or poor, low scores; Morgan Hill and Milpitas, middle-class towns, middling scores. The SAT scores reflect the basic test scores.

The same pattern shows up in Alameda County. The schools in the poorer neighborhoods of Oakland score low; well-to-do Piedmont scores high. And the pattern shows up around the Bay Area, the country and in other countries. The federal study, "Japanese Education Today," notes a "solid correlation

Top SAT math scores
22 public high schools in California scoring over 600 in math

High School	County	City	Math
Albany	Alameda	Albany	603
Mission San Jose	Alameda	Fremont	616
Piedmont	Alameda	Piedmont	613
Acalanes	Contra Costa	Lafayette	600
Campolindo	Contra Costa	Moraga	610
Miramonte	Contra Costa	Orinda	610
Cerritos	Los Angeles	Cerritos	604
Whitney	Los Angeles	Cerritos	680
Arcadia	Los Angeles	Arcadia	619
La Cañada	Los Angeles	La Cañada	619
Palos Verdes	Los Angeles	Rolling Hills Est.	618
San Marino	Los Angeles	San Marino	626
South Pasadena	Los Angeles	South Pasadena	601
Sunny Hills	Orange	Fullerton	613
University	Orange	Irvine	637
Mira Loma	Sacramento	Sacramento	603
Lynbrook	Santa Clara	San Jose	636
Monta Vista	Santa Clara	Cupertino	652
Saratoga	Santa Clara	Saratoga	636
Gunn	Santa Clara	Palo Alto	641
Palo Alto	Santa Clara	Palo Alto	629
Lowell	San Francisco	San Francisco	620

Source: California Dept. of Education, 1997-98 tests.

between poverty and poor school performance ...."

Family and Culture

In its refined form, socioeconomics moves away from the buck and toward culture and family influence.

Note the chart on Page 21. The towns with the highest number of college educated are generally also the towns with the highest scores. If your mom or dad attended college, chances are you will attend college or do well at school because in a thousand ways while you were growing up they and their milieu pushed you in this direction. Emphasis on "chances are." Nothing is certain when dealing with human beings.

What if mom and dad never got beyond the third grade? Or can't even speak English? Historically, many poor and immigrant children have succeeded at school because their parents badgered, bullied and encouraged them every step of the way and made sacrifices so they would succeed. Asian kids are the latest example of poor kids succeeding but we can also point to the children of peasant Europeans and Africans brought to this country as slaves.

Does it make a difference if the child is English proficient? Immigrant children unfamiliar with English will have more difficulties with literature and language-proficient courses than native-born children. They will need extra or special help in schools.

National Scholastic Aptitude Test (SAT) Scores

State	*Tested (%)	Verbal	Math
Alabama	8	562	558
Alaska	52	521	520
Arizona	32	525	528
Arkansas	6	568	555
California	**47**	**497**	**516**
Colorado	31	537	542
Connecticut	80	510	509
Delaware	70	501	493
Dist. of Columbia	83	488	476
Florida	52	500	501
Georgia	64	486	482
Hawaii	55	483	513
Idaho	16	545	544
Illinois	13	564	581
Indiana	59	497	500
Iowa	5	593	601
Kansas	9	582	585
Kentucky	13	547	550
Louisiana	8	562	558
Maine	68	504	501
Maryland	65	506	508
Massachusetts	77	508	508
Michigan	11	558	569
Minnesota	9	585	598
Mississippi	4	562	549
Missouri	8	570	573
Montana	24	543	546
Nebraska	8	565	571
Nevada	33	510	513
New Hampshire	74	523	520
New Jersey	79	497	508
New Mexico	12	554	551
New York	76	495	503
North Carolina	62	490	492
North Dakota	5	590	599
Ohio	24	536	540
Oklahoma	8	568	564
Oregon	53	528	528
Pennsylvania	71	497	495
Rhode Island	72	501	495
South Carolina	61	478	473
South Dakota	5	584	581
Tennessee	13	564	557
Texas	51	494	501
Utah	4	572	570
Vermont	71	508	504
Virginia	66	507	499
Washington	53	524	526
West Virginia	18	525	513
Wisconsin	7	581	594
Wyoming	10	548	546
Nationwide	**43**	**505**	**512**

Source: California Dept. of Education, 1998 tests. This chart includes public and private schools and differs slightly from the preceding chart, which presents only public school scores. *Percentage of class taking the test.

Nonetheless, the home-school correlation retains much validity: The stronger the educational support the child receives at home, the better he or she will do at school.

Role of Schools

If you carry the logic of socioeconomics too far, you come to the conclusion that schools and teachers and teaching methods don't matter: Students succeed or fail according to their family or societal backgrounds.

Just not the case. No matter how dedicated or well-intentioned the parent, if the teacher is grossly inept the child probably will learn little. If material or textbooks are out-of-date or inaccurate, what the student learns will be useless or damaging. Conversely, if the teacher is dedicated and knowledgeable, if the material is well-presented and appropriate, what the child comes away with will be helpful and, to society, more likely to be beneficial. Almost every one of us can recall a favorite teacher who worked with us and influenced our lives.

The late Albert Shanker, president of the American Federation of Teachers, argued that U.S. students would improve remarkably if schools refused to tolerate disruptive behavior, if national or state academic standards were adopted, if external agencies (not the schools themselves) tested students and if colleges and employers, in admissions and hiring, rewarded academic achievement and penalized failure. These four reforms do little or nothing to address socioeconomics but many educators believe they have merit.

Admittedly, however, this is a contentious area. Theories abound as to what is wrong with our schools and what should be done to fix them.

Where the Confusion Enters

It's very difficult, if not impossible, to separate the influence of home and schools.

When scores go up, often principals or superintendents credit this or that instructional program, or extra efforts by teachers.

But the scores may have risen because mom and dad cracked down on excessive TV. Or a city with old and faded low-income housing (low scores) approves a high-end development. The new residents are more middle class, more demographically inclined to push their kids academically.

One last joker-in-the-deck, mobility. Johnny is doing great at his school, which has low to middling scores, but programs that seem to be working. And his family is doing better. Mom has a job, Dad a promotion. What does the family do? It moves. Happens all the time in the U.S.A. and this also makes precise interpretation of scores difficult.

Back to Scores

If a school's scores are middling, it may still be capable of doing an excellent job, if it has dedicated teachers and sound programs. The middling scores may reflect socioeconomics, not instructional quality.

Don't judge us by our overall scores, many schools say. Judge us by our ability to deliver for your son or daughter.

This gets tricky because children do influence one another and high-income parents often interact differently with schools than low-income parents. To some extent, the school must structure its programs to the abilities of the students. But schools with middling and middling-plus grades can point to many successes.

Basic Instruction-Ability Grouping

California and American schools attempt to meet the needs of students by providing a good basic education and by addressing individual and subgroup needs by special classes and ability grouping.

In the first six years in an average school, children receive some special help according to ability but for the most part they share the same class experiences and get the same instruction.

About the seventh grade, until recently, students were divided into classes for low achievers, middling students and high achievers, or low-middle and advanced — tracking. Texts, homework and expectations were different for each group. The high achievers were on the college track, the low, the vocational.

Pressured by the state, schools are curtailing this practice, but many schools retain accelerated English and math classes for advanced seventh and eighth graders. Parents can always request a transfer from one group to another (whether they can get it is another matter). The reality often is, however, that remedial and middle children can't keep pace with the high achievers.

In the last 30 years or so schools introduced into the early grades special programs aimed at low achievers or children with learning difficulties. Although they vary greatly, these programs typically pull the children out of class for instruction in small groups then return them to the regular class.

Many schools also pull out gifted (high I.Q.) students and a few cluster them in their own classes.

College Influence

So many local students attend the University of California and California State University schools that public and private high schools must of necessity teach the classes demanded by these institutions.

So the typical high school will have a prep program that meets University of California requirements. The school also will offer general education classes in math and English but these will not be as tough as the prep courses and will not be recognized by the state universities. And usually the school will teach some trades so those inclined can secure jobs upon graduation.

California College Admissions of Public School Graduates

High School	UC	CSU	Com	Total
Cupertino	40	23	137	200
Del Mar	15	29	123	167
Fremont	24	21	139	184
Gilroy	17	22	190	229
Gunderson	8	28	88	124
Gunn	77	21	64	162
Hill	18	69	78	165
Homestead	90	28	164	282
Independence	43	109	1,042	1,194
Leigh	21	45	188	254
Leland	99	53	133	285
Lick	3	25	61	89
Lincoln	14	35	83	132
Live Oak	36	48	245	329
Los Altos	61	25	93	179
Los Gatos	51	36	120	207
Lynbrook	108	26	89	223
Milpitas	50	62	187	299
Monta Vista	136	49	139	324
Mt. Pleasant	21	32	78	131
Mtn. View	46	34	105	185
Oak Grove	23	39	163	225
Overfelt	10	42	79	131
Palo Alto	76	23	60	159
Piedmont Hills	26	58	176	260
Pioneer	14	27	99	140
Prospect	16	22	147	185
San Jose	9	25	53	87
Santa Clara	19	48	157	224
Santa Teresa	30	46	191	267
Saratoga	81	24	48	153
Silver Creek	18	67	124	209
Westmont	19	29	131	179
Wilcox	30	33	165	228
Willow Glen	24	28	93	145
Yerba Buena	11	48	122	181

Source: California Department of Education. The chart lists the local public high schools and shows how many students they advanced in 1997 into California public colleges and universities. The state does not track graduates enrolling in private or out-of-state colleges. Continuation schools not included in list. Key: UC (University of California system); CSU (Cal State system); Com (Community Colleges); Total (total number of graduates attending California colleges).

Can a school with mediocre or even low basic scores field a successful college prep program? With comprehensive programs, the answer is yes.

How "Mediocre" Schools Succeed — College Admissions

Freshmen attending a California State University, a public community college or a University of California (Berkeley, Los Angeles, San Diego, Davis, etc.) are asked to identify their high schools. In this way and others, the state finds out how many students individual high schools are advancing to college.

The chart on the previous page breaks out the high schools in Santa Clara County (data collected fall 1997) and shows how many students from each school went on to the public colleges. For an idea of the size of the graduating class, see the SAT chart on Page 65.

The UCs generally restrict themselves to the top 13 percent in the state. The Cal States take the top third.

Every school on the chart is graduating kids into college but obviously some are more successful at it than others. Does this mean that the 'lesser" schools have awful teachers or misguided programs? We have no idea. It simply may be demographics at work.

Parents with college ambitions for their children should find out as much as possible about prospective schools and their programs and make sure that their kids get into the college-track classes.

Where does the chart mislead? For starters, the Cal States and UCs run on academics, the community colleges run on academics and vocational classes. Just because a student attends a community college does not mean he or she is pursuing a bachelor's degree.

Secondly, students who qualify for a Cal State or even a UC often take their freshman and sophomore years at a community college. It's cheaper and closer to home. The chart suggests that middle- and low-income communities send more kids proportionally to community colleges than high-income towns.

To attract minority students, the universities, in some instances, have modified their admission policies, a practice that has critics and supporters. The numbers mentioned previously and listed in the accompanying chart may not consist of the top students. This policy, because of a recently passed state initiative, is being changed.

The chart does not track private colleges. It doesn't tell us how many local students went to Mills College or the University of San Francisco or Stanford or Harvard. Or public colleges out of the state.

Many college students drop out. These numbers are not included.

The chart does confirm the influence of socioeconomics: the rich towns, the educated towns or neighborhoods, send more kids to the UCs than the poorer ones.

But socioeconomics does not sweep the field. Not every student from a high-scoring school goes on to college. Many students from low- and middle-income towns come through.

Dissatisfaction

If high schools can deliver on college education and train students for

Assessing High Schools

The California Department of Education recently put together a new assessment package for public high schools. The chart on the opposite page presents the new assessment tools. All the numbers are in percentile rankings, comparing California high schools against one another. The highest ranking is 99, the lowest 1.

• **A-F.** High schools teach a variety of academic courses but not all count toward meeting the admission requirements of the University of California or California State universities. Those that do are termed "A -F." A high number indicates that as a percentage of school enrollment, many students are enrolled in college-prep courses.

• **National Average.** Based on scores from Scholastic Assessment Test (SAT) and American College Testing, tests designed to measure ability to do college work. This assessment breaks out scores above the national average, then ranks the numbers from each California public school. A high number suggests that students are scoring high on these tests (compared to other California students).

• **AP.** Top-notch high school students often take Advanced Placement (AP) or International Baccalaureate exams. A high number in these rankings suggests that the school offers many tough courses and has many top students (as compared to other high schools).

Contradictions: A school with high National Average figures and high Advanced Placement figures but middling college-bound figures (see other charts in this chapter) may be sending many students to out-of-state colleges or private institutions. The highest-scoring schools usually are located in the high-income towns; parents would have the means to send the kids out of state or to USC, Stanford, etc. The state has sparse data on students who attend private or out-of-state colleges. For a more rounded picture of an individual school, see the rankings in the previous chapters.

vocations, why are so many people dissatisfied with public schools? These schools can cite other accomplishments: Textbooks and curriculums have been improved, the dropout rate has been decreased and proficiency tests have been adopted to force high school students to meet minimum academic standards.

Yet almost every year or so, some group releases a study showing many California children are scoring below expectations or doing poorly as compared to Japanese or European children.

Employers report that many high school grads are unable to understand

High School Assessments

High School	A-F	Nat. Avg.	AP
Cupertino	62	85	81
Del Mar	38	57	67
Fremont	81	63	31
Gilroy	18	39	35
Gunderson	43	34	62
Gunn	94	99	99
Hill	20	22	64
Homestead	93	94	88
Independence	44	39	62
Leigh	52	72	81
Leland	91	96	96
Lick	28	19	41
Lincoln	40	52	87
Live Oak	55	62	37
Los Altos	84	95	97
Los Gatos	93	97	97
Lynbrook	94	98	96
Milpitas	38	70	59
Monta Vista	91	98	96
Mt. Pleasant	51	28	49
Mtn. View	73	94	96
Oak Grove	93	46	57
Overfelt	35	21	49
Palo Alto	95	98	98
Piedmont Hills	62	54	54
Pioneer	54	68	71
Prospect	51	53	73
San Jose	29	34	80
Santa Clara	77	60	66
Santa Teresa	71	68	65
Saratoga	96	99	99
Silver Creek	19	33	59
Westmont	63	61	70
Wilcox	37	69	69
Willow Glen	44	46	76
Yerba Buena	89	30	17

Source: California Department of Education, High School Performance Report, 1996-97.

instructions or write competently. Colleges complain that honor high school students often need remedial math and English.

The California system is expensive, over $30 billion annually for just the kindergarten-through-twelfth schools.

Comparisons between countries are tricky. If Japanese or European high school students fail or do poorly on their tests, they are often denied admission to college. Those who do well, however, are marked not only for college but the higher-paying jobs. Our system gives second and third chances and allows

UCs Chosen by Public School Graduates

School	Berk	Davis	Irv	UCLA	SD	SB	River	SC	Total
Cupertino	14	14	0	2	3	4	0	3	40
Del Mar	2	3	2	0	1	4	0	3	15
Fremont	2	6	1	4	2	5	0	4	24
Gilroy	1	3	1	0	0	8	0	4	17
Gunderson	1	4	0	0	0	1	0	2	8
Gunn	27	14	3	5	13	9	3	3	77
Hill	1	6	1	1	2	2	2	3	18
Homestead	19	16	4	14	10	16	2	9	90
Independence	3	16	4	7	2	1	3	7	43
Leigh	6	3	0	2	2	1	2	5	21
Leland	28	20	1	15	17	12	3	3	99
Lick	0	1	0	0	0	0	0	2	3
Lincoln	0	3	1	1	3	0	0	6	14
Live Oak	5	11	2	5	5	7	1	0	36
Los Altos	11	6	0	11	17	9	0	7	61
Los Gatos	7	14	0	6	5	13	0	6	51
Lynbrook	40	18	6	17	15	6	5	1	108
Milpitas	6	17	8	2	5	4	3	5	50
Monta Vista	33	18	5	13	31	20	9	7	136
Mt. Pleasant	4	4	1	5	1	2	1	3	21
Mtn. View	13	9	0	6	11	4	0	3	46
Oak Grove	7	10	1	3	0	1	0	1	23
Overfelt	3	1	1	2	0	1	0	2	10
Palo Alto	17	8	2	9	11	16	0	13	76
Piedmont Hills	3	6	1	7	2	4	1	2	26
Pioneer	1	1	0	4	1	5	0	2	14
Prospect	6	3	1	1	0	1	1	3	16
San Jose	0	4	0	1	0	0	1	3	9
Santa Clara	3	5	4	3	0	3	0	1	19
Santa Teresa	4	12	1	7	1	2	2	1	30
Saratoga	25	15	3	10	16	5	3	4	81
Silver Creek	1	5	1	5	1	0	0	5	18
Westmont	1	5	0	2	2	5	0	4	19
Wilcox	6	6	3	3	2	2	2	6	30
Willow Glen	2	4	1	4	0	3	0	10	24
Yerba Buena	4	3	0	2	0	0	1	1	11

Source: California Dept. of Education. The chart shows the University of California choices of 1997 local public high school graduates. The state does not track graduates enrolling in private colleges or out-of-state colleges. **Key**: Berk (Berkeley), Irv (Irvine), SD (San Diego), SB (Santa Barbara), River (Riverside), SC (Santa Cruz).

easy admission to colleges, but bears down on students during college and after they graduate. Then they have to prove themselves at work to get ahead, and this forces many to return to college or get training. Their system pressures teenagers; ours pressures young adults. Some studies suggest that by age 30 the differences even out.

As intriguing as this theory is, many parents and teachers would feel much better if the learning curve showed a sharper rise for the high-school scholars and, of course, our top universities — Cal, Stanford, Harvard — demand top scores for admission.

Registering For School

To get into kindergarten, your child must turn five before Dec. 3 of the year he or she enters the grade.

For first grade, your child must be six before Dec. 3. If he is six on Dec. 4, if she is a mature Jan. 6 birthday girl, speak to the school. There may be some wiggle room.

For registration, you are required to show proof of immunization for polio, diphtheria, hepatitis B, tetanus, pertussis (whooping cough), measles, rubella and mumps. If the kid is seven or older, you can skip mumps and whooping cough.

Register Early

Just because you enroll your child first does not necessarily mean that you will get your first choice of schools or teachers.

But in some school districts first-come does mean first-served. Enrollment and transfer policies change from year to year in some districts, depending on the number of children enrolled and the space available. When new schools are opened, attendance boundaries are often changed.

Even if the school district says, "There's plenty of time to register," do it as soon as possible. If a dispute arises over attendance — the school might get an unexpected influx of students — early registration might give you a leg up in any negotiations. Persistence sometimes helps in trying for transfers.

Choosing the "Right" School

Almost all public schools have attendance zones, usually the immediate neighborhood. The school comes with the neighborhood; often you have no choice. Your address determines your school.

Always call the school district to find out what school your children will be attending. Sometimes school districts change attendance boundaries and do not inform local Realtors. Sometimes crowding forces kids out of their neighborhood schools. It's always good to go to the first source.

Just say something like, "I'm Mrs. Jones and we're thinking about moving into 1234 Main Street. What school will my six-year-old attend?"

Ask what elementary school your child will attend and what middle school and high school. In Santa Clara County, many children attend elementary and middle school or junior high in one school district then move up to a high school in a different district.

Keep in mind that although a district scores high, not all the schools in the district may score high. In some districts, scores vary widely.

Several districts may serve one town, another reason to nail down your

Cal States Chosen by Public School Graduates

School	Cal Poly	Chico	Hay	Sac	S.D.	S.F.	S.J.	Son	Fres
Cupertino	0	1	0	0	0	3	14	2	0
Del Mar	6	1	0	0	0	4	14	1	1
Fremont	2	0	0	0	2	0	16	0	0
Gilroy	4	4	0	0	1	0	5	4	1
Gunderson	1	0	1	1	2	1	19	0	1
Gunn	0	1	0	0	6	2	4	3	1
Hill	2	0	1	0	2	0	63	0	1
Homestead	1	5	1	0	5	2	12	1	0
Independence	6	0	1	3	1	1	93	1	0
Leigh	3	5	0	1	7	1	20	0	0
Leland	7	6	0	1	5	2	29	0	1
Lick	4	0	0	0	0	1	18	0	2
Lincoln	0	3	3	0	0	0	25	0	0
Live Oak	7	9	0	0	9	2	15	1	0
Los Altos	7	5	0	0	2	1	6	1	1
Los Gatos	11	6	0	2	6	1	5	1	0
Lynbrook	2	3	0	0	1	4	11	3	0
Milpitas	5	2	1	1	4	2	41	3	0
Monta Vista	9	6	0	0	12	3	10	1	0
Mt. Pleasant	1	1	0	0	3	1	25	0	1
Mtn. View	6	3	0	0	8	3	10	1	0
Oak Grove	0	3	1	0	3	1	25	0	2
Overfelt	1	0	1	0	0	1	38	0	0
Palo Alto	7	5	0	0	0	1	6	1	0
Piedmont Hills	3	0	1	0	0	6	43	1	0
Pioneer	3	3	0	0	0	2	15	1	2
Prospect	2	1	0	1	2	0	13	1	0
San Jose	1	1	0	0	0	1	20	0	0
Santa Clara	7	5	0	1	1	1	30	0	0
Santa Teresa	3	4	0	0	3	2	31	1	1
Saratoga	5	2	0	0	7	0	6	2	0
Silver Creek	0	0	0	1	0	5	57	0	0
Westmont	4	3	0	3	0	1	14	0	2
Wilcox	2	1	0	1	2	1	25	1	0
Willow Glen	1	0	0	0	0	2	21	2	0
Yerba Buena	3	0	1	0	0	1	43	0	0

Source: California Dept. of Education. The chart shows the most popular choices of 1997 local public high school graduates. The chart does not include all Cal State universities. The state does not track graduates enrolling in private or out-of-state colleges. Continuation schools not included in list. Key: Cal Poly (San Luis Obispo), Hay (Hayward), Sac (Sacramento), S.D. (San Diego), S.F. (San Francisco), S.J. (San Jose), Son (Sonoma), Fres (Fresno).

school of attendance.

Transfers

If you don't like your neighborhood school, you can request a transfer to another school in the district or to a school outside the district. But the school won't provide transportation.

Dropout Rates — High School Districts

District	*1995	*1996	*1997	**No.
Campbell	3%	3%	3%	172
East Side	5%	8%	4%	926
Fremont	2%	2%	2%	167
Gilroy	8%	5%	3%	62
Los Gatos-Saratoga	***0%	***0%	***0%	6
Milpitas	1%	1%	2%	44
Morgan Hill	3%	4%	4%	102
Mt.View-Los Altos	1%	***0%	***0%	5
Palo Alto	***0%	1%	1%	15
San Jose	2%	2%	1%	106
Santa Clara	7%	1%	1%	44
County	3%	4%	3%	1,699

Source: California Dept. of Education. *Percentages are single-year droput rate; includes grades 9-12. **No. is the actual number of dropouts in 1997. ***Less than 0.5%. NA (not available).

Transfers to schools inside the district are easier to get than transfers outside the district. New laws supposedly make it easier to transfer children to other districts. In reality, the more popular (high scoring) districts and schools, lacking space, rarely — very rarely — accept "outside" students.

A few parents use the address of a friend or relative to smuggle their child into a high-scoring school or district. Some districts make an effort to ferret out these students and give them the boot.

If your child has a special problem that may demand your attention, speak to the school administrators about a transfer to a school close to your job. If your child's ethnicity adds some diversity to a school or district, it might bend its rules. Never hurts to ask.

Does a Different School Make a Difference?

This may sound like a dumb question but it pays to understand some of the thinking behind choosing one school or school district over another. Two stories:

Researching earlier editions, we contacted a school district (not in this county) that refused to give us test results. This stuff is public information. By law, we (and you) should be able to obtain it routinely.

In so many words, the school administrator said, look, our scores are lousy because our demographics are awful: low income, parents poorly educated, etc. But our programs and staff are great. I'm not giving out the scores because parents will get the wrong idea about our district and keep their kids out of our schools (He later changed his mind and gave us the scores.)

Second story, while working as a reporter, one of our editors covered a large urban school district and heard about a principal who was considered top

(Continued on page 80)

School Accountability Report Card

Want more information about a particular school or school district?

Every public school and district in the state is required by law to issue an annual School Accountability Report Card. The everyday name is the SARC report or the SARC card. SARCs are supposed to include:

• The ethnic makeup of the school and school district.

• Test results. The results may be presented in several ways but almost without exception the formats follow the presentation methods of the California Dept. of Education.

• Dropout rates for high schools.

• A description of the curriculum and the programs.

• Class sizes, teacher-pupil ratios.

• Description of the teaching staff. How many have teaching credentials.

• Description of facilities.

To obtain a SARC, call the school and if the person answering the phone can't help you, ask for the superintendent's secretary or the curriculum department. Some schools want you to pick up the report in person; others will mail it to you. It sometimes helps if you mail the school a stamped, self-addressed envelope or simply $3 worth of stamps and a cover letter. If you don't know the name of the neighborhood school, start with the school district. Here are the phone numbers:

Alum Rock Union Elementary	(408) 928-6800
Berryessa Union Elementary	(408) 923-1800
Cambrian Elementary	(408) 377-2103

(Continued on page 80)

School Districts, opposite page. Unified school districts include elementary, middle and high schools, the whole ball of wax. Palo Alto, San Jose, Santa Clara, Morgan Hill and Gilroy run unified districts. In the other arrangements, elementary school districts, as individual political agencies, educate the children up to the eighth grade. Then the students move up to high schools run by high school districts, also politically independent. For example, students from Los Altos, Mountain View and Whisman elementary districts move up to high schools in the Mountain View/Los Altos High School District. Attendance policies vary by district. For information about attendance, call the school districts.

Santa Clara County

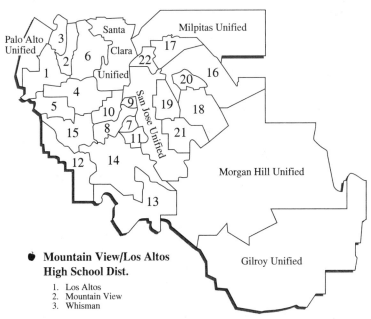

ELEMENTARY, HIGH SCHOOL & UNIFIED SCHOOL DISTRICTS

Palo Alto Unified

Santa Clara Unified

Milpitas Unified

San Jose Unified

Morgan Hill Unified

Gilroy Unified

Mountain View/Los Altos High School Dist.

1. Los Altos
2. Mountain View
3. Whisman

Fremont Union High School Dist.

4. Cupertino
5. Montebello
6. Sunnyvale

Campbell High School Dist.

7. Cambrian
8. Campbell
9. Luthur Burbank
10. Moreland
11. Union

Los Gatos-Saratoga School Dist.

12. Lakeside
13. Loma Prieta
14. Los Gatos
15. Saratoga

Gilroy Unified School Dist.

East Side Union High School Dist.

16. Alum Rock
17. Berryessa
18. Evergreen
19. Franklin McKinley
20. Mount Pleasant
21. Oak Grove
22. Orchard

Palo Alto Unified School Dist.

San Jose Unified School Dist.

Santa Clara Unified School Dist.

Morgan Hill Unified School Dist.

Milpitas Unified School Dist.

(School Accountability Report Card, Continued from page 78)

Campbell Union Elementary	(408) 364-4200
Campbell Union High	(408) 371-0960
Cupertino Union	(408) 252-3000
East Side Union High	(408) 272-6400
Evergreen Elementary	(408) 270-6800
Franklin-McKinley Elementary	(408) 283-6000
Fremont Union High	(408) 522-2200
Gilroy Unified	(408) 847-2700
Lakeside Joint	(408) 354-2372
Loma Prieta Joint Union Elementary	(408) 353-1101
Los Altos Elementary	(650) 941-4010
Los Gatos-Saratoga Joint High	(408) 354-2520
Los Gatos Union Elementary	(408) 395-5570
Luther Burbank	(408) 295-2450
Milpitas Unified	(408) 945-2300
Montebello Elementary	(408) 867-3628
Moreland Elementary	(408) 379-1370
Morgan Hill Unified	(408) 779-5272
Mt. Pleasant Elementary	(408) 223-3700
Mountain View Elementary	(650) 526-3500
Mountain View-Los Altos Union High	(650) 940-4650
Oak Grove Elementary	(408) 227-8300
Orchard Elementary	(408) 998-2889
Palo Alto Unified	(650) 329-3700
San Jose Unified	(408) 944-0388
Santa Clara Unified	(408) 983-2000
Saratoga Union Elementary	(408) 867-3424
Sunnyvale Elementary	(408) 522-8200
Union Elementary	(408) 377-8010
Whisman Elementary	(650) 903-6900

(Continued from page 77)

notch. An interview was set up and the fellow seemed as good as his reputation: friendly, hardworking, supportive of his staff, a great role model for his students, many of whom he knew by their first names. But scores at the school were running in the 10th to 20th percentiles, very low.

The reason: the old failing of demographics, crime high, family structures weak, and so on.

Although neither person said this, the clear implication was that if the demographics were different, scores would be much higher. And they're probably right. If these schools got an influx of middle- and upper middle-class children, their scores would dramatically increase.

Why don't schools tell this to the public, to parents? Probably because socioeconomics is difficult to explain. Teachers want to work with parents, not alienate them with accusations of neglect. Some educators argue that even with poor socioeconomics, teachers should be able to do an effective job — controversy. Socioeconomics focuses attention on the problems of home and society to the possible detriment of schools (which also need help and funds). School, after all, is a limited activity: about six hours a day, about 172 teaching days a year (to be expanded to 180).

When you strip away the fluff, schools seem to be saying that they are in the business of schools, not in reforming the larger society, and that they should be held accountable only for what they can influence: the children during the school day, on school grounds.

For these reasons — this is our opinion — many teachers and school administrators think that scores mislead and that parents often pay too much attention to scores and not enough to programs and the background and training of personnel. This is not to say that teachers ignore scores and measurements of accomplishment. They would love to see their students succeed. And schools find tests useful to determine whether their programs need changes.

No matter how low the scores, if you, as a parent, go into any school and ask — can my child get a good education here — you will be told, probably invariably, often enthusiastically, yes. First, there's the obvious reason: if the principal said no, his or her staff and bosses would be upset and angry. Second, by the reasoning common to public schools, "yes" means that the principal believes that the school and its teachers have the knowledge, training and dedication to turn out accomplished students. And the programs. Schools stress programs.

Is all this valid? Yes. Programs and training are important. Many schools with middling scores do turn out students that attend the best universities.

But this approach has its skeptics. Many parents and educators believe that schools must be judged by their scores, that scores are the true test of quality.

Some parents fear that if their child or children are placed in classes with low-achieving or even middle-achieving children they will not try as hard as they would if their friends or classmates were more academic, or that in some situations their children will be enticed into mischief. In some inner-city districts, the children, for misguided reasons, pressure each other not to do well in school.

Some parents do not believe that a school with many low-scoring students can do justice to its few middle- and high-scoring students. To meet the needs of the majority, instruction might have to be slowed for everyone.

Discipline is another problem. Teachers in low-scoring schools might have to spend more time on problem kids than teachers in high-scoring schools.

There's much more but basically it comes down to the belief that schools do not stand alone, that they and their students are influenced by the values of parents, of classmates and of the immediate neighborhood.

To continue this logic, schools and school districts are different from one another and for this reason it pays to move into a neighborhood with high-scoring schools or one with at least middling-plus scores. Or to somehow secure a transfer to one of the schools in these neighborhoods.

To an unknown extent, the marketplace has reinforced this belief. It rewards neighborhoods and towns with high-scoring schools by increasing the value (the price) of their homes.

Woven into all this is the suspicion, held by many in California, that public schools have failed to dismiss incompetent teachers and have become inflexible and unable to address problems. California for decades has been wracked by arguments over the power of the teachers' union, and over testing and teaching methods, and curriculum.

For the first time in decades, the state in 1999 will have a Democratic governor, a Democratic legislature and a Democratic superintendent of education. Will the arguments disappear? Don't hold your breath.

The parents who seem to do best at this business find out as much as possible about the schools, make decisions or compromises based on good information and work with the schools and teachers to advance their children's interests. Each school should be publishing an "accountability report." Ask for it.

Year-Round Schools

Year-round schools are becoming popular, especially in fast-growing towns, as a way to handle rapidly increasing enrollments. Schedules, called "tracks," vary from district to district but all students attend a full academic year.

Traditional holidays are observed. One group may start in summer, one in late summer and so on. A typical pattern is 12 weeks on, four weeks off. One track is always off, allowing another track to use its class space. Some school districts run a "year-round" program called modified traditional: two months summer vacation, three two-week breaks in the school year.

Families with several children on different tracks are sometimes forced to do quite a bit of juggling for vacation and child care. A new game is being played: how to get the tracks you want. Call your school for information.

Ability Grouping

Ask about the school's advancement or grouping policy or gifted classes.

Without getting into the pros and cons of these practices, schools often tiptoe around them because they upset some parents and frankly because some children have to be slighted. Say the ideal in a middle school is three levels of math: low, middle and high. But funds will allow only two levels. So low is combined with middle or middle with high. If you know the school is making compromises, you might choose to pay for tutoring to bridge the gap.

Miscellaneous

• Because state spending on education was skimped for years, many school districts have asked their voters to approve parcel taxes or bonds, which require two-thirds of the votes cast. Within the last 10 years, many school districts in the county have won approval for at least one construction bond and a few have passed several financial measures. In 1998 voters passed a state bond to spend $9.2 billion on school construction and renovation. Of this, $6.7 billion will go to kindergarten-through-twelfth schools, and $2.9 billion for community colleges and universities.

• Private vs. public. A complex battle, it boils down to one side saying public schools are the best and fairest way to educate all children versus the other side saying public education is inefficient and will never reform until it has meaningful competition. The state has allowed about 130 schools to restructure their programs according to local needs — an effort at eliminating unnecessary rules. These institutions are called charter schools. Generally, they are found in low-income neighborhoods. Legislation was recently passed to raise the number of charter schools to 250.

• Once tenured, teachers are almost impossible to fire, which opens schools to accusations of coddling incompetents. If your child gets a sour teacher, request a transfer. Better still, become active in the PTA or talk to other parents and try to identify the best teachers. Then ask for them.

• Educational methods. Arguments rage over what will work. In a recent lurch, California schools tilted back to phonics to teach reading.

• New math. A novel approach to teaching math gives students several ways to view problems and to get a "correct" answer. Supporters say it is much more effective than traditional methods. Opponents say that in the guise of boosting self-esteem, the program fails to teach math. Many districts, according to newspapers, mix the two methods.

• Over the past three years, the state Dept. of Education has adopted standards for science, history, math and reading. These standards define what the students are supposed to master at every grade level. Next to come are textbooks that reflect the new standards and after that tests based on the new standards. If students don't pass the tests, they may not be promoted. How much of this will be implemented remains to be seen. Testing is a touchy topic in California.

Community College Transfers

ALTHOUGH PRIMARILY trade schools, community colleges are a major source of students for the University of California and for the California State universities. The students usually take freshman and sophomore classes at a community college, then transfer to a university.

Community colleges are cheap ($39 for average class) and, often, conveniently located. Many community colleges have worked out transfer agreements with local state universities and with the UCs. The data below shows how many students each sector advances.

Tracking All Santa Clara County Students to UCs & CSUs
By High Schools and Community Colleges

Student Sector	Graduates	To UC	To CSU
Public High School	12,393	1,387	1,374
Private High School	1,623	274	279
Community Colleges	NA	824	3,165

By Community College Campus

Community College	To UC	To CSU
De Anza College	394	1,122
Evergreen College	22	335
Foothill College	181	385
Gavilan College	15	185
Mission College	42	272
San Jose City College	36	296
West Valley College	134	570

Source: California Postsecondary Education Commission. **Note**: Enrolling students counted in fall 1997 by UCs and Cal States.

• Courts and school districts are sorting out Proposition 227, which curtailed non-English instruction in public schools. Parents can request a waiver, which under certain conditions allows instruction in the native language. Some school districts are asking to be exempted from the proposition's requirements.

• In well-to-do neighborhoods and rich towns, parents are informally "taxing" themselves to raise money for schools. If you are new to one of these districts, you might be approached by the parents' group — never the school — and asked to contribute $100, $200 or $300 per child to the parents' group. Often the money is used to hire aides to help the teachers in the classroom.

• What if you or your neighborhood can't afford voluntary fees? Shop for bargains. Community colleges, in the summer, often run academic programs for children. Local tutors might work with small groups. Specific tutoring, say just in math, might be used to get the student over the rough spots. For information on tutors, look in the Yellow Pages under "Tutoring."

• Busing. School districts can charge and several do. Some low-income and special education kids ride free.

• High school changes. Many have switched to "block" instruction. The traditional six 50-minute classes are replaced by three blocks of 90 minutes.

• Uniforms. Schools have the discretion to require uniforms, an effort to discourage gang colors and get the kids to pay more attention to school than to how they look. "Uniforms" are generally interpreted to mean modest dress; for example, dark pants and shirts for boys, plaid skirts and light blouse for girls.

• Closed campus vs. open campus. The former stops the students from leaving at lunch or at any time during the school day. The latter allows the kids to leave. Kids love open, parents love closed.

• Grad night. Not too many years ago, graduating seniors would whoop it up on grad night and some would drink and then drive and get injured or killed. At many high schools now, parents stage a grad night party at the school, load it with games, raffles and prizes, and lock the kids in until dawn. A lot of work but it keeps the darlings healthy.

• T-P. California tradition. Your son or daughter joins a school team and it wins a few games or the cheerleaders win some prize — any excuse will do — and some parent will drive the kids around and they will fling toilet paper over your house, car, trees and shrubs. Damn nuisance but the kids love it.

• The number of teaching days is being increased, from about 172 to 180 but some of these days are coming at the expense of preparation time for teachers.

• Open Houses, Parents Nights. One study, done at Stanford, concluded that if parents will attend these events, the students, or at least some of them, will be impressed enough to pay more attention to school.

• Magnet Schools. Some school districts, notably San Jose Unified, use magnet or enriched schools to promote integration. With the enriched programs, educators open to draw the students out of neighborhood schools that have too many of one ethnic group and too few of another. For information about magnet programs, contact the school district.

Chapter 4

SANTA CLARA COUNTY
Private Schools

ALTHOUGH PRIVATE SCHOOLS often enjoy a better reputation than public, they are not without problems. The typical private or parochial school is funded way below its public school counterpart. In size, facilities and playing fields, and in programs, public schools usually far outstrip private schools. Private school teachers earn less than public school teachers.

"Typical" has to be emphasized. Some private schools are well-equipped, offer exceptional programs, pay their teachers competitively and limit class sizes to fewer than 15 students. Private schools vary widely in funding.

But even when "typical," private schools enjoy certain advantages over public schools.

The Advantages

Public schools must accept all students, have almost no power to dismiss incompetent teachers and are at the mercy of their neighborhoods for the quality of students — the socioeconomic correlation. The unruly often cannot be expelled or effectively disciplined.

Much has been said about the ability of private schools to rid themselves of problem children and screen them out in the first place. But tuition, even when modest, probably does more than anything else to assure private schools quality students.

Parents who pay extra for their child's education and often agree to work closely with the school are, usually, demanding parents. The result: fewer discipline problems, fewer distractions in the class, more of a willingness to learn.

When you place your child in a good private school, you are, to a large extent, buying him or her scholastic classmates. They may not be the smartest children — many private schools accept children of varying ability — but generally they will have someone at home breathing down their necks to succeed in academics.

The same attitude, a reflection of family values, is found in the high-

Work Can Be Child's Play

At Rainbow Montessori, our work has been child's play for two decades. At our Sunnyvale facility, we take child care and education to a new level.

Programs include computer education & gymnastics, a curriculum from infants to the sixth grade, music, dance, corporate child care programs, hot meals available and much more. Rainbow Montessori is the largest Montessori facility in the Bay Area, located in Sunnyvale, near Lawrence and Central Expressways, Highway 101 & Wolfe. We're currently accepting enrollment for all ages, so call us today for an appointment.

Rainbow Montessori
Child Development Centers

...Because You Care

Rainbow Montessori

790 E. Duane Ave.
Sunnyvale 408-738-3261

Public Colleges-Univ. Chosen by Private School Graduates

School	UC	CSU	Com	Total
Archbishop Mitty	34	77	72	183
Bellarmine	91	50	15	156
Castilleja	17	1	2	20
Mid-Pen. Ctr.	2	3	11	16
Mtn. View	0	3	1	4
Notre Dame	23	22	21	66
Pinewood	0	2	4	6
Presentation	34	32	27	93
St. Francis	64	48	57	169
St. Lawrence	2	8	28	38
Valley Christian	4	16	51	71

Source: California Dept. of Education. The chart tracks California public colleges or universities, and high school graduates from private schools. It shows how many students from these high schools enrolled as college freshmen in fall 1997. The state does not track graduates enrolling in private colleges or out-of-state colleges. **Key**: UC (University of California), CSU (California State University), Com (community college).

achieving public schools. When a child in one of these schools or a private school turns to his left and right, he will see and later talk to children who read books and newspapers.

A child in a low-achieving school, public or private, will talk to classmates who watch a lot of television and rarely read.

(These are, necessarily, broad generalizations. Much depends on whom a child picks for friends. High-achieving students certainly watch television but, studies show, much less than low-achieving students. Many critics contend that even high-scoring schools are graduating students poorly prepared for college.)

The Quality of Teaching

Do private schools have better teachers than public schools? Impossible to tell. Both sectors sing the praises of their teachers.

Private schools, compared to public, have much more freedom to dismiss teachers but this can be abused. The private schools themselves advise parents to avoid schools with excessive teacher turnover.

Although most can't pay as much as public schools, private institutions claim to attract people fed up with the limitations of public schools, particularly restrictions on disciplining and ejecting unruly children. Some proponents argue that private schools attract teachers "who really want to teach."

Religion and Private Schools

Some private schools are as secular as any public institution. But many are religious-oriented and talk in depth about religion or ethics, or teach a specific creed. Or possibly they teach values within a framework of western civilization or some other philosophy.

(Continued on Page 91)

A Profile of Catholic Schools

THE LARGEST PRIVATE school system in Santa Clara County, Catholic schools enroll 16,057 students. The following information is based on interviews with Catholic educators and reviewed by San Jose diocese. Data from 1997-98 school year.

• Statistics. 28 elementary schools, one kindergarten, six high schools.

"The Catholic community values Catholic education, and they want it," according to a Catholic education administrator.

• All races, creeds welcome. Where schools are full, preference is given first to Catholic children from families active in parish. After that, to active Catholics unable to get into own parish schools.

High schools recruit regionally for students. Admissions and placement tests but all accept average students. Standards vary by school. Recommendations by parish pastors, principals, eighth-grade teachers carry clout.

• Non-Catholic students for both elementary and secondary schools total 2,482 or 15 percent of system.

Ethnic breakdown elementary: Asian, 7 percent ; Af. American, 2; Filipino, 12; Hispanic, 18; Causasian, 59 (percentages rounded).

Ethnic breakdown secondary: Asian, 9 percent; Af. American, 3; Filipino, 7; Hispanic, 12; Causasian, 63 percent.

• Why parents send kids to Catholic schools. A survey: 1. Religious tradition, moral and spiritual values. 2. Academics. 3. Discipline.

• Curriculum. Elementary schools cover same basic subjects as public schools but weave in religious-moral viewpoint. "Philosophy based in Jesus Christ. Religious values are integral to learning experience." State textbooks often used. Each school picks texts from list approved by diocese. High school instruction, although varied, is greatly influenced by requirements of University of California. Strong emphasis on technology in elementary and secondary schools.

Educators advise parents to approach high schools as they would any educational institution: ask about grades, what percentage of students go on to college.

• Non-Catholics. Get same instruction as Catholics, including history of Church and scripture. Attend Mass but not required to take sacraments. "We don't try to convert them," said one nun.

(Continued on Next Page)

Catholic Schools

(Continued from Previous Page)

• Corporal punishment. Thing of past. More aware now of child abuse. Stress positive discipline, name on board, detention, probation. Try to work problems through, few expulsions.

• Class sizes. Before 40, now 30 to 32. Somewhat smaller for high schools because of special classes, e.g. French.

Would like smaller but point out that with well-behaved students, teachers can accomplish a lot. Matter of economics. If parents wanted smaller classes, they would have to pay more. "We want to keep affordable prices so all people can choose us, not just rich."

• Tuition. See directory of private schools at the end of this chapter.

• Schedule. Similar to public schools. 180 teaching days, minimum of five hours, 10 minutes a day. Many go longer.

• Ability grouping. In elementary grades (K-8) not done by class. Grouping within classes, advanced children working at one level, slow children at another. Tutoring after class. "You're not going to walk in and find 35 children on the same page."

All high schools run prep programs, tend to attract prep students, but will accept remedial students, if they have remedial instruction. Admission standards vary by high school.

• Homework. Each school sets policy but diocese suggests guidelines: Grades one and two, 20 minutes; three and four, 30-45 minutes; five and six, 45 to 60 minutes; seven and eight, 60-90 minutes. None on weekends and vacations. High schools require more homework, may assign on weekends and holidays. Teacher's choice.

• Report cards. Four a year plus results of diocesan tests. Parents are expected to attend conferences, back-to-school nights.

• Teacher quality. Bachelor's degree required. Most credentialed. Hired for competence, commitment to Catholic educational philosophy. A few non-Catholic teachers but system tends to attract Catholic educators.

• Uniforms. Yes. Generally plaid skirts, blouses and sweaters for girls, collared shirts, sweaters and cords for boys.

• Extended care. Most schools offer before- and after-school care, 7 a.m. to 6 p.m. Ask.

(Continued on Next Page)

CATHOLIC SCHOOLS (Continued from Previous Page)

• Drugs. "Not major problem but when it happens we do everything to work with student."

• Extracurricular activities. Although campuses small, schools try to offer variety of activities, sports, arts, music. At elementary school, much depends on work of parents. "Parents are expected to do a lot." High schools offer good variety: music, band, arts, intramural sports, many club activities, computers, science. Catholic high schools usually field very competitive football and basketball teams.

• For more information, admissions, call school directly. Most registrations in spring but earlier for high schools. Waiting list for many primary grades. Education office at diocese, (408) 983-0185.

(Continued from Page 88)

Until recently public schools almost never talked about religion or religious figures. They now teach the history of major religions and the basic tenets of each, and they try to inculcate in the children a respect for all religions.

It's hard, if not impossible, however, for public schools to talk about values within a framework of religion or a system of ethics. Often, it's difficult for them to talk about values. Some people argue that this is a major failing.

Many religious schools accept students of different religions or no religion. Some schools offer these students broad courses in religion — less dogma. Ask about the program.

Money

Private-school parents pay taxes for public schools and they pay tuition. Public-school parents pay taxes but not tuition. Big difference.

Ethnic Diversity

Many private schools are integrated and the great majority of private-school principals — the editor knows no exceptions — welcome minorities. Some principals fret over tuition, believing that it keeps many poor students out of private schools.

Money, the lack of it, weighs heavily on private schools. Scholarships, however, are awarded, adjustments made, family rates offered. Ask.

What's in Santa Clara County

Santa Clara County has more than 100 private schools. Here is a brief overview:

UCs Chosen by Private School Graduates

School	Berk	Davis	Irv	UCLA	Riv	SD	SB	SC	Total
Archbishop Mitty	2	11	0	3	0	0	9	9	34
Bellarmine	32	21	2	9	3	8	10	6	91
Castilleja	4	2	0	8	0	0	0	3	17
Mid-Pen. Ctr.	0	0	0	0	0	0	1	1	2
Mtn. View	0	0	0	0	0	0	0	0	0
Notre Dame	7	6	0	1	4	3	2	0	23
Pinewood	0	0	0	0	0	0	0	0	0
Presentation	3	7	1	6	1	7	4	5	34
St. Francis	6	17	3	9	0	11	9	9	64
St. Lawrence	0	1	0	0	0	1	0	0	2
Valley Christian	0	2	0	0	0	2	0	0	4

Source: Calif. Dept. of Education. The chart tracks Universities of California and high school graduates from private schools. It shows how many students from these schools enrolled as UC freshmen in fall 1997. The state does not track graduates enrolling in private colleges or out-of-state colleges. **Key**: Berk (Berkeley), Irv (Irvine), SD (San Diego), SB (Santa Barbara), Riv (Riverside), SC (Santa Cruz).

Many are one-family schools, mother and father teaching their own children at home. A support network that supplies books and materials has grown up for these people.

Some regular private schools have low teacher-pupil ratios, fewer than 15 students per teacher, occasionally around 10 to 1. Public school classes usually go 25 to 30 per teacher, sometimes higher (new funding has reduced sizes in grades 1-3). Class sizes in Catholic schools, in the upper grades, run close to the public-school ratio, and in some schools higher. Catholic schools, nonetheless, are the most popular, a reflection in part of the high number of Catholics in Santa Clara County. Some Catholic schools have waiting lists.

Private schools in Santa Clara County come in great variety, Christian, Jewish, Montessori, Carden (schools with different teaching approaches), prep schools, schools that emphasize language or music, boarding and day schools, schools that allow informal dress, schools that require uniforms.

Choosing a Private School

1. Inspect the grounds, the school's buildings, ask plenty of questions. "I would make myself a real pest," advised one private school official. The good schools welcome this kind of attention.

2. Choose a school with a philosophy congenial to your own, and your child's. Carden schools emphasize structure. Montessori schools, while somewhat structured, encourage individual initiative and independence.

Ask whether the school is accredited. Private schools are free to run almost any program they like, to set any standards they like, which may sound enticing but in some aspects might hurt the schools. A few bad ones spoil the reputation of the good.

To remedy this, many private schools sign up for inspections by independent agencies, such as the Western Association of Schools and Colleges and the California Association of Independent Schools. These agencies try to make sure that schools meet their own goals. Some good schools do not seek accreditation.

3. Get all details about tuition carefully explained. How is it to be paid? Are there extra fees? Book costs? Is there a refund if the student is withdrawn or dropped from the school?

4. Progress reports. Parent conferences. How often are they scheduled?

5. What are the entrance requirements? When must they be met? Although many schools use entrance tests, often they are employed to place the child in an academic program, not exclude him from the school.

6. For prep schools, what percentage of the students go on to college and to what colleges?

7. How are discipline problems handled?

8. What are the teacher qualifications? What is the teacher turnover rate?

9. How sound financially is the school? How long has it been in existence? There is nothing wrong inherently with new schools. But you want a school that has the wherewithal to do the job.

10. Do parents have to work at school functions? Are they required to "volunteer"?

11. Don't choose in haste but don't wait until the last minute. Some schools fill quickly, some fill certain classes quickly. If you can, call the school the year before your child is to enter, early in the year.

12. Don't assume that because your child attends a private school you can expect everything will go all right, that neither the school nor the student needs your attention. The quality of private schools in California varies widely.

Susan Vogel has written "Private High Schools of the San Francisco Bay Area." (1998) Check with bookstores or call (415) 267-5978.

Directory of Private Schools

The directory contains the most current information available at press time but it may not include all the private school offerings. Some institutions mix day care with, say, a kindergarten program and come under the vague category of day care-private school. Consult the local phone directory.

In California, tuition ranges widely in private schools. Many Catholic elementaries charge from about $2,000 to $2,800. Some nondenominational schools go as high as $10,000. High schools range from $5,000 to $12,000, with the Catholic schools running from $5,000-$6,000 (plus fees and books).

Discounts are often given for siblings. If strapped, ask about financial help. Many schools offer family rates. Religious schools often charge more for nonmembers. Day care costs extra.

Campbell

Campbell Christian 1075 W. Campbell Ave. (408) 374-7260 Enroll: 170 K-6th.

Covenant Life Acad. 1300 Sheffield Ave. (408) 371-5141 Enroll: 56 K-8th.

Old Orchard Elem. 400 West Campbell Ave. (408) 378-5935 Enroll: 221 K-8th.

Pioneer Family Acad. 1799 S. Winchester Blvd. #100 (408) 265-4386 Enroll: 199 K-12th.

Primary Plus 1125 W. Campbell Ave. (408) 379-3184 Enroll: 55 K-2nd.

San Jose Christian 1300 Sheffield Ave. (408) 371-7741 Enroll: 201 K-8th.

St. Lucy's 76 E. Kennedy Ave. (408) 378-7454 Enroll: 318 K-8th.

West Valley Seventh-Day Adventist Elem. 95 Dot Ave. (408) 378-4327 Enroll: 118 K-8th.

Cupertino

Bethel Lutheran Elem. 10181 Finch Ave. (408) 252-8512 Enroll: 98 K-4th.

Lutheran School of Our Savior 5825 Bollinger Rd. (408) 252-0250 Enroll: 108 K-8th.

Monarch Christian School Inc. 1196 Lime Dr. (408) 773-8543 Enroll: 100 K-6th.

One World Montessori 20220 Suisun Dr. (408) 255-3770 Enroll: 106 K-6th.

St. Joseph of Cupertino 10120 N. DeAnza Blvd. (408) 252-6441 Enroll: 309 K-8th.

Tican Institute 220 Blake Ave. No. D (408) 554-8787 Enroll: 43 K-6th.

Gilroy

Cornerstone Christian 1020 Hoesch Wy. (408) 848-5895 Enroll: 83 K-12th.

Gavilan Hills Acad. 2080 Pacheco Pass Rd. (408) 842-7455 Enroll: 34 K-12th.

Pacific West Christian Acad. 1575 Mantelli Dr. (408) 847-7922 Enroll: 156 K-6th.

St. Mary's 7900 Church St. (408) 842-2827 Enroll: 311 K-8th.

Los Altos Hills

Pinewood Private School of Fremont Hills 26800 Fremont Rd. (650) 941-1532 Enroll: 305 7th-12th.

St. Nicholas Elem. 12816 So. El Monte Ave. (650) 941-4056 Enroll: 286 K-8th.

Los Altos

Canterbury Christian Elem. 101 N. El Monte Ave. (650) 949-0909 Enroll: 104 K-6th.

Los Altos Christian 625 Magdalena Ave. (650) 948-3738 Enroll: 229 K-6th..

Miramonte Elem. 1175 Altamead Dr. (650) 967-2783 Enroll: 161 K-8th.

Morgan Center 201 Covington Rd. (650) 948-6834 Enroll: 48 Ungraded.

Pinewood Private School of Los Altos 327 Fremont Ave. (650) 948-5438 Enroll: 177 3rd-6th.

Pinewood Private School-Lower Campus 477 Fremont Ave. (650) 962-9076 Enroll: 141 K-2nd.

St. Simon Elem. 1840 Grant Rd. (650) 968-9952 Enroll: 611 K-8th.

Waldorf School of the Peninsula 11311 Mora Dr. (650) 948-8433 Enroll: 177 K-8th.

Los Gatos

Academy of Our Mother of Perpetual Help 19101 Bear Creek Rd. (408) 354-7703 Enroll: 26 K-8th.

Hillbrook 16000 Marchmont Dr. (408) 356-6116 Enroll: 252 K-8th.

Los Gatos Acad. 220 Belgatos Rd. (408) 358-1046 Enroll: 108 K-12th.

Los Gatos Christian 16845 Hicks Rd. (408) 268-1502 Enroll: 559 K-8th.

St. Mary's Elem. 30 Lyndon Ave. (408) 354-3944 Enroll: 279 1st-8th.

Valley Christian Elem. 220 Kensington Way (408) 559-4400 Enroll: 348 K-5th.

Yavneh Day 14855 Oka Rd. (408) 358-3413 Enroll: 136 K-5th.

Milpitas

Children's World Learning Centers 860 N. Hillview Dr. (408) 263-0444 Enroll: 32 K-1st.

Milpitas Foothill Seventh-Day Adventist 1991 Landess Ave. (408) 263-2568 Enroll: 137 K-8th.

Rainbow Bridge Ctr. 1500 Yosemite Dr. (408) 945-9090 Enroll: 330 K-6th.

St. John the Baptist Catholic 360 S. Abel St. (408) 262-8110 Enroll: 314 K-8th.

Morgan Hill

South Valley Christian Elem. 145 Wright Ave. (408) 779-8850 Enroll: 285 K-8th.

St. Catherine Elem. 17500 S. Peak Ave. (408) 779-9950 Enroll: 298 K-8th.

Mountain View

Mountain View Acad. 360 S. Shoreline Blvd. (650) 967-2324 Enroll: 99 9th-12th.

Southbay Christian 1134 Miramonte Ave. (650) 961-9485 Enroll: 390 K-8th.

St. Francis High 1885 Miramonte Ave. (650) 968-1213 Enroll: 1459 9th-12th.

St. Joseph's Elem. 1120 Miramonte Ave. (650) 967-1839 Enroll: 299 K-8th.

Palo Alto

Ananda School on the Peninsula 2171 El Camino Real (650) 462-8151 Enroll: 34 K-5th.

Castilleja High 1310 Bryant St. (650) 328-3160 Enroll: 375 6th-12th.

Children's International 4000 Middlefield Rd. (650) 813-9131 Enroll: 31 K-5th.

Heads Up Elem. 445 E. Charleston Rd. (650) 424-1267 Enroll: 37 K-6th.

International School of the Peninsula 3233 Cowper St. (650) 852-0264 Enroll: 275 K-6th.

Keys 2890 Middlefield Rd. (650) 328-1711 Enroll: 166 K- 8th.

Mid-Peninsula Education Ctr. 870 N. California Ave. (650) 493-5910 Enroll: 140 9th-12th.

Mid-Peninsula Jewish Community Day 655 Arastradero Rd. (650) 424-8482 Enroll: 135 K-5th.

Palo Alto Preparatory 4000 Middlefield Rd. (650) 493-7071 Enroll: 53 8th-12th.

Peninsula Children's Ctr. 3800 Blackford Ave. (650) 494-1200 Enroll: 33 Ungraded.

St. Elizabeth Seton Catholic Community 1095 Channing Ave. (650) 326-9004 Enroll: 249 K-8th.

Stanford Chinese 2347 Williams St. (650) 813-1720 Enroll: 94 1st-3rd.

San Jose

Achiever Christian 820 Ironwood Dr. (408) 264-6789 Enroll: 439 K-6th.

Almaden Country 6835 Trinidad Dr. (408) 997-0424 Enroll: 363 K-8th.

Almaden Valley Christian 6291 Vegas Dr. (408) 997-0290 Enroll: 73 K-12th.

Apostles Lutheran Elem. 5828 Santa Teresa Blvd. (408) 578-4800 Enroll: 190 K-8th.

Archbishop Mitty High 5000 Mitty Ave. (408) 252-6610 Enroll: 1330 9th-12th.

Beacon 5670 Camden Ave. (480) 265-8611 Enroll: 30 7th-12th.

Bellarmine College Prep. 850 Elm St. (408) 294-9224 Enroll: 1355 9th-12th.

Bridge Acad. 5308 Cedar Grove Cir. (408) 365-7654 Enroll: 76 1st-12th.

Calvary Cathedral Acad. 2165 Lucretia Ave. (408) 298-7622 Enroll: 116 K-8th.

Casa Di Mir Montessori Elem. 4300 Bucknall Rd. (408) 866-7758 Enroll: 59 1st-6th.

Challenger 1325 Bouret Dr. (408) 723-0111 Enroll: 434 K-8th.

Challenger 880 Wren Dr. (408) 448-3010 Enroll: 220 K-5th.

Christ the King Academy 2530 Berryessa Rd. (408) 298-2969 Enroll: 46 K-12th.

Christian Community Acad. 1523 McLaughlin Ave. (408) 279-0846 Enroll: 260 K-12th.

De Young 3001 Ross Ave. #3 (408) 445-2760 Enroll: 43 K-12th.

East Valley Christian School 2715 S. White Road (408) 274-6644 Enroll: 124 K-12th.

Five Wounds Elem. 1390 Five Wounds Ln. (408) 293-0425 Enroll: 275 K-8th.

For His Joy Christian 228 Purple Glen Dr. (408) 578-9289 Enroll: 35 K-12th.

Harker 500 Saratoga Ave. (408) 249-2510 Enroll: 799 K-8th.

Holy Family Educational Ctr. 4850 Pearl Ave. (408) 978-1355 Enroll: 608 K-8th.

Learning Acad. 5670 Camden Ave. (408) 723-1131 Enroll: 141 K-6th.

Liberty Baptist 2790 S. King Rd. (408) 274-5613 Enroll: 502 K-12th.

Little Scholars 3703 Silver Creek Rd. (408) 238-2500 Enroll: 46 K-4th.

Milpitas Christian 3435 Birchwood Ln. (408) 945-6530 Enroll: 658 K-8th.

Most Holy Trinity Elem. 1940 Cunningham Ave. (408) 729-3431 Enroll: 305 K-8th.

Mulberry 1980 Hamilton Ave. (408) 377-1595 Enroll: 86 K-5th.

Notre Dame High 596 S. Second St. (408) 294-1113 Enroll: 485 9th-12th.

Olive Tree 4586 Shadowhurst Ct. (408) 265-3621 Enroll: 73 K-12th.

Piedmont Hills Montessori 1425 Old Piedmont Rd. (408) 923-5131 Enroll: 32 K.

Pine Hill School 1975 Cambrianna Dr. (408) 371-5881 Enroll: 56 1st-12th.

Plantation Christian 209 Herlong Ave. (408) 972-8211 Enroll: 111 1st-12th.

Presentation High 2281 Plummer Ave. (408) 264-1664 Enroll: 685 9th-12th.

Primary Plus 3500 Amber Dr. (408) 248-2464 Enroll: 412 K-8th.

Private Educational Network 461 Park Ave. (408) 280-1122 Enroll: 63 1st-12th.

Queen of Apostles Elem. 4950 Mitty Way (408) 252-3659 Enroll: 310 K-8th.

Rainbow Bridge Ctr. 750 N. Capitol Ave. (408) 254-1280 Enroll: 243 K-4th.

San Jose Community Christian 480 S. McCreery Ave. (408) 729-9300 Enroll: 48 K-12th.

South Valley Carden 1921 Clarinda Wy. (408) 879-1000 Enroll: 215 K-8th.

St. Christopher Elem. 2278 Booksin Ave. (408) 723-7223 Enroll: 625 K-8th.

St. Elizabeth Day Home 1544 McKinley Ave. (408) 295-3456 Enroll: 39 K-2nd.

St. Frances Cabrini 15325 Woodard Rd. (408) 377-6545 Enroll: 621 K-8th.

St. John Vianney 4601 Hyland Ave. (408) 258-7677 Enroll: 624 K-8th.

St. Leo the Great 1051 W. San Fernando St. (408) 293-4846 Enroll: 297 K-8th.

St. Martin of Tours Elem. 300 O'Connor Dr. (408) 287-3630 Enroll: 361 K-8th.

St. Patrick Elem. 51 N. Ninth St. (408) 283-5858 Enroll: 305 K-8th.

St. Stephen's Elem. 500 Shawnee Ln. (408) 365-2927 Enroll: 207 K-6th.

St. Thomas More 12000 Berryessa Rd. (408) 453-6086 Enroll: 126 K-12th.

St. Timothy's Lutheran 5100 Camden Ave. (408) 265-0244 Enroll: 130 K-5th.

St. Victor Elem. 3150 Sierra Rd. (408) 251-1740 Enroll: 317 K-8th.

Tower Acad. 2887 McLaughlin Ave. (408) 578-2830 Enroll: 71 K-3rd.

Valley Christian High 1570 Branham Ln. (408) 978-9950 Enroll: 636 9th-12th.

Valley Christian Jr. High 1570 Branham Ln. (408) 978-9830 Enroll: 307 6th-8th.

White Road Baptist Acad. 480 S. White Rd. (408) 272-7713 Enroll: 58 K-12th.

Santa Clara

Adventures in Learning 890 Pomeroy Ave. (408) 247-4769 Enroll: 53 K-6th.

Carden El Encanto Day 615 Hobart Ter. (408) 244-5041 Enroll: 412 K-8th.

Delphi Acad. of S.F. Bay 890 Pomeroy Ave. (408) 260-2300 Enroll: 47 K-8th.

Granada Islamic 3003 Scott Blvd. (408) 980-1161 Enroll: 269 K-8th.

Neighborhood Christian 1290 Pomeroy Ave. (408) 241-8837 Enroll: 94 K-6th.

New Covenant Christian 220 Blake Ave. #A (408) 249-3993 Enroll: 54 K-4th.

Our Lady of Peace 2800 Mission College Blvd. (408) 988-4160 Enroll: 38 K.

Pioneer Montessori 400 N. Winchester Blvd. (408) 241-5077 Enroll: 103 K-6th.

Santa Clara Christian 3421 Monroe St. (408) 246-5423 Enroll: 72 K-3rd.

Sierra Elem. & High 220 Blake Ave. (408) 247-4740 Enroll: 109 K-12th.

St. Clare Elem. 725 Washington St. (408) 246-6797 Enroll: 302 K-8th.

St. Justin's 2655 Homestead Rd. (408) 248-1094 Enroll: 311 K-8th.

St. Lawrence Acad. 2000 Lawrence Ct. (408) 296-3013 Enroll: 308 9th-12th.

St. Lawrence Elem. & Middle 1971 St. Lawrence Dr. (408) 296-2260 Enroll: 417 K-8th.

Stanbridge Acad. 890 Pomeroy Ave. (408) 261-6610 Enroll: 72 K-12th.

Saratoga

Challenger 18811 Cox Ave. (408) 378-0444 Enroll: 52 K.

Primary Plus 18720 Bucknall Rd. (408) 370-0357 Enroll: 51 K-2nd.

Sacred Heart Elem. 13718 Saratoga Ave. (408) 867-9241 Enroll: 300 K-8th.

St. Andrews 13601 Saratoga Ave. (408) 867-3785 Enroll: 400 K-8th.

Sunnyvale

Challenger 1185 Hollenbeck Ave. (408) 245-7170 Enroll: 573 K-8th.

French 1510 Lewiston Dr. (408) 746-0460 Enroll: 54 K-3rd.

Jubilee Academy 560 Britton Ave. (408) 730-4777 Enroll: 34 K-3rd.

King's Acad. 562 N. Britton Ave. (408) 481-9900 Enroll: 468 K-12th.

Rainbow Montessori Child Dev. Ctr. 790 E. Duane Ave. (408) 738-3261 Enroll: 220 K-6th.

Resurrection Elem. 1395 Hollenbeck Ave. (408) 245-4571 Enroll: 285 K- 8th.

South Peninsula Hebrew Day 1030 Astoria Dr. (408) 738-3060 Enroll: 250 K-8th.

St. Cyprian 195 Leota Ave. (408) 738-3444 Enroll: 292 K-8th.

St. Martin's Elem. 597 Central Ave. (408) 736-5534 Enroll: 334 K-8th.

Sunnyvale Christian 445 S. Mary Ave. (408) 736-3286 Enroll: 114 K-5th.

Chapter **5**

SANTA CLARA COUNTY
Baby Care

FOR LICENSING, CALIFORNIA divides child-care facilities into several categories:

- Small family: up to 6 children in the providers's home.
- Large family: 7-12 children in the provider's home.
- Nursery Schools or Child-Care centers.

A child is considered an infant from birth to age 2. No category at this time has been established for toddler.

Individual sitters are not licensed and neither are people whom parents arrange for informally to take care of their children but if a person is clearly in the business of child care from more than one family he or she should be licensed. Each of the three categories has certain restrictions. For example, the small-family provider with six children cannot have more than three under the age of 2.

In everyday reality, many of the larger facilities tend to limit enrollments to children over age 2, and some have even higher age limits.

The state and its local umbrella agencies maintain referral lists of local infant and day-care providers. All you have to do is call and they will send a list of the licensed providers and suggestions on how to make a wise choice.

The names of the agencies and their numbers are:

4 Cs Community Coordinated Child Care Development Council of Santa Clara County, Inc., 111 East Gish Road, San Jose 95112. (408) 487-0747.

Community Coordinated Child Development Council of San Mateo County, Inc., 700 S. Claremont, No. 107, San Mateo. Ph: (650) 696-8787.

Here's some advice from one licensing agency:

- Plan ahead. Give yourself one month for searching and screening.
- Contact the appropriate agencies for referrals.
- Once you have identified potential caregivers, phone them to find out

about their services and policies. For those that meet your needs, schedule a time to visit while children are present.

• At the site, watch how the children play and interact with one another.

• Contact other parents using the programs. Ask if they are satisfied with the care and if their children are happy and well-cared-for.

• Select the program that best meets your needs. "Trust your feelings and your instincts."

This is a bare-bones approach. The referral centers can supply you with more information.

To get you started, we are listing here the names of the infant centers in the county. For the older children, please refer to the directory in the following chapter.

The infant centers:

Campbell
A Special Place-Camden, 1260 Erin Way, (408) 559-1566

Executive Sweet , 2323 S. Bascom Ave., (408) 559-6090

Kiderwood Children's Ctr. #2, 1190 W. Latimer, (408) 374-4442

Kinder Care Learning Ctr., 1806 W. Campbell, (408) 379-8152

Noah's Ark , 560 N. Harrison Ave., (408) 378-3212

Primary Plus, 1125 W. Campbell Ave., (408) 379-3198

Primary Plus, Inc., 1125 W. Campbell Ave., (408) 379-3198

Cupertino
Apple CCCtr., 10253 Portal Ave., (408) 862-6170

Bethel Lutheran Nursery & Learning Ctr, 10181 Finch Ave., (408) 252-8512

Good Samaritan, 19624 Homestead Rd., (408) 996-8290

Gilroy
Countryside DCC, 8985 Monterey Rd., (408) 848-3448

Goldsmith Seeds Ctr., 2280 Hecker Pass Hwy., (408) 847-7333

Happy Place Montessori, 7360 & 7350 Alexander St., (408) 848-3819

Ochoa Infant Migrant CDCtr., 915 Southside Dr., (408) 842-5066

Los Altos Hills
Foothill College Campus CCtr., 12345 El Monte Rd., (650) 949-7777

Los Altos
Baby World, 1715 Grant Rd., (650) 988-8627

Early Horizons, 201 Covington Rd., (650) 941-2548

Pebbles, 211 Covington Rd., (650) 435-8823

Los Gatos
Addison Penzak Jewish Comm. Ctr., 14855 Oka Rd, Rm 25, (408) 358-3636

Kiddie Kampus DCCtr., 16330 Los Gatos Blvd., (408) 356-6776

Magic Rock CDC, 14969 Los Gatos-Almaden Rd., (408) 559-8531

Milpitas
Bright Beginnings, 1331 E. Calaveras Blvd., (408) 744-9280

Children's World-Medallion Sch. Partnerships, 860 Hillview Rd., (408) 263-0444

KinderCare Learning Ctr, 400 So. Abel St., (408) 263-7212

Rainbow Bridge Ctr., 1500 Yosemite Dr., (408) 945-9090

Moffett Field
Ames CCCtr., Bldg. T20-D, (650) 604-4184

Morgan Hill
KinderCare Learning Ctr. , 605 E. Dunne Ave., (408) 778-1237

Linda's Place DCC, 17535 Del Monte, (408) 779-7678

Top 25 Baby Names

Santa Clara County

Boys	Girls
Michael (232)	Jessica (193)
Christopher (200)	Jennifer (148)
Daniel (194)	Emily (128)
David (183)	Samantha(120)
Jose (181)	Sarah (120)
Anthony (177)	Ashley (107)
Andrew (176)	Michelle (104)
Kevin (172)	Elizabeth (102)
Alexander (170)	Vanessa (102)
Jonathan (167)	Stephanie (100)
Matthew (161)	Jasmine (98)
Brandon (149)	Hannah (92)
Nicholas(149)	Megan (90)
Joshua (146)	Nicole (90)
Justin (143)	Maria (83)
Jacob (141)	Alyssa (81)
Ryan (132)	Lauren (76)
Joseph (125)	Alexandra (73)
John (110)	Amanda (73)
Luis (109)	Katherine (73)
Eric (108)	Melissa (71)
Christian (106)	Sabrina (68)
Kyle (104)	Taylor (68)
Tyler (99)	Rachel (67)
Brian (97)	Brianna (66)

California

Boys	Girls
Daniel (4,384)	Jessica (3,185)
Michael (4,252)	Jennifer (2,782)
Jose (4,116)	Ashley (2,608)
Anthony (3,862)	Emily (2,527)
Christopher (3,690)	Samantha (2,479)
David (3,674)	Stephanie (2,153)
Andrew (3,535)	Sarah (2,135)
Jacob (3,218)	Vanessa (1,977)
Matthew (3,213)	Elizabeth (1,974)
Jonathan (3,188)	Alexis (1,884)
Joshua (3,079)	Maria (1,816)
Joseph (2,856)	Jasmine (1,794)
Brandon (2,822)	Alyssa (1,723)
Nicholas(2,608)	Melissa (1,716)
Christian (2,581)	Hannah (1,620)
Kevin (2,546)	Kimberly(1,573)
Luis (2,463)	Victoria (1,442)
Ryan (2,351)	Taylor (1,427)
Juan (2,324)	Amanda (1,400)
Alexander (2,165)	Lauren (1,355)
Justin (2,140)	Natalie (1,342)
Jesus (2,010)	Madison (1,339)
Austin (1,940)	Michelle (1,329)
Tyler (1,863)	Megan (1,321)
John (1,807)	Diana (1,264)

Source: California Department of Health Services, 1997 birth records. Shown in parentheses is the number of children with the given name. Some names would move higher on the list if the state grouped essentially same names with slightly different spellings, for example, Sarah and Sara. But state computer goes by exact spellings.

Tutor Time Child Care/Learning Ctr., 610 Dunne Ave., (408) 778-1977 *See ad on page 111*

Young Explorer, 25 Wright Ave., (408) 778-2529

Mountain View

Kiddie Acad. CC Learning Ctr., 205 E. Middlefield Rd., (650) 960-6900

Kidstown CDC, 180 No. Rengstorff, (650) 964-5006

KinderCare, 2065 W. El Camino Real, (650) 967-4430

Primary Plus, 333 Eunice Ave., (650) 967-3780

Walnut Grove CCtr., 84 Murlagan Ave., (650) 960-1826

Palo Alto

Casa dei Bambini, 463 College, (650) 858-0892

Children's Ctr of Stanford Comm. Big Kids, 695 Pampas Lane, (650) 853-3090

Children's Presch., 4000 Middlefield, T-1, (650) 855-5770

Covenant Children's Ctr., 670 E. Meadow Dr., (650) 493-9505

Good Neighbor Montessori, 4000 Middlefield Road, (650) 493-2777

Headsup CDCtr., 4251 El Camino Real Bldg A, (650) 424-1155

Learning Center, 459 Kingsley, (650) 325-6683

Lilliput Infant TRoddler Ctr., 3789 Park Blvd., (650) 857-1736

Mini Infant Ctr., 3149 Waverly St., (650) 424-9170

Neighborhhod Infant Toddler Ctr., 2185 Bryant St., (650) 321-3493

Santa Clara County Births — History & Projections

1970s		1980s		1990s	
Year	Births	Year	Births	Year	Births
1970	19,721	1980	21,299	1990	28,080
1971	17,596	1981	21,902	1991	27,881
1972	16,598	1982	22,538	1992	27,481
1973	16,161	1983	22,698	1993	26,530
1974	16,800	1984	23,681	1994	26,022
1975	16,660	1985	24,110	1995	25,576
1976	17,414	1986	24,400	1996	25,014
1977	18,156	1987	24,518	1997	24,517
1978	18,519	1988	26,274	1998	24,021
1979	19,827	1989	26,805	1999	23,518

Source: California Dept. of Finance, Demographic Research Unit.

Palo Alto Infant Toddler Ctr., 4111 Alma St., (650) 493-2240

Sojourner Truth CDCtr., 3990 Ventura Ct., (650) 493-5990

Whistle Stop, 3801 Miranda Ave. #T6B, (650) 852-3497

San Jose

A Special Place-Mobile West, 295 Nicholson Ln., (408) 433-5242

A Special Place-Williamsburg, 3124 Williamsburg Dr., (408) 374-4980

Action Day Nursery, 3000 Moorpark Ave., (408) 249-0668

Atypical Infant Motivation, 4115 Jacksol Dr., (408) 559-1400

Bright Horizons, 6120 Liska Ln., (408) 225-3276

Center for Employment Training-DCCtr, 701 Vine St., (408) 295-4566

CET Montessori, 1212 McGinness, (408) 929-4627

Children's Presch Ctr.- Evergreen, 3403 Yerba Buena Rd., (408) 239-2633

Familiar Footsteps, 301 Cottle Rd., (408) 225-0289

Future Assests CD, 7245 Sharon Dr., (408) 252-0203

Good Samaritan Hospital CDCtr., 2425 Samaritan Dr., (408) 264-1275

Headsup CDCtr., 2841 Junction Ave., (408) 424-1155

KinderCare Learning Ctr., 3320 San Felipe Rd., (408) 270-0980

KinderCare Learning Ctr.-Foxworthy, 1081 Foxworthy Ave., (408) 265-7380

Kinderwood Childrens Ctr., 5560 Entrada Cedros, (408) 363-1366

Montessori Acad., 1188 Wunderlich Dr., (408) 255-4710

Neighborhood Christian Presch., 2575 Coit Dr., (408) 371-4222

One World Montessori Sch., 5331 Dent Ave., (408) 723-5140

Orchard Sch. Dist./Early Learning Ctr., 921 Fox Ln., (408) 044-0395

Primary Plus-Hibiscus, 801 Hibiscus Ln., (408) 248-2464

Rainbow Bridge Ctr., 750 N. Capitol Ave., (408) 254-1280

San Jose Day Nursery, 33 No. 8th St., (408) 295-2752

San Jose Job Corps, 3485 E. Hills Dr., (408) 923-1200

San Juan Bautista CDCtr., 1945 Terilyn Ave., (408) 259-4796

Santa Familia CDCtr., 4758 Joseph Speciale Dr., (408) 264-1012

Santa Teresa Village CDCtr., 7026 Santa Teresa Blvd., (408) 225-5437

St. Elizabeth's Day Home, 1544 McKinley Ave. Rm 6,9 & Aud., (408) 295-3456

Tamian CCCtr., 1197 Lick Ave., (408) 271-1980

TLC Child Care Ctr., 2466 Almaden Rd., (408) 264-3707

Trinity Presbyterian CCtr., 3151 Union Ave., (408) 377-2342

Tutor Time Child Care/Learning Ctr., 5891 Santa Teresa Blvd., (408) 224-8687 *See ad on page 111.*

Valley Medical Ctr., 569 Thorton Way, (408) 297-9044
Voyager's DCCtr., 1590 Las Plumas Ave., (408) 926-8885
Wonder Years, 1411 Piedmont Rd., (408) 946-8728
YWCA-Eden Palms CCCtr, 5398 Monterey Rd., (408) 227-9858
YWCA-Villa Nueva, 375 S. 3rd St., (408) 295-4011

Santa Clara
Beautiful Beginnings Presch., 890 Pomery, (408) 247-4234
Happy Days CD Ctr., 220 Blake Ave., (408) 296-5770
Kinder Care Learning Ctr., 840 Bing Dr., (408) 246-2141
Martinson CDCtr., Bldg 8, Circle Dr. S/Mesa Ln., (408) 988-8296
Monticello CDCtr., 3401 Monroe St., (408) 261-0494
Neighborhood Christian Presch., 1290 Pomeroy Ave., (408) 984-3418
Small World-Sutter, 3200 Forbes Ave. #5, (408) 985-5990
YMCA-Millikin, 2720 Sonoma Pl., (408) 243-6577

Saratoga
Magic Years Child Care, 1472 Saratoga Ave., (408) 376-0385

Primary Plus, 12211 Titus Ave., Rm 19, (408) 996-1437
Primary Plus, 18720 Bucknall Rd., (408) 370-0350

Stanford
Children's Ctr. of Stanford, 695 Pampas Ln., (650) 853-3090
Stanford Arboretum, 211 Quarry Rd., (650) 725-6322

Sunnyvale
Calif. Young World #5, 1110 Fairwood Ave., (408) 245-7285
Caring Hearts CD Ctr., 645 W. Fremont Ave., (408) 245-6356
Children's Creative Learning Ctr., 794 E. Duane Ave., (408) 732-2288
De Lor Montessori Sch., 1510 Lewiston Dr., (408) 773-0200
Early Horizons, 1510 Lewiston Dr., (408) 746-3020
Feeling Better Ctr. (Ill Child), 335 Moffett Park Dr., (408) 745-1400
Little Rascals CCCtr., 494 S. Bernardo Ave., (408) 730-9900
Mothers Day Out, 728 W. Fremont Ave., (408) 736-2511
Prodigy CDCtr., 1155 E. Arquez Ave., (408) 245-3276
Rainbow Montessori, 790 Duane Ave., (408) 738-3261
Sunnyvale CDCtr., 1500 Partridge Ave., (408) 730-9600

Chapter 6

SANTA CLARA COUNTY
Day Care

SEE THE PRECEDING chapter on baby care for more information about how local baby and child care is provided and who provides it.

For insights on how to pick a day-care center or provider, here is some advice offered by a person who runs a day-care center.

• Ask about age restrictions. Many centers and family-care providers will not take care of children under age two or not toilet trained. See previous chapter for infant centers.

• Give the center or home a visual check. Is it clean? In good condition or in need of repairs? Is there a plan for repairs when needed?

• Find out if the person in charge is the owner or a hired manager. Nothing wrong with the latter but you should know who is setting policy and who has the final say on matters.

• Ask about the qualifications of the people who will be working directly with your child. How long have they worked in day care? Training? Education? Many community colleges now offer training in early childhood and after-school care.

• What philosophy or approach does the center use. The Piaget approach believes children move through three stages and by exploring the child will naturally move through them. The job of the teacher is to provide activities appropriate to the right stage. For example, from age 2-7, many children master drawing and language; from 7-11, they begin to think logically. For the younger child art and sorting and language games would be appropriate; multiplication would not.

Montessori believes that if given the right materials and placed in the right setting, children will learn pretty much by themselves through trial and error. Montessorians employ specific toys for teaching.

Traditional emphasizes structure and repetition.

These descriptions are oversimplified and do not do justice to these approaches or others. Our only purpose here is to point out that day-care providers vary in methods and thinking, and in choosing a center, you also choose a distinct philosophy of education.

• For family day-care providers. Some set up a small preschool setting in the home. Often your child will be welcomed into the family as an extended member. Is this what you want?

• Discipline. Johnny throws a snit. How is it handled? Does the provider have a method or a plan? Do you agree with it?

• Tuition. How much? When it is due? Penalty for picking up child late? Penalty for paying late?

• Hours of operation. If you have to be on the road at 5:30 a.m. and the day-care center doesn't open until 6, you may have to look elsewhere or make different arrangements. Some centers limit their hours of operation, e.g., 10 hours.

• Holidays. For family providers, when will the family take a vacation or not be available? For the centers, winter breaks? Summer vacations?

• Communication. Ask how you will be kept informed about progress and problems. Regular meetings? Notes? Calls? Newsletters?

• Classes-Tips for parents. Opportunities to socialize with other parents? Activities for whole family?

• Field trips and classes. Outside activities. Your son and daughter play soccer, an activity outside the day-care center. How will they get to practice? What's offered on site? Gymnastics? Dance?

• Siestas. How much sleep will the children get? When do they nap? Does this fit in with your child's schedule?

• Activities. What are they? How much time on them? Goals?

• Diapers, bottles, cribs, formula, extra clothes. Who supplies what?

• Food, lunches. What does the center serve? What snacks are available?

Remember, day-care centers and providers are in business. The people who staff and manage these facilities and homes may have the best intentions toward the children but if they can't make a profit or meet payrolls, they will fail or be unable to provide quality care. Even "nonprofits" must be run in a businesslike way or they won't survive.

Some centers may offer a rich array of services but for fees beyond your budget. You have to decide the tradeoffs.

For licensing, the state divides child care into several categories, including infant, licensed family, child-care centers, and school-age centers for older children. The previous chapter lists the infant providers. This chapter will list the large day-care centers, for both pre-school and school-age children.

For a list of family-care providers, please call the Community Coordinated Child Development Council of Santa Clara at (408) 487-0747.

Alviso (San Jose)

Geo. Mayne St. Presch., 5030 N. First St., (408) 983-2150

Campbell

A Special Place-Camden, 1260 Erin Way, (408) 559-1566

Aurora CDCtr., 995 Apricot Ave., (408) 371-2605

Bright Days CDCtr., 1675 Winchester Blvd., (408) 378-8422

Bright Ideas, 1063 Fewtrell Dr., (408) 371-9310

Campbell Parents Nursery, 528 N. Harrison St., (408) 866-7223

Capri Extended Day, 850 Chapman Dr., (408) 370-9646

Castlemont Sch.-Age CDCtr., 3040 E. Payne Ave., (408) 378-2143

Christian Day Nursery Sch., 1075 W. Campbell Ave., (408) 378-0879

Discoveryland, 600 W. Campbell Ave., (408) 379-6636

Early Years CDC, 3225 S. Winchester Vlvd., (408) 378-9000

Executive Sweet , 2323 S. Bascom Ave., (408) 559-6090

Hazelwood Extd. Day , 775 Waldo Rd., (408) 370-9699

Hazelwood Head Start, 775 Waldo Rd., (408) 453-6900

Kiderwood Children's Ctr. #2, 1190 W. Latimer, (408) 374-4442

Kids at Play Presch., 124 Latimer, (408) 370-3745

Kinder Care Learning Ctr., 1806 W. Campbell, (408) 379-8152

Montessori Acad.-Campbell, 177 E. Rincon, (408) 378-9244

Moreland Area Comm. Ctr., 1125 W. Campbell Ave., Rm 2, (408) 374-4103

Noah's Ark , 560 N. Harrison Ave., (408) 378-3212

Primary Plus, 1125 W. Campbell Ave., (408) 379-3198

Primary Plus, Inc., 1125 W. Campbell Ave., (408) 379-3198

Raggedy Ann and Andy Presch., 1291 Elam Ave., (408) 866-5422

Rosemary Sch.-Age CDCtr, 401 W. Hamilton Ave., (408) 725-1717

Rosemary State Presch., 401 W. Hamilton Ave., (408) 374-1158

San Jose Montessori Sch., 1300 Sheffield Ave., (408) 377-9888

Cupertino

Apple CCCtr., 10253 Portal Ave., (408) 862-6170

Bethel Lutheran Nursery & Learning Ctr, 10181 Finch Ave., (408) 252-8512

Calif. Children's Comm.-Regnart, 1180 Yorkshire Dr., (408) 253-8820

Children's Creative Learning Ctr., 10931 Maxine Dr., (408) 736-7334

Collins Schoolage CDC, 10401 Vista Dr., (408) 446-5428

De Anza CDCtr., 21250 Stevens Creek Blvd., (408) 864-8822

Faria Schoolage CDC, 10155 Barbara Ln., (408) 973-0325

Garden Gate CDCtr., 10500 Ann Arbor Ave., (408) 725-0269

Good Samaritan, 19624 Homestead Rd., (408) 996-8290

Little People Christian DCCtr., 20900 McClellan Rd., (408) 257-1212

Play and Learn, 10067 Byrne Ave., (408) 253-7081

Portal School CDC, 10300 Blaney Ave., (408) 996-1540

Sedgwick CDCtr., 19200 Phil Ln., (408) 725-0909

TLC , 10038 Bret Ave., (408) 996-1866

Vallco CDCtr., 10123 N. Wolfe Rd., (408) 446-4136

Villa Montessori Sch., 20900 Stevens Creek Rd., (408) 257-3374

Village Little, 10100 N. Stelling Rd., (408) 252-2050

YMCA-Lincoln, 21710 McClellan Rd., (408) 996-9260

YMCA-Northwest, 20803 Alves Dr., (408) 257-7160

YMCA-Stevens Creek, 10300 Ainsworth Dr., (408) 736-5041

Gilroy

Christopher Ranch Head Start, 305 Bloomfield Ave., (408) 847-3110

Countryside DCC, 8985 Monterey Rd., (408) 848-3448

Fourth St. Head Start, 7600 Church St., (408) 848-5093
Gavilan College CD Lab, 5055 Santa Teresa Blvd., (408) 848-4815
Gilroy CDCtr., 8387 Wren Ave., (408) 842-8447
Gilroy Head Start Ctr., 7151 Hanna St., (408) 842-3022
Gilroy Unified State Presch., 475 W. Ninth St., (408) 842-4486
Goldsmith Seeds Ctr., 2280 Hecker Pass Hwy., (408) 847-7333
Happy Place Montessori, 7360 & 7350 Alexander St., (408) 848-3819
Medallion Sch. Partnerships, 8755 Kern Ave., (408) 847-1932
Medallion Sch. Partnerships, 9225 Calle Del Rey, (408) 842-7150
Medallion Sch. Partnerships, 930 3rd St., (408) 842-1093
Ochoa Infant Migrant CDCtr., 915 Southside Dr., (408) 842-5066
Vineyard Presch., 1735 Hecker Pass, (408) 842-2713
YMCA-Las Animas, 8450 Wren Ave., Portable, (408) 842-5245

Los Altos Hills
Foothill College Campus CDC, 12345 El Monte Rd., (650) 941-7500
YMCA Kid's Place-Bullis, 25890 Fremont Rd., (650) 941-3876

Los Altos
Almond Extended Day, 550 Almond Ave., (650) 949-4075
Altos Oaks Presch., 625 Magdalena, (650) 948-2907
Children's House of Los Altos, 770 Berry Ave., (650) 968-9052
Joan Bourriague's Presch., 1040 Border Rd., (650) 941-1662
Los Altos-Mtn. View Children's Corner, 97 Hillview Ave., (650) 948-8950
Monarch Christian Sch., 2420 Foothill Blvd., (650) 773-8543
Montclaire Sch.-Age CDC, 1160 St. Joseph Ave., (650) 965-7169
Montecito Presch., 1468 Grant Road, (650) 968-5957
Montessori School of Los Altos, 201 Covington Rd., (650) 948-2329
New Horizons Presch., 211 Covington Rd., (650) 948-8265
Oak Extended Day Prgm., 1501 Oak Ave., (650) 969-2751

Santa Rita Extended Day, 700 Los Altos Ave., (650) 968-3756
Stepping Stones, 201 Covington Rd., (650) 435-8823

Los Gatos
Addison Penzak Jewish Comm. Ctr., 14855 Oka Rd, Rm 25, (408) 358-3636
Casa Maria Montessori, 200 Prospect Ave., (408) 354-8475
Green Hills Presch., 16195 George St., (408) 356-8911
Growing Footprints & Growing Footsteps, 16575 Shannon Rd., (408) 356-4442
Harwood Hills Country Sch., 16220 Harwood Rd., (408) 266-2400
Hillbrook Presch., 16000 Marchmont Dr., (408) 356-6511
Holy Cross Lutheran CCtr., 15885 Los Gatos-Almaden Rd., (408) 356-6828
JCC Afterschool-Kidsspace, 14855 Oka Rd, Rm 20 & 23, (408) 356-0814
Kiddie Kampus DCCtr., 16330 Los Gatos Blvd., (408) 356-6776
Little Oak Presch., 16837 Placer Oaks Rd., (408) 356-2444
Los Gatos Acad., 220 Belgatos Road, #K2, (408) 358-1046
Magic Rock CDC, 14969 Los Gatos-Almaden Rd., (408) 559-8531
Oak Tree Children's Club, 17765 Daves Ave., (408) 395-6144
Open Doors CDCtr., 630 W. Parr Ave., (408) 370-7064
Peppertree Presch., 16035 Los Gatos-Almaden Rd., (408) 356-3211
Rinconada Hills Charmer Presch.-DC, 1975 Pollard Rd., (408) 378-7805
Shannon Nursery, 16575 Shannon Rd., (408) 356-6156
YMCA-Alta Vista, 200 Blossom Valley Dr., (408) 356-1866

Milpitas
Children's World-Medallion Sch. Partnerships, 860 Hillview Rd., (408) 263-0444
Day Star Montessori, 215 Dempsey Rd., (408) 263-1618
Elan Esprit Presch., 40 E. Carlo St., (408) 493-2441
First Years, 1400 S. Main St. CCC, (408) 730-9900

Hands on Learning Ctr., 637 So. Main St., (408) 946-5622

KinderCare Learning Ctr, 400 So. Abel St., (408) 263-7212

Milpitas Christian Presch.-DC, 10 Dempsey Rd., (408) 957-0523

Milpitas Christian Presch.-DC, 200 Abbott Rd., (408) 946-5795

Milpitas Christian Sch., 1435 Clear Lake, (408) 262-2630

Milpitas Discoveryland, 1991 Landess Ave., (408) 263-7626

Milpitas Montessori, 1500 Yosemite Dr., (408) 720-3913

Milpitas Parents Presch., 355 E. Dixon Rd., (408) 263-3950

Milpitas-Rose Head Start, 250 Roswell Dr., (408) 262-3641

Monarch Christian , 1715 Calaveras Blvd., (408) 263-4840

Rainbow Bridge, 123 Corning Ave., (408) 946-2812

Rainbow Bridge Ctr., 1500 Yosemite Dr., (408) 945-9090

Randall Schoolage , 1300 Edsel Dr., (408) 945-5585

Rose CDCtr., 250A Roswell Dr., (408) 262-3535

Spangler CD, 140 N. Abbott Ave., (408) 945-5591

St. John The Baptist Sch., 360 S. Abel St., (408) 262-8110

Sunnyhills CDCtr., 356 Dixon Rd., (408) 945-5577

Tri-Cities Sunnyhills Children's Ctr., 297 Autrey St., (408) 263-9576

YMCA Pomeroy, 1505 Escuela, (408) 298-3888

Moffett Field

Ames CCCtr., Bldg. T20-D, (650) 604-4184

Morgan Hill

Burnett Schoolage CDC, 85 Tilton, (408) 779-6016

Countryside DC #2, 174 W. Main Ave., (408) 779-1220

El Toro CDC-State Presch., 455 E. Main St., (408) 778-1402

Galvan Park CDCtr., 17666 Crest Ave., (408) 779-6553

KinderCare Learning Ctr. , 605 E. Dunne Ave., (408) 778-1237

Linda's Place DCC, 17535 Del Monte, (408) 779-7678

Little Sonshine, 16970 DeWitt Ave., (408) 779-6788

Montessori Learning for Living, 16900 De Witt Ave., (408) 358-2032

Morgan Hill Children's Ctr., 17720 Peak Ave., (408) 779-9924

Morgan Hill Parent-Child Nursery, 16870 Murphy Ave., (408) 779-4515

Morgan Hill PreSch Acad., 17780 Monterey Rd., (408) 226-2857

Noah's Ark, 18980 Monterey Rd., (408) 776-3262

Nordstrom State Presch., 1425 E. Dunne Ave., (408) 778-2821

P.A. Walsh CDC, 353 W. Main St., (408) 778-2896

Tutor Time Child Care/Learning Ctr., 610 Dunne Ave., (408) 778-1977 *See ad on page 111.*

YMCA-Jackson, 2700 Fountain Oaks Dr., (408) 779-8854

YMCA-Paradise Valley , 1400 La Crosse Dr., (408) 778-5711

Young Explorer, 25 Wright Ave., (408) 778-2529

Mountain View

Abracadabra Child Care Ctrs., 1120 Rose Ave, (650) 965-0695

Castro State Presch., 505 Escuela Ave., (650) 964-7555

Hobbledehoy Montessori Presch., 2321 Jane Ln., (650) 968-1155

Kiddie Acad. CC Learning Ctr., 205 E. Middlefield Rd., (650) 960-6900

Kidstown CDC, 180 No. Rengstorff, (650) 964-5006

KinderCare, 2065 W. El Camino Real, (650) 967-4430

Little Acorn, 1667 Miramonte Ave., (650) 964-8445

Mt. View Parent Nursery, 1299 Bryant Ave., (650) 969-9506

Mt. View Sch. Dist. State Presch., 325 Gladys Ave., (650) 526-3530

Oaktree III, 2100 University Ave., (650) 493-1905

Primary Plus, 333 Eunice Ave., (408) 967-3780

Southbay Christian Ctr., 1134 Miramonte Ave., (650) 961-5781

St. Paul Lutheran CDCtr., 1075 El Monte Ave., (650) 967-0667

St. Timothy's Nursery, 2094 Grant Rd., (650) 967-4724

Walnut Grove CCtr., 84 Murlagan Ave., (650) 960-1826

Western Montessori Day Sch., 323 Moorpark Way, (650) 961-4131

Whisman Head Start, 750-A San Pierre Way #1, (650) 960-3427

YMCA Kid's Place-Bubb, 525 Hans St., (650) 965-2922

YMCA Kid's Place-Castro, 505 Escuela, (650) 965-1436

YMCA Kid's Place-Landels, 115 W. Dana St., (650) 965-2008

YMCA Kid's Place-Monta Loma, 460 Thompson Ave., (650) 966-1120

YMCA Kid's Place-Slater, 325 Gladys Ave., (650) 965-8002

YMCA Kid's Place-Theuerkauf, 1625 San Luis Ave., Portable 18, (650) 961-7076

YMCA of the East Bay, 750 San Pierre Way, (650) 964-3809

YMCA-Way to Grow Presch.-El Camino, 115 W. Dana St., (650) 965-2008

Palo Alto

Addison Kids Corner, 650 Addison Ave, (650) 323-6806

Albert L. Schultz Jewish Comm. Ctr, 655 Arastradero Rd., (650) 493-9400

Barron Park Presch., 3650 La Donna Ave., (650) 493-7597

Besse Bolton CCtr., 500 E. Meadow Dr., (650) 856-0847

Besse Bolton CD, 4120 Middlefield Rd., (650) 856-0876

Casa dei Bambini, 463 College, (650) 858-0892

Children's Ctr of Stanford Comm. Big Kids, 695 Pampas Lane, (650) 853-3090

Children's Presch., 4000 Middlefield, T-1, (650) 855-5770

College Terrace Presch., 2300 Wellesley, (650) 858-1580

Community Assoc. for Rehabilitation, 3864 Middlefield Road, (650) 494-0550

Country Day Little School, 3990 Ventura Ct., (650) 464-8044

Covenant Children's Ctr., 670 E. Meadow Dr., (650) 493-9505

Discovery Montessori, 303 Parkside Dr., (650) 570-5038

Downtown Children's Ctr., 555 Waverly, (650) 321-9578

Duveneck Kids Club, 705 Alester Ave., (650) 328-8356

El Carmelo Kids Corner, 3024 Bryant St., (650) 856-6150

Ellen Thacher CCtr., 505 E. Charleston Rd., (650) 493-2361

Escondido Kid's Club, 890 Escondido Rd.., (650) 855-9828

First Congregational Church Nursery, 1985 Louis Rd., (650) 856-6662

First School, 625 Hamilton Ave., (650) 323-6167

Good Neighbor Montessori, 4000 Middlefield Road, (650) 493-2777

Grace Lutheran Presch., 3149 Waverly St., (650) 494-1212

Headsup CDCtr., 4251 El Camino Real Bldg A, (650) 424-1155

Heffalump Coop., 3990 Ventura Ct., (650) 856-4321

Hoover Kids Corner, 800 Barron Ave., (650) 856-3177

Int'l School of the Peninsula, 870 N. California, (650) 328-2338

Learning Center, 459 Kingsley, (650) 325-6683

Love-N-Care Christian Presch., 2490 Middlefield Rd., (650) 322-1872

Mid-Peninsula YWCA CCC, 4161 Alam St., (650) 494-0972

Midtown Nursery, 855 Bruce Dr., (650) 856-7461

Ohlone Kids Club, 950 Amarillo Ave., (650) 493-2361

Palo Alto Comm. CC, 4100 Orme St., (650) 856-0877

Palo Alto Friends Nursery, 957 Colorado St., (650) 856-0744

Palo Alto Montessori, 575 Arastradero Rd., (650) 493-5930

Palo Verde Kid's Corner, 3450 Louise Rd., (650) 856-1337

Peninsula Day Care Ctr., 525 San Antonio Rd., (650) 494-1880

Piccolo, 888 Boyce Ave., (650) 322-9668

Redwood Enrichment Ctr., 500 E. Meadow Dr., (650) 858-1006

Sojourner Truth CDCtr., 3990 Ventura Ct., (650) 493-5990

Walter Hayes Kids Club, 1525 Middlefield Rd., (650) 325-5350

Whistle Stop, 3801 Miranda Ave. #T6B, (650) 852-3497

Young Life Christian Presch., 687 Arastradero Rd., (650) 494-7885

San Jose

A Brand New World, 2174 Lincoln Ave, (408) 978-1116

A Place to Grow, 3001 Ross Avenue, (408) 265-2994

A Special Place-Mobile West, 295 Nicholson Ln., (408) 433-5242

A Special Place-Williamsburg, 3124 Williamsburg Dr., (408) 374-4980

A.T.L.C. Presch., 1855 Curtner Ave., (408) 264-3151

A.T.L.C. Presch., 1975 Cambrianna Dr, (408) 371-2573

Achieve Therapeutic Presch., 3800 Blackbird Ave., (408) 494-1200

Achiever Christian, 800 Ironwood Dr., (408) 264-2345

Action Day Nursery, 2146-2148 Lincoln Ave., (408) 266-8952

Action Day Nursery, 3000 Moorpark Ave., (408) 249-0668

After School Adventures-Steindorf Play Society, 3001 Ross Ave., #10 &12, (408) 264-8400

Almaden Head Start, 1200 Blossom Hill Rd., (408) 265-6251

Almaden Parents Presch., 5805 Cahalan Ave., (408) 225-7211

Alphabet Soup, 1191 DeAnza Blvd., (408) 253-6660

Anderson Head Start, 4000 Rhoda Dr., (408) 248-6697

Anderson Schoolage CDC, 6800 Calpine Dr., (408) 972-5373

Andrew Hill CCtr., 3200 Senter Rd., (408) 226-5822

Applegate School, 890 Meridian Way, (408) 947-1221

Arbuckle CDCtr., 1910 Cinderella Ln., (408) 259-8340

Arbuckle-Sunset Head Start, 1970 Cinderella Ln., (408) 251-4062

Astroland Presch., 3993 Will Rogers Dr., (408) 247-4510

Bachrodt CDCtr., 1471 Keoncrest Rd., (408) 453-0511

Bachrodt Schoolage CDCtr., 102 Sonora Ave., (408) 453-7533

Berryessa CDCtr., 2760 Trimble Rd., (408) 923-1943

Berryessa Presch.-Northwood Elem., 2760 Trimble Rd., (408) 923-1944

Bethel CCCtr., 1201 S. Winchester, (408) 246-6790

Blackford Sch.-Age CDCtr., 1970 Willow St., (408) 371-9900

Blackford State Presch., 3800 Blackford Ave., (408) 248-6661

Blossom Hill-Southside State Presch., 5585 Cottle Rd., (408) 225-6885

Bright Beginnings, 635 Calero Ave., (408) 227-1771

Bright Horizons, 6120 Liska Ln., (408) 225-3276

Building Blocks, 6350 Rainbow Dr., (408) 996-2477

C.A.R. Creative Rec. , 780 Thornton Way, (408) 298-2009

Carter Ave. Nursery Sch., 5303 Carter Ave., (408) 265-3580

CAS-Los Arboles Head Start, 455 Los Arboles Ave., (408) 363-9016

Cathedral of Faith Learning, 2315 Canoas Garden Ave., (408) 267-4691

Center for Employment Training-DCCtr, 701 Vine St., (408) 295-4566

Central Nursery, 1177 Naglee Ave., (408) 287-0266

CET Montessori, 1212 McGinness, (408) 929-4627

Challenger Presch. #3, 4977 Dent Ave., (408) 266-7073

Challenger School, 880 Wren Dr., (408) 448-3010

Cherrywood Extended DCCtr., 2550 Greengate Dr., (408) 259-9739

Child Kingdom, 4160 Senter Rd., (408) 365-1236

Childcare Ctr. at Calvary Chapel, 1175 Hillsdale Ave., (408) 269-8331

Children's Presch Ctr.- Evergreen, 3403 Yerba Buena Rd., (408) 239-2633

Church of the Chimes CCtr., 1447 Bryan Ave., (408) 723-3600

Clement Presch., 955 Branham Ln., (408) 256-2226

College of the Crayons CDC, 4390 Narvaez Ave., (408) 723-8650

Congregation Sinai, 1556 Willowbrae, (408) 264-8486

Cornerstone Presch., 6601 Camden Ave., (408) 268-7595

Cory Sch. CDCtr., 897 Broadleaf Ln., (408) 296-5975

Crayon Ctr., 1590 Minnesota Ave., (408) 269-8026

Creative Beginnings, 14834 Leigh Ave.,
(408) 559-3247

Cupertino House of Montessori, 1211 D
& E Kentwood Ave., (408) 255-8905

De Vargas Sch.-Age CDC, 5050
Moorpark, (408) 725-0278

Del Roble CDCtr., 5345 Avenida
Almendros, (408) 371-9900

Dilworth Sch.-Age CDC, 101 Strayer Dr.,
(408) 446-5285

Discovery Ctr., 4645 Albany Dr., (408)
985-1460

Discovery Parent-Child Presch., 1919
Gunston Way, (408) 377-5390

Discovery School, 801 Hibiscus, (408)
556-1040

East Hills Presch., 14845 Story Rd.,
(408) 923-8616

Easthills/Lyndale Head Start, 13901
Nordyke Dr., (408) 258-1523

Eastside CDC, 2490 Story Rd., (408)
251-7516

**Eastside Parents Participating Nursery
Sch.,** 935 Piedmont Rd., (408) 926-
1264

Edenvale/Discovery Head Start, 285
Azucar Ave., (408) 363-1823

Eitz Chaim Acad., 1532 Willowbrae Ave.,
(408) 978-5822

El Rancho Verde CDCtr., 3l8 El Rancho
Verde Dr., (408) 254-1717

Emmanuel's CDC, 467 N. White Rd.,
(408) 272-9310

**Empire Gardens At Waston Park
Annex,** 550 N. 22nd St., (408) 535-
6083

Enchanted Land Montessori, 667 N.
First St., (408) 275-1720

Enchanted Land Montessori II, 712 Elm
St., (408) 293-9669

Evergreen Valley College CDCtr., 3095
Yerba Buena Rd., (408) 270-6452

Evergreen Valley Presch., 3122 Fowler
Rd., (408) 238-4001

Explorer Presch., 15040 Union Ave.,
(408) 879-0181

Familiar Footsteps, 301 Cottle Rd., (408)
225-0289

Familiar Footsteps, 420 Calero Ave.,
(408) 227-3464

Foothill Christian Presch., 5301 McKee Rd., (408) 258-8133

Forest Hill Extended Day, 4450 McCoy, (408) 370-9697

Foxdale-Story Road Head Start, 1250 Foxdale Loop, (408) 251-8796

Frances Gulland CDCtr., 405 S. 10th St., (408) 924-6988

Frances Presley CDCtr., 1990 Kammerer Ave., (408) 258-4923

Franklin House Head Start, 451 Baltic, (408) 293-3558

Fred Marten Head Start, 14265-B Story Rd., Rm. 1, (408) 254-2035

Future Assests CD, 7245 Sharon Dr., (408) 252-0203

Gardner Children's Ctr., 611 Willis Ave., (408) 998-1343

Gardner's River Glen , 1610 Bird Ave., (408) 998-1343

Gardner/Washington at CET, 701 Vine St., (408) 534-5227

Gloria Dei Lutheran, 121 S. White Rd., (408) 258-7563

Good Samaritan Hospital CDCtr., 2425 Samaritan Dr., (408) 264-1275

Goss Presch., 2475 Van Winkle Ln., (408) 258-4923

Grace Head Start, 2650 Aborn Rd., (408) 274-8193

Grant CDC Schoolage, 470 E. Jackson St., Rm F26, (408) 998-4204

Grant Presch., 470 E. Jackson St., (408) 293-7955

Graystone CDCtr., 6982 Shearwater Dr., (408) 997-1980

Green Hills Presch. Downtown, 571 N. 3rd St., (408) 286-1533

Green Valley CDCtr., 302 Checkers Dr., (408) 923-1130

Green Valley CDCtr., 525 Giuffrieda Ave., (408) 371-9900

Grove CDCtr., 510 E. Branham Ln., (408) 226-3640

Hacienda Presch., 1290 Kimberly Dr., (408) 998-6259

Hayes CDCtr., 5035 Poston Dr., (408) 371-9900

Head Start-Chandler Tripp, 780 Thornton Way, (408) 293-8404

Headsup CDCtr., 2841 Junction Ave., (408) 424-1155

Hellyer Head Start, 725 Hellyer Ave., (408) 225-8534

Hillview Glen CDCtr., 880 Hillsdale Ave., (408) 265-8329

Holy Cross Lutheran CCtr., 5410 Taft Dr., (408) 356-4777

Holy Family Ed. Ctr., 4850 Pearl Ave., (408) 978-1355

Hubbard Presch., 1745 June Ave., (408) 258-4923

James Lick CCtr., 2955 Alum Rock Ave., (408) 251-8400

Jordan Presch., 5102 Alum Rock Ave., (408) 258-7387

Julian/26th St. Head Start, 333 No. 26th St., (408) 995-6735

K's Quality Children Ctr., 3621 Bercaw Ln., (408) 377-6660

Kid Connection, 410 Sautner Dr., (408) 226-8600

Kiddie Kollege, 5386 Alum Rock Ave., (408) 259-1188

Kiddie Kountry, 2701 So. White Rd., (408) 274-2040

Kids Extended Care, 280 Martinvale Ln., (408) 926-6532

Kids Korner, 1515 Kooser Rd., (408) 267-3706

Kidspark, 1600 Saratoga Ave. #431, (408) 374-2229

Kidspark, 2858 Stevens Creek Blvd., (408) 281-8880

Kidspark, 5440 Thornwood Dr., (408) 356-3721

KinderCare Learning Ctr., 3320 San Felipe Rd., (408) 270-0980

KinderCare Learning Ctr.-Foxworthy, 1081 Foxworthy Ave., (408) 265-7380

Kinderwood Childrens Ctr., 5560 Entrada Cedros, (408) 363-1366

Las Casitas Head Start, 632 N. Jackson Ave., (408) 259-4670

Las Plumas Head Start, 1590 Las Plumas Dr., (408) 926-8885

Latimer Head Start, 4250 Latimer Ave. #8, (408) 453-6900

Learning Co. #2, 5670 Camden Ave., (408) 723-1131

Linda Vista CDCtr., 65 Gordon Ave., (408) 258-4923

Little Friends, 2720 S. Bascom Ave., (408) 377-8541

Little Kiddles/Swing Set Groups, 286 Sorrento Way, (408) 227-5758

Little Scholar Presch., 3560 Kettmann Rd., (408) 238-1474

Little Scholars Schools, 3703 Silvercreek Rd., (408) 274-4726

Los Alamitos Presch., 6130 Silberman Dr., (408) 535-6297

Lotus Presch., 639 N. Fifth St., (408) 293-9292

Luther Burbank CDCtr., 4 Wabash Ave., (408) 295-1731

MACSA Ext. DCtr., 848 E. Williams St., (408) 295-6054

MACSA Youth Ctr., 660 Sinclair Dr., (408) 929-1080

Mandala Children's House, 5038 Hyland Ave., (408) 251-8633

McGinness Head Start, 1212 McGinnis, (408) 453-6900

McKinley Shea Presch., 651 Macredes Ave., (408) 283-6300

Medallion Sch. Partnerships, 6044 Vera Cruz Dr., (408) 997-9821

Meyer Presch., 1824 Daytona Dr., (408) 258-4923

Miller Presch., 1250 S. King Rd., (408) 258-4923

Minigym Explorations, 4115 Jacksol Dr., (408) 559-4616

Monte Alban Head Start, 1324 Santee Dr., (408) 298-2164

Montessori Acad., 1188 Wunderlich Dr., (408) 255-4710

Montessori Acad. III, 495 Massar Ave., (408) 259-5736

Montessori Acad. Saratoga, 480 Saratoga Ave., (408) 244-1420

Mt. Pleasant CCtr., 1650 S. White Rd., (408) 259-2331

Mulberry Coop. Nursery Sch., 1980 Hamilton Ave., (408) 377-1595

Neighborhood Christian Presch., 2575 Coit Dr., (408) 371-4222

New Frontier Presch., 1980 Fruitdale Ave., (408) 295-6687

Noble Extended DC., 3466 Grossmont Dr., (408) 251-8952

Olinder Presch., 890 E. William St., Rm K32, (408) 286-4198

One World Montessori Sch., 5331 Dent Ave., (408) 723-5140

Orchard Sch. Dist./Early Learning Ctr., 921 Fox Ln., (408) 044-0395

Over the Rainbow, 3001 Ross Ave., (408) 978-5454

Pacific Montessori Acad. #1, 4115 Jacksol Dr., (408) 246-5432

Park Ave. Presch., 1080 The Alameda, (408) 294-4807

Parkview CDC, 330 Bluefield Dr., (408) 371-9900

Parkway CDCtr., 1800 Fruitdale Ave., (408) 297-7717

Phelan Tiny Tots, 801 Hibiscus Ln., (408) 446-4166

Piedmont Hills Montessori Acad., 1425 Old Piedmont Rd., (408) 923-5151

Pioneer Montessori Presch., 1010 University Ave., (408) 295-8140

Pioneer Montessori Sch., 3520 San Felipe Rd., (408) 238-8445

Play-n-Learn Presch., 3800 Narvaez Ave., (408) 269-9004

Precious Presch., 12360 Redmond Ave., (408) 268-9000

Preschool DC Dom Dinis, 1395 E. Santa Clara St., (408) 993-0383

Primary Plus-Hibiscus, 801 Hibiscus Ln., (408) 248-2464

Rainbow Bridge Ctr., 750 N. Capitol Ave., (408) 254-1280

Rainbow of Knowledge, 1718 Andover Ln., (408) 377-5730

Rainbow/McKinley Head Start, 651 Macredes, (408) 993-0403

Randol School-Age CDC, 762 Sunset Glen Dr., (408) 224-4505

Redmond CDC, 11843 Redmond Ave., (408) 268-5165

Regard CCCtr., 2021 Lincoln Ave., (408) 971-2308

Rex and Lee Lindsey's CDC, 1315 McLaughlin Ave., (408) 279-1388

River Glen Presch., 1619 Bird Ave., (408) 998-6240

Rouleau Head Start, 1875 Monrovia Dr., (408) 270-4873

San Antonio Presch., 1855 E. San Antonio St., (408) 259-3020

San Jose City College, 2100 Moorpark Ave., (408) 288-3759

San Jose Day Nursery, 33 No. 8th St., (408) 295-2752

San Jose Day Nursery, 890 East William, Rm 6 & K33, (408) 288-7855

San Jose Job Corps, 3485 E. Hills Dr., (408) 923-1200

San Jose Parents Participating, 2180 Radio Ave., (408) 265-3202

San Jose State University CDC, 1 Washington Sq., (408) 924-3727

San Juan Bautista CDCtr., 1945 Terilyn Ave., (408) 259-4796

Santa Familia CDCtr., 4758 Joseph Speciale Dr., (408) 264-1012

Santa Maria CCtr., 437 N. 10th St., (408) 729-1490

Santa Teresa CDC, 6200 Encinal Dr., (408) 972-4396

Santa Teresa Children's Ctr., 6150 Snell Rd., (408) 578-4510

Santa Teresa Village CDCtr., 7026 Santa Teresa Blvd., (408) 225-5437

Santee Sch.-Age CDC, 1313 Audobon Dr., (408) 280-6739

Seven Trees Head Start, 3975 Mira Loma, (408) 363-8944

Shea Pre-K Santee School, 1313 Audubon Dr., (408) 283-6450

Shepherd of the Valley Lutheran, 1281 Redmond Rd., (408) 997-4846

Shields Presch., 2851 Gay Ave., (408) 258-4923

Slonaker Ext. Day, 1601 Cunningham Ave., (408) 259-4796

Small World-Athenour #A, 5200 Dent Ave., (408) 257-7320

Small World-Baker, 4845 Bucknall Rd., (408) 257-3757

Small World-Country Lane, 5140 Country Ln., (408) 379-3200

Small World-Latimer, 4250 Latimer Ave., (408) 379-7459

Small World-Noddin, 1755 Gilda Way, (408) 257-7320

Small World-Payne, 3750 Gleason Ave., (408) 246-1028

Small World-Strawberry Park, 730 Camina Escuela, (408) 379-2300

Small World-Valley Vista, 2400 Flint Ave., (408) 238-3525

Solari Park Head Start, 3590 Cas Dr., (408) 578-0283

South Valley Children's Ctr. at Carlton Elem., 2421 Carlton Ave., (408) 356-1453

South Valley Children's Ctr. at Oster Elem., 1855 Lencar Way, (408) 269-1676

South Valley Children's Ctr., 4949 Harwood Rd. #19 & 20, (408) 448-1438

St. Elizabeth's Day Home, 1544 McKinley Ave. Rm 6,9 & Aud., (408) 295-3456

St Frances Cabrini Sch., 15325 Woodard Ave., (408) 377-6545

St. Patrick Sch. , 51 N. 9th St., (408) 283-5858

St. Stephen's School, 500 Shawnee Ln., (408) 227-1235

St. Timothy's Lutheran, 5100 Camden Ave., (408) 265-0244

Steindorf Head Start, 3001 Ross Dr, Rm 5, (408) 266-0953

Strawberry Park Tiny Tots, 730 Camina Escuela, (408) 446-4166

Sunnymont Nursery, 1188 Wunderlich Dr., (408) 253-8125

Sunrise Kiddie Korral, 5860 Blossom Ave., (408) 227-0831

Tamian CCCtr., 1197 Lick Ave., (408) 271-1980

Tinytown, 1133 Piedmont Rd., (408) 923-0441

TLC Child Care Ctr., 2466 Almaden Rd., (408) 264-3707

Tom Thumb Presch., 668 No. First St., (408) 288-8832

Tower Academy, 2887 McLaughlin Ave., (408) 578-2830

Toyon Partners CDCtr., 995 Bard St., (408) 729-8239

Trace Presch., 651 Dana Ave., (408) 535-6257

Trinity Presbyterian CCtr., 3151 Union Ave., (408) 377-2342

Tully Head Start, 420 Tully Rd., (408) 971-7362

Tutor Time Child Care/Learning Ctr., 5891 Santa Teresa Blvd., (408) 224-8687 *See ad on page 111.*

Valley Medical Ctr., 569 Thorton Way, (408) 297-9044

Villa San Pedro Head Start, 282 Danze Dr., (408) 453-6900

Voyager's DCCtr., 1590 Las Plumas Ave., (408) 926-8885

W.C. Overfelt CCtr., 1835 Cunningham Ave., (408) 258-3654

Westside Coop., 3257 Payne Ave., (408) 374-1232

Williams Sch.-Age CDC, 1150 Rajkovich Way, (408) 371-9900

Willow Glen Comm. Ext. Day, 1425 Lincoln Ave., (408) 286-6999

Willow Glen United Meth. Church., 1420 Newport Ave., (408) 294-9796

Willow Vale Christian CC, 1730- Curtner Ave., (408) 448-0656

Willow/Sacred Heart Head Start, 310 Edwards, (408) 286-8826

Winnie the Pooh, 1321 Miller Ave., (408) 996-0851

Wonder Years, 1411 Piedmont Rd., (408) 946-8728

Woolcreek Head Start, 645 Woolcreek Rd., (408) 283-6118

Yerba Buena CCtr., 1855 Lucretia Ave., (408) 279-2760

YMCA-Anderson, 4000 Rhoda Dr., (408) 244-1962

YMCA-Autumn Wonderland, 505 W. Julian, (408) 298-1717

YMCA-Booksin, 1590 Dry Creek Rd., (408) 266-4454

YMCA-Brooktree, 1781 Olivetree Dr., (408) 923-1910

YMCA-Central Presch., 1717 The Alameda , (408) 298-1717

YMCA-East Valley, 1975 S. White Rd., (408) 258-4419

YMCA-Easterbrook, 4660 Eastus Dr., (408) 257-4505

YMCA-Fammatre, 2800 New Jersey Ave., (408) 370-1877

YMCA-Farnham, 15711 Woodard Rd., (408) 370-1877

YMCA-Hacienda Valley View, 1290 Kimberly Dr., (408) 978-1156

YMCA-Hester, 1100 Shasta Ave., (408) 295-1717

YMCA-Holly Oak, 2995 Rossmore Way, (408) 258-4419

YMCA-Laneview, 2095 Warmwood Ln., (408) 923-1920

YMCA-Lietz, 5300 Carter Ave., (408) 298-3888

YMCA-Los Paseos, 121 Avenida Grande, (408) 225-2686

YMCA-Lowell, 625 S. 7th St., (408) 287-8776

YMCA-Majestic Way, 1855 Majestic Way, (408) 923-1925

YMCA-Meyerholz, 6990 Melvin Dr., (408) 996-2308

YMCA-Muir, 6550 Hanover Dr., (408) 253-7440

YMCA-Reed, 1524 Jacob Ave., (408) 978-3002

YMCA-Ruskin, 1363 Turlock Ln., (408) 251-6222

YMCA-Sakamoto, 6280 Shadelands Dr., (408) 227-3605

YMCA-Silver Oak, 1 Farnsworth Dr., (408) 258-4419

YMCA-Simonds, 6515 Grapevine Way, (408) 268-7125

YMCA-Terrell, 5925 Pearl Ave., (408) 226-9622

YMCA-Vinci Park, 1131 Vinci Park Way, (408) 259-0127

YWCA-Christopher, 565 Coyote Rd., (408) 578-1733

YWCA-Eden Palms CCCtr, 5398 Monterey Rd., (408) 227-9858

YWCA-Ext. Program—Lynhaven, 881 S. Cypress Ave., (408) 246-7538

YWCA-Frost, 530 Gettysburg Dr., (408) 225-1881

YWCA-Hillsdale, 3200 Water St., (408) 295-4011

YWCA-Kennedy, 1602 Lucretia Ave., (408) 286-2530

YWCA-O.B. Whaley, 2655 Alvin Ave., (408) 223-8952

YWCA-Villa Nueva, 375 S. 3rd St., (408) 295-4011

YWCA-West Valley, 4343 Leigh Ave., (408) 269-7543

San Martin

San Martin CDC, 100 North St., (408) 683-2808

San Martin Head Start, 13570 Depot Ave., (408) 6783-2800

Santa Clara

A Special Place-Stevens Creek, 5041 Stevens Creek Blvd., (408) 248-0148

Action Day Nursery, 2001 Pruneridge Ave., (408) 244-2909

Alameda Day Nursery, 810 Washington St., (408) 296-7064

Angels Montessori Presch., 1000 Kiely Blvd., (408) 241-8434

Beautiful Beginnings Presch., 890 Pomery, (408) 247-4234

Bowers State Presch., 2755 Barkley Ave., (408) 983-2150

Bracher Children's Ctr., 2401 Bowers Ave., (408) 983-2106

Briarwood Children's Ctr., 1940 Townsend Ave., Rms 25-27, (408) 983-2095

Bright Beginnings Presch., 2445 Cabrillo Ave., (408) 247-7777

Carden El Encanto Day Sch., 615 Hobart Terr., (408) 244-5041

Christian Day Care, 3111 Benton Ave., (408) 241-8964

Family Living Ctr. Head Start, Agnew State Hosp. Circle Dr. #7, (408) 748-8627

First Step Presch., 1515/1525 Franklin St., (408) 554-9591

Happy Days CD Ctr., 220 Blake Ave., ⸱ (408) 296-5770

Hughes State Presch., 4949 Calle de Escuela, (408) 983-2174

Joyful Noise Presch., 1700 Lincoln St., (408) 247-3600

Kids on Campus, Santa Clara University, (408) 554-4771

Kidsville Presch. & DCC, 1247 Benton St., (408) 296-7442

Kinder Care Learning Ctr., 840 Bing Dr., (408) 246-2141

Laurelwood Presch., 955 Teal Dr., (408) 554-1390

Little Lambs Christian Presch., 2499 Homestead Rd., (408) 736-3286

Martinson CDCtr., Bldg 8, Circle Dr. S/ Mesa Ln., (408) 988-8296

MCA Granada Islamic Sch., 3003 Scott Blvd., (408) 980-1161

Mission College Campus CC, (408) 748-2712

Monroe & Pacific Head Start, 2383 Pacific Dr., Rm 3 & 5, (408) 261-2701

Montague State Presch., 750 Laurie Ave., Rm 12, (408) 983-2145

Monticello CDCtr., 3401 Monroe St., (408) 261-0494

Neighborhood Christian Presch., 1290 Pomeroy Ave., (408) 984-3418

One World Montessori Sch., 2495 Cabrillo Ave., (408) 615-1254

Pioneer Montessori Presch., 400 N. Winchester, (408) 241-5077

Santa Clara Christian Pres., 3421 Monroe St., (408) 246-5423

Santa Clara Parents Nursery, 471 Monroe St., (408) 248-5131

Scott Lane State Presch., 1925 Scott Blvd., (408) 983-2150

St. Lawrence Presch., 1971 St. Lawrence Dr., (408) 248-1966

St. Mark's Episcopal Church, 1957 Pruneridge Ave., (408) 247-2223

Warburton Parent-CCtr., 2545 Warburton Ave., (408) 296-2774

YMCA-Eisenhower, 277 Rodonovan Dr., (408) 249-5330

Saratoga

Action Day Nursery, 13560 S. Saratoga-Sunnyvale Rd., (408) 867-4515

Challenger Presch. #2, 18811 Cox Ave., (408) 378-0444

Magic Years Child Care, 1472 Saratoga Ave., (408) 376-0385

Marshall Lane School-Age CDC, 14114 Marilyn Ln., (408) 374-1156

Next Generation CDC, 19190 Austin Way, (408) 927-7250

Notre Dame Montessori Presch., 15100 Norton Rd., (408) 867-1663

Primary Plus, 12211 Titus Ave., Rm 19, (408) 996-1437

Primary Plus, 18720 Bucknall Rd., (408) 370-0350

Saratoga Presbyterian Presch., 20455 Herriman Ave., (408) 741-5770

St. Andrew's School, 13601 Saratoga Ave., (408) 867-3785

Village Presch., 20390 Park Pl., (408) 867-3181

West Valley College CDCtr., 14000 Fruitvale Ave., (408) 741-2007

West Valley Comm. College Dist., 14000 Fruitvale Ave., (408) 867-2200

YMCA-Blue Hill, 12300 De Sanka Ave., (408) 257-7160

YMCA-Southwest Presch., 13500 Quito Rd., (408) 370-1877

Stanford

Bing Nursery, 850 Escondido Rd., (650) 723-4865

Children's Creative Learning Ctr., 1711 Stanford Ave., (650) 493-6006

Peppertree After School, 845 Escondido Rd., (650) 723-0217

Rainbow Sch. at Escondido Village, 859 Escondido Rd., (650) 723-0217

Stanford Arboretum, 211 Quarry Rd., (650) 725-6322

Sunnyvale

Alan S. Maremont CDCtr., 1601 Tenaka Pl., (408) 732-0648

Appleseed Montessori, 1095 Dunford Way #B, (408) 260-7333

Bishop CDCtr., 440 N. Sunnyvale Ave., (408) 739-2611

Calif. Young World #5, 1110 Fairwood Ave., (408) 245-7285

Calif. Young World-Ellis, 550 East Olive St., Rm K1&K2, (408) 774-0405

Calif. Young World-Lakewood, 750 Lakechime, (408) 734-8400

Calif. Young World-San Miguel, 777 San Miguel Ave., (408) 245-7285

Caring Hearts CD Ctr., 645 W. Fremont Ave., (408) 245-6356

Challenger Sch., 1185 Hollenbeck Ave., (408) 245-7170

Cherry Chase Sch.-Age CDC, 1138 Heatherstone, (408) 736-0168

Children's Creative Learning Ctr., 794 E. Duane Ave., (408) 732-2288

Community Presch., 1098 Remington Dr., Rms 2-9, (408) 739-2022

Cumberland Sch.-Age CDC, 824 Cumberland Ave., (408) 371-9900

Cupertino Coop., 563 W. Fremont Ave., (408) 739-8963

De Lor Montessori Sch., 1510 Lewiston Dr., (408) 773-0200

Early Horizons, 1510 Lewiston Dr., (408) 746-3020

Fairwood Elem. Sch., 1110 Fairwood Ave., (408) 522-8200

Fairwood Head Start, 1110 Fairwood Ave., (408) 749-8404

Feeling Better Ctr. (Ill Child), 335 Moffett Park Dr., (408) 745-1400

French-American Sch. of Silicon Valley, 1510 Lewiston Dr., (408) 746-0460

Fun Learning Presch., 1194 Fairwood Ave., (408) 735-1776

Jamil Islamic Ctr/ Silicon Valley Acad., 1095 Dunford Way, Bldg C, (650) 326-0400

Jubilee Academy, 560 Britton Ave., (408) 730-4777

Little Rascals CCCtr., 494 S. Bernardo Ave., (408) 730-9900

Monarch Montessori, 1196 Lime Dr., (408) 749-0239

Montessori House of Children, 582 Dunholme Way #A, (408) 749-1602

Mothers Day Out, 728 W. Fremont Ave., (408) 736-2511

Nimitz School-Age CDC., 545 E. Cheyenne Dr., (408) 736-6176

Ponderosa Dist. Presch., 804 Ponderosa Ave., (408) 736-7647

Presbyterian Early Learning Ctr., 728 W. Fremont Ave., (408) 245-2253

Prodigy CDCtr., 1155 E. Arquez Ave., (408) 245-3276

Rainbow Montessori, 790 Duane Ave., (408) 738-3261

Rainbow Presch., 878 Lakewood Dr., (408) 738-2737

Resurrection Sch., 1395 HBollenbeck Ave., (408) 245-4571

South Peninsula Hebrew Day Sch., 1030 Astoria Dr., (408) 738-3060

St. Martin Sch., 597 Central Ave., (408) 736-5534

Stocklmeir-Ortega Sch.-Age CDC, 592 Dunholme Way, (408) 732-2008

Sunnyvale CDCtr., 1500 Partridge Ave., (408) 730-9600

Sunnyvale Christian Sch., 445 So. Mary Ave., (408) 736-3286

Sunnyvale Parent Presch., 1515 Partridge Ave., (408) 736-8043

Sunnyvale Sch. Dist. Presch., 739 Morse Ave., (408) 522-8213

Triumphant Learning Ctr., 420 Carroll St., (408) 737-7450

Vargas Sch.-Age CDCtr., 1054 Carson Dr., (408) 736-0174

Village Campus CDC, 649 E. Homestead Rd., (408) 732-5611

Wedgwood School, 1025 The Dalles, (408) 720-9080

YMCA-West Valley, 1635 Belleville Way, (408) 245-0148

Chapter **7**

SANTA CLARA COUNTY
Hospitals & Health Care

GOOD HEALTH CARE. You want it. Where, how, do you get it? The question is particularly puzzling these days because so many changes are taking place in medicine and medical insurance.

The "operations" of a few years ago are the "procedures" of today, done in the office not the surgery room, completed in minutes not hours, requiring home care, not hospitalization. Large insurance companies, through their health maintenance plans, are setting limits on what doctors and hospitals can charge, and — critics contend — interfering with the ability of doctors to prescribe what they see fit. The companies strongly deny this, arguing they are bringing reforms to a profession long in need of reforming.

Many hospitals are now setting up their own insurance plans, structured according to the needs of local residents. Many hospitals are also merging, the better to avoid unnecessary duplication and to save money by purchasing supplies and medicine in larger amounts.

Universal health insurance having failed to clear congress, about 43 million Americans are not covered by any medical plan. Unable to afford medical bills, many ignore ailments and illnesses.

This chapter will give you an overview of Northern California health care and although it won't answer all your questions — too complex a business for that — we hope that it will point you in the right directions.

For most people, health care is twined with insurance, in systems that are called "managed care." But many individuals, for a variety of reasons, do not have insurance. This is a good place to start: with nothing, all options open. Let's use as our seeker for the best of all health care worlds — on a tight budget — a young woman, married, one child. Her choices:

No Insurance — Cash Care

The woman is self-employed or works at a small business that does not offer health benefits. She comes down with the flu. When she goes into the doctor's office, she will be asked by the receptionist, how do you intend to pay? With no insurance, she pays cash (or credit card), usually right there. She

WE HAVE FIVE CORE VALUES.
Financial gain isn't one.

How do you know if a hospital values you, or just your insurance payments?

Since 1889, under the inspired leadership of the Daughters of Charity of St. Vincent de Paul, our mission has been to provide our community with the best possible medical care in the most caring environment.

As a member of Catholic Healthcare West, these are our Core Values:

1 **DIGNITY.** "Respecting the inherent value and worth that each person possesses as a member of the human family." Dignity salves the emotional wounds at our VISTAS program for seniors with mental and emotional challenges.

2 **COLLABORATION.** "Working together with people who support common values and vision to achieve shared goals." Our many collaborative efforts include our hospice services which are offered in affiliation with Mid-Peninsula HomeCare and Hospice.

3 **JUSTICE.** "Advocating for change of social structures which undermine human dignity and demonstrating

special concern for the poor." As Catholic hospitals, we place special emphasis on welcoming, serving, comforting and standing up for those less fortunate.

4 **STEWARDSHIP.** "Cultivating the resources entrusted to us to promote healing and wholeness." While making money isn't one of our core values, we manage our finances very carefully. We do this so we can put any surplus back into needed technology or additional services for our community.

Through modern financial management systems and new environmental programs for recycling and safe-guarding our environment, we can better serve and live in harmony in our community.

5 **EXCELLENCE.** "Exceeding expectations through teamwork and innovation." When you visit our hospitals, you may notice that some of our people wear a special pin. The pin is a reward to those who exemplify our core values. Clearly though, the ones who benefit most are our patients.

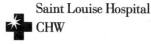

O'Connor Hospital
✚ CHW

2105 FOREST AVENUE, SAN JOSE, CA 95128
(408) 947-2500

Saint Louise Hospital
✚ CHW

18500 SAINT LOUISE DRIVE, MORGAN HILL, CA 95037
(408) 779-1500

Population by Age Groups in Santa Clara County

City or Area	Under 5	5-18	19-29	30-54	55+
Campbell	2,584	4,507	8,329	14,278	6,021
Cupertino	2,383	6,413	6,037	17,494	7,463
Gilroy	2,942	7,353	5,735	10,697	4,284
Los Altos	1,343	4,066	2,176	10,325	8,135
Los Altos Hills	297	1,289	703	3,064	2,084
Los Gatos	1,386	3,725	4,136	11,540	6,289
Milpitas	4,229	9,250	10,436	20,572	5,555
Monte Sereno	135	571	327	1,404	802
Mountain View	4,441	7,531	16,083	27,410	11,394
Palo Alto	2,696	7,188	9,221	22,619	13,700
San Jose	65,666	143,262	163,990	288,971	108,966
San Martin	184	330	381	585	214
Santa Clara	5,880	11,703	23,107	34,602	16,907
Saratoga	1,317	4,507	2,839	11,436	7,608
Stanford	506	867	10,768	2,461	1,167
Sunnyvale	7,538	14,919	25,791	45,146	22,679
Remainder	3,860	9,337	9,368	20,878	10,100
County Total	111,821	247,386	308,400	565,180	243,030

Source: 1990 Census.

takes her prescription, goes to the pharmacy and pays full cost.

If her child or husband gets sick and needs to see a doctor, the same procedure holds. Also the same for treatment of a serious illness, to secure X-rays or hospitalization. It's a cash system.

Medi-Cal

If an illness strikes that impoverishes the family or if the woman, through job loss or simply low wages, cannot afford cash care, the county-state health system will step in. The woman fills out papers to qualify for Medi-Cal, the name of the system (it's known elsewhere as Medicaid), and tries to find a doctor that will treat Medi-Cal patients. If unable to find an acceptable doctor, the woman could turn to a county hospital or clinic. There she will be treated free or at very low cost.

Drawbacks-Pluses of Medi-Cal

County hospitals and clinics, in the personal experience of one of the editors — who has relatives who work at or use county facilities — have competent doctors and medical personnel. If you keep appointments promptly, often you will be seen with little wait. If you want immediate treatment for, say, a cold, you register and you wait until an urgent-care doctor is free.

If you need a specialist, often the county facility will have one on staff, or will be able to find one at a teaching hospital or other facility. You don't choose the specialist; the county physician does.

County facilities are underfunded and inconveniently located — a major drawback. Some counties, lacking clinics and hospitals, contract with adjoining counties that are equipped. You have to drive some distance for treatment.

County hospitals and clinics are not 100 percent free. If you have money or an adequate income, you will be billed for service. Some county hospitals run medical plans designed for people who can pay. These people can ask for a "family" doctor and receive a higher (usually more convenient) level of care.

Let's say the woman lacks money but doesn't want to hassle with a long drive and, possibly, a long wait for treatment of a minor ailment. She can sign up for Medi-Cal to cover treatment of serious illnesses, and for the colds, etc., go to a private doctor for treatment and pay in cash, ignoring Medi-Cal. There are many ways to skin the cat, and much depends on circumstances. For the poor and low-income, Medi-Cal is meant to be a system of last resort.

Medicare — Veterans Hospital

If our woman were elderly, she would be eligible for Medicare, the federal insurance system, which covers 80 percent, with limitations, of medical costs or allowable charges. Many people purchase supplemental insurance to bring coverage up to 100 percent (long-term illnesses requiring hospitalization may exhaust some benefits.) If the woman were a military veteran with a service-related illness, she could seek care at a Veteran's clinic or hospital.

Indemnity Care

Usually the most expensive, this insurance allows complete freedom of choice. The woman picks the doctor she wants. If her regular doctor recommends a specialist, she can decide which one, and if she needs hospital treatment, she can pick the institution. In reality, the choice of hospital and specialist will often be strongly influenced by her regular doctor but the patient retains control. Many indemnity plans have deductibles and some may limit how much they pay out in a year or lifetime. Paperwork may be annoying.

Managed Care

This divides into two systems, Preferred Provider Organizations (PPO) and Health Maintenance Organizations (HMO). Both are popular in California and if your employer provides health insurance, chances are almost 100 percent you will be pointed toward, or given a choice of, one or the other.

PPOs and HMOs differ among themselves. It is beyond the scope of this book to detail the differences but you should ask if coverage can be revoked or rates increased in the event of serious illness. Also, what is covered, what is not. Cosmetic surgery might not be covered. Psychiatric visits or care might be limited. Ask about drug costs and how emergency or immediate care is provided.

Preferred Provider

The insurance company approaches certain doctors, clinics, medical facilities and hospitals and tells them: We will send patients to you but you must agree to our prices — a method of controlling costs — and our rules. The young woman chooses her doctor from the list, often extensive, provided by the PPO.

The physician will have practicing privileges at certain local hospitals. The young woman's child contracts pneumonia and must be hospitalized. Dr. X is affiliated with XYZ hospital, which is also signed up with the PPO plan. The child is treated at XYZ hospital.

If the woman used an "outside" doctor or hospital, she would pay extra — the amount depending on the nature of the plan. It is important to know the doctor's affiliations because you may want your hospital care at a certain institution.

Hospitals differ. A children's hospital, for instance, will specialize in children's illnesses and load up on children's medical equipment. A general hospital will have a more rounded program. For convenience, you may want the hospital closest to your home.

If you need specialized treatment, you must, to avoid extra costs, use the PPO-affiliated specialists. The doctor will often guide your choice.

Complaints are surfacing from people who started out with a general physician, who was affiliated with their PPO, then moved on to a specialist who was not affiliated with the PPO. When the second doctor submits a bill, people are shocked. Each time you see a doctor you should ask if he or she is affiliated with your PPO.

Besides the basic cost for the policy, PPO insurance might charge fees, co-payments or deductibles. A fee might be $5 or $10 a visit. With co-payments, the bill, say, comes to $100. Insurance pays $80, the woman pays $20.

Deductible example: The woman pays the first $250 or the first $2,000 of any medical costs within a year, and the insurer pays bills above $250 or $2,000. With deductibles, the higher the deductible the lower the cost of the policy. The $2,000 deductible is really a form of catastrophic insurance.

Conversely, the higher the premium the more the policy covers. Some policies cover everything. (Dental care is usually provided through a separate insurer.) The same for prescription medicines. You may pay for all, part, or nothing, depending on the type plan.

The PPO doctor functions as your personal physician. Often the doctor will have his or her own practice and office, conveniently located. If you need to squeeze in an appointment, the doctor usually will try to be accommodating.

Drawback: PPOs restrict choice.

Health Maintenance Organization (HMO)

Very big in California because Kaiser Permanente, one of the most popular medical-hospital groups, is run as an HMO. The insurance company and medical provider are one and the same. All or almost all medical care is given by the HMO. The woman catches the flu. She sees the HMO doctor at the HMO clinic or hospital. If she becomes pregnant, she sees an HMO obstetrician at the HMO hospital or clinic and delivers her baby there.

With HMOs you pay the complete bill if you go outside the system (with obvious exceptions; e.g., emergency care).

HMOs encourage you to pick a personal physician. The young woman wants a woman doctor; she picks one from the staff. She wants a pediatrician as her child's personal doctor; the HMO, usually, can provide one.

HMO clinics and hospitals bring many specialists and services together under one roof. You can get your eyes examined, your hearing tested, your prescriptions filled, your X-rays taken within an HMO facility (this varies), and much more.

If you need an operation or treatment beyond the capability of your immediate HMO hospital, the surgery will be done at another HMO hospital within the system or at a hospital under contract with the HMO. Kaiser recently started contracting with other facilities to provide some of the services that it used to do in its own hospitals or clinics.

HMO payment plans vary but many HMO clients pay a monthly fee and a small ($5-$15) per visit fee. Often the plan includes low-cost or reduced-cost or free prescriptions.

Drawback: Freedom of choice limited. If HMO facility is not close, the woman will have to drive to another town.

Point of Service (POS)

Essentially, an HMO with the flexibility to use outside doctors and facilities for an extra fee or a higher deductible. POS systems seem to be popular with people who don't feel comfortable limiting themselves to an HMO.

They pay extra but possibly not as much as other alternatives.

Which is Better: a PPO, an HMO or a POS?

This is a competitive field with many claims and counter claims. In recent years, PPOs have signed up many doctors and facilities — increasing the choices of members. Kaiser Permanente, however, remains very popular.

Point of Service (POS) seems to be catching on but some experts predict it will fade when people become more familiar with HMOs.

If you are receiving medical insurance through your employer, you will be limited to the choices offered. In large groups, unions often have a say in what providers are chosen. Some individuals will base their choice on price, some on convenience of facilities, others on what's covered, and so on.

Many private hospitals offer Physician Referral Services. You call the hospital, ask for the service and get a list of doctors to choose from. The doctors will be affiliated with the hospital providing the referral. Hospitals and doctors will also tell you what insurance plans they accept for payment and will send you brochures describing the services the hospital offers.

For Kaiser and other HMOs, call the local hospital or clinic.

A PPO will give you a list of its member doctors and facilities.

Ask plenty of questions. Shop carefully.

Common Questions

The young woman is injured in a car accident and is unconscious. Where will she be taken?

Generally, she will be taken to the closest emergency room or trauma center, where her condition will be stabilized. Her doctor will then have her admitted into a hospital. Or she will be transferred to her HMO hospital or, if indigent, to a county facility.

If her injuries are severe, she most likely will be rushed to a regional trauma center. Trauma centers have specialists and special equipment to treat serious injuries. Both PPOs and HMOs offer urgent care and emergency care.

The young woman breaks her leg. Her personal doctor is an internist and does not set fractures. What happens?

The personal doctor refers the case to a specialist. Insurance pays the specialist's fee.

In PPO, the woman would generally see a specialist affiliated with the PPO. In an HMO, the specialist would be employed by the HMO.

The young woman signs up for an HMO then contracts a rare disease or suffers an injury that requires treatment beyond the capability of the HMO. Will she be treated?

Often yes, but it pays to read the fine print. The HMO will contract treatment out to a facility that specializes in the needed treatment.

The young woman becomes despondent and takes to drink. Will insurance pay for her rehabilitation?

Depends on her insurance. And often her employer. Some may have drug and alcohol rehab plans. Some plans cover psychiatry.

The woman becomes pregnant. Her doctor, who has delivered many babies, wants her to deliver at X hospital. All the woman's friends say, Y Hospital is much better, nicer, etc. The doctor is not cleared to practice at Y Hospital. Is the woman out of luck?

With a PPO, the woman must deliver at a hospital affiliated with the PPO

— or pay the extra cost. If her doctor is not affiliated with that hospital, sometimes a doctor may be given courtesy practicing privileges at a hospital where he or she does not have staff membership. Check with the doctor.

With HMOs, the woman must deliver within the HMO system.

Incidentally, with PPOs and HMOs you should check that the doctors and specialists listed in the organization's booklets can treat you. Some plans may restrict access to certain doctors. Some booklets may be out-of-date and not have an accurate list of doctors.

The young woman goes in for minor surgery, which turns into major surgery when the doctor forgets to remove a sponge before sewing up. Upon reviving, she does what?

Some medical plans require clients to submit complaints to a panel of arbitrators, which decides damages, if any. Read the policy.

The woman's child reaches age 18. Is she covered by the family insurance?

All depends on the insurance. Some policies will cover the children while they attend college. (But attendance may be defined in a certain way, full-time as opposed to part-time.) You should read the plan thoroughly.

At work, the woman gets her hand caught in a revolving door and is told she will need six months of therapy during which she can't work. Who pays?

Insurance will usually pay for the medical costs. Workers Compensation, a state plan that includes many but not all people, may compensate the woman for time lost off the job and may pay for medical costs. If you injure yourself on the job, your employer must file a report with Workers Comp.

Ask also how emergency or immediate care is provided.

The woman wakes up at 3 a.m. with a sore throat and headache. She feels bad but not bad enough to drive to a hospital or emergency room. She should:

Many hospitals and medical plans offer 24-hour advice lines. This is something you should check on when you sign up for a plan.

The woman wins a vacation to Switzerland where she falls off a mountain, breaks a leg, and spends three days in a Swiss hospital. Her HMO or PPO is 7,000 miles away. Who pays?

Usually the insurance company, but it is wise to check out how to obtain medical services before going on vacation. The woman may have to pay out-of-pocket and then file for reimbursement on her return home.

While working in her kitchen, the woman slips, bangs her head against the stove, gets a nasty cut and becomes woozy. She should:

Call 9-1-1, which will send an ambulance. 9-1-1 is managed by police dispatch. It's the fastest way to get an ambulance — with one possible exception. Lately in the Bay Area, 9-1-1 calls placed on cellular phones have been running into delays. In a pinch, try one of the emergency call boxes. San Jose Police Dept. has opened an easy-dial line for non-emergencies. Phone 3-1-1.

What's the difference between a hospital, a clinic, an urgent-care center and a doctor's office?

The hospital has the most services and equipment. The center or clinic has several services and a fair amount of equipment. The office, usually, has the fewest services and the smallest amount of equipment but in some places "clinic-office" means about the same.

Hospitals have beds. If a person must have a serious operation, she goes to a hospital. Hospitals have coronary-care and intensive-care units, emergency care and other specialized, costly treatment units. Many hospitals also run clinics for minor ailments and provide the same services as medical centers.

Urgent care or medical centers are sometimes located in neighborhoods, which makes them more convenient for some people. The doctors treat the minor, and often not-so-minor, ailments of patients and send them to hospitals for major surgery and serious sicknesses.

Some doctors form themselves into groups to offer the public a variety of services.

Some hospitals have opened neighborhood clinics or centers to attract patients. Kaiser has hospitals in some towns and clinic-offices in other towns.

The doctor in his or her office treats patients for minor ailments and uses the hospital for surgeries, major illnesses. Many illnesses that required hospitalization years ago are now treated in the office or clinic.

Some hospitals offer programs outside the typical doctor-patient relationships. For example, wellness plans — advice on how to stay healthy or control stress or quit smoking.

Major Hospitals & Medical Facilities

Alexian Brothers Hospital, 225 N. Jackson Ave., San Jose, 95116. Phone: (408) 259-5000. ICU, CCU, 24-hour emergency services, family birthing center, pediatrics, neonatal intensive care, outpatient surgery, physical occupational & speech therapy, radiology & laboratory services, diagnostic imaging, diagnostic & vascular ultrasound, home health care, community education seminar & wellness programs, maternal child health classes in English, Vietnamese and Spanish, parish nurse program, senior health center, pediatric Medi-Cal clinic, OB Medi-Cal clinic, community benefit programs, physician referral. 204 beds.

Community Hospital of Los Gatos, 815 Pollard Rd., Los Gatos, 95032. Phone: (408) 378-6131. ICU, CCU, 24-hour emergency care services, Family Birth Place, perinatal education program, physician referral services, pediatrics, Community Home Health, diagnostic imaging, Joint Care Program, acute and subacute rehabilitation, Center for Spinal Deformity & Injury, Arthritis Center, Physical Performance Institute, sports medicine program, occupational medicine, transitional care, outpatient surgery, comprehensive endoscopy, advanced surgical procedures, community education preventive medicine lecture program, Women's Cancer Center, dietary and nutritional services, diabetes services, Western Kidney Stone Center. 153 beds.

El Camino Hospital, 2500 Grant Rd., Mountain View, 94040. Ph: (650) 940-7000. 24-hour emergency services, ambulatory surgery, behavioral medicine, breast screening, cancer care, cardiovascular, chemical dependency, community health education, critical care, critical care nursery, dialysis services, emergency heart services, employee assistance programs, endoscopy, interventional diagnostic radiology, laser surgery, maternal child health services, MRI, nutritional therapy, occupational and physical therapy, Older Adult Resource Center, radiation therapy. 426 beds.

Good Samaritan Hospital, 2425 Samaritan Dr., San Jose, 95124. Phone: (408) 559-2011. General and tertiary acute care services; 24-hour emergency care; cardiology, cardiovascular surgery; cancer care center; comprehensive women and children services including family birthing center, level III neonatal intensive care nursery, maternal transport program, perinatology services, diabetes screening, childbirth and parenting education, breastfeeding services; Center for Children's Surgery; surgery, including endoscopic surgery; orthopedics; critical care; adult psychiatric services; alcohol and substance abuse, skilled nursing unit; diagnostic imaging, including MRI, CT Scan; home health care. 511 beds. Outpatient surgery, Columbia Breast Center on the Mission Oaks Hospital Campus, 15891 Los Gatos-Almaden Rd., Los Gatos. For physician referral, call 1-800-COLUMBIA.

Kaiser Medical Center, 900 Kiely Blvd., Santa Clara, 95051. Phone: (408) 236-6400. Kaiser Permanente is a group practice prepayment plan which provides comprehensive medical and hospital services to its Kaiser Foundation Health Plan members. Full range of hospital services including alcohol and drug abuse program, CCU, craniofacial and pediatric surgery, CT scan and MRI, emergency services, gynecological oncology, hospice, ICU, neonatal intensive care, high risk OB, internal medicine, neurosurgery, pediatric ICU, pediatrics, plasmapheresis, sports medicine center, surgery. Kaiser Permanente is an affiliated teaching hospital for Stanford University School of Medicine and has independent residency programs in Internal Medicine, OB and GYN, podiatry and emergency medicine. 337 licensed beds.

Kaiser Permanente-Santa Teresa Medical Center, 250 Hospital Pkwy., San Jose, 95119. Phone: (408) 972-3000 Kaiser Permanente is a group practice prepayment plan which provides comprehensive medical and hospital services to its Kaiser Foundation Health Plan members. Full range of hospital services including cardiac catheterization, emergency services, genetics, ICU, CCU, internal medicine, OB, GYN, pediatrics, surgery. 228 licensed beds.

Kaiser Permanente Medical Offices—Gilroy, 7520 Arroyo Cir., Gilroy, 95020. Ph. (408) 848-4001. Outpatient medical office providing pediatrics, internal medicine, OB, GYN, allergy, dermatology, optometry, health education and urgent care.

Kaiser Permanente Medical Offices—Milpitas, 770 E. Calaveras Blvd., Milpitas, 95035. Ph. (408) 945-2900. Outpatient medical office providing pediatrics, internal medicine, OB, GYN, allergy, dermatology, optometry, health education and urgent care.

Kaiser Permanente Medical Offices—Mountain View, 555 Castro St., Mountain View, 94041. Ph. (650) 903-3000. Outpatient medical office providing pediatrics, internal medicine, OB, GYN, allergy, dermatology, optometry, health education and urgent care.

Lucille Salter Packard Children's Hospital at Stanford, 725 Welch Rd., Palo Alto, 94304. Phone: (650) 497-8000. Primary care and specialty outpatient clinics, child psychiatry, neonatology, oncology/bone marrow transplantation, kidney and liver transplantation, heart and heart/lung transplantation, intensive care, cardiology, pediatric general surgery, neurosurgery, orthopedics, and other full-service medical and surgical services for children. Pediatric diagnostic, treatment and support services. Home pharmacy service, rehabilitation engineering, Parent Information & Referral Center (PIRC), Kidcall program. 162 beds.

O'Connor Hospital, 2105 Forest Ave., San Jose, 95128. Phone: (408) 947-2500. Heart center, family center, cancer care center, recovery center for alcohol and chemical dependency, mental health program for seniors, wound care center, transitional care center, ICU, surgical services, 24-hour emergency department, physical, occupational and speech therapy, O'Connor MRI and all other diagnostic imaging services. Home health, pharmacy, physician referral service, community education seminars and wellness programs. Member of Catholic Healthcare West. 360 beds.

Saint Louise Hospital, 18500 Saint Louise Dr., Morgan Hill, 95037. Phone: (408) 779-1500. 24-hour emergency care, ICU, OB, GYN, surgical services, physical therapy, skilled nursing, birthing suites, outpatient surgery, Center for Life prenatal care and delivery program, comprehensive diagnostic imaging, community health education, home health care, physician referral service. Urgent care center, cancer care center, family clinic and MRI located on campus. Member of Catholic Healthcare West. 60 beds.

San Jose Medical Center, 675 E. Santa Clara St., San Jose, 95112. Phone: (408) 998-3212. ICU, CCU, OB, GYN, emergency services, county-designated trauma center with helicopter service, family health center, family birthing center, women's wellness services, cancer care center, neurosurgery center, comprehensive cardiology services, center for rehabilitation, skilled nursing facility, home health care, comprehensive diagnostic imaging and therapeutic services, pediatric ICU, outpatient surgery, replantation and microvascular surgery, physician referral service. 295 beds.

Santa Clara Valley Health & Hospital System, 751 S. Bascom Ave., San Jose, 95128. Phone: (408) 885-5000. Recently rebuilt, $197 million job. Surgical ICU, medical ICU, CCU, OB, GYN, Trauma Center, Emergency Care, Regional Burn Center, Physical Rehab including Brain & Spinal Injury Center, Physician Referral, Pediatrics, Psychiatry, Poison Center, Neonatal Intensive Care, Pediatrics Intensive Care. Outpatient clinics. Helicopter transportation. 302 beds.

South Valley Hospital, 9400 No Name Uno, Gilroy, 95020. Phone: (408) 848-2000 or (800) 423-2032. 24-hour emergency services with emergency helicopter, ICU/CCU, medical, surgical and pediatric services; outpatient surgery, family-oriented birth suites, breast-care center; physical, occupational and speech therapy; diagnostic services include X-ray services, MRI and CT scan, ultrasound, home-health services. Skilled nursing facility. 21 beds.

Stanford University Hospital, 300 Pasteur Dr., Stanford, 94305. Ph: (650) 723-4000. ICU, CCU, OB, GYN, emergency care & prompt care, trauma center, cardiovascular, stroke center, epilepsy, bone marrow transplantion, psychiatric care, physician referral, radiology, home health care, cancer treatment, ambulatory surgery center, multi-organ transplant center, comprehensive rehabilitation center, helicopter transportation. 663 beds.

Veterans Affairs Palo Alto Health Care System, 3801 Miranda Ave., Palo Alto, 94304. Phone: (650) 493-5000. ICU, CCU, GYN, psychiatric care, physical therapy, skilled nursing, home health care, trauma center, physician referral, chemical dependency, radiology, geriatric services, emergency care, alcohol treatment, eating disorders, cancer treatment, MRI, PET, PTSD, blind rehab, BIRU, spinal cord injury center, 1,264 beds (Palo Alto, Menlo Park and Livermore facilities combined).

Key: ICU, intensive care unit; CCU, coronary care unit; OB, obstetrics; GYN, gynecology; MRI, magnetic resonance imaging; PET, position emission tomography; PTSD, post-traumatic stress disorder; BIRU, brain injury rehabilitation unit.

Chapter 8

SANTA CLARA COUNTY
Newcomers Guide

Voter Registration

You must be 18 years and a citizen. Go to post office and ask for a voter registration postcard. Fill it out and pop it into the mail box. Or pick up the form when you register your vehicle or secure a driver's license. Before every election, the county will mail you a sample ballot with the address of your polling place. For more information call the elections office (408) 299-8302.

Change of Address — Mail

The change-of-address form can also be picked up at the post office. To assure continuity of service, fill out this form 30 days before you move.

Dog Licensing-Spaying

If you live in a city, call city hall for information about dog licensing and pet vaccinations and spaying-neutering. City hall numbers are listed at the beginning of your phone book.

If you live in the county jurisdiction, phone (800) 215-2555.

For licensing, bring proof of rabies vaccination. Some jurisdictions will discount the license fee if Rover or Fifi has been fixed.

Driving

California has the most stringent smog requirements in the country. If your car is a few years old, you may have to spend a couple of hundred dollars to bring it up to code.

You have 20 days from the time you enter the state to register your vehicles. After that you pay a penalty, and face getting a ticket-fine.

For registration, go to any office of the Department of Motor Vehicles. Bring your smog certificate, your registration card and your license plates.

Registration is simple but the fees can be hefty. The basic use tax is 2 percent of market value, as estimated by the state. A $10,000 car would cost $200, a $15,000 car, $300, a $20,000 car $400 — plus about $40 in miscellaneous costs. In 1998, the governor pushed through legislation that slightly lowered these fees.

If you are a California resident, all you need to do is complete a change-of-address form, which can be obtained by calling (800) 777-0133 or visiting one of the following Dept. of Motor Vehicles offices:

- Campbell: 430 Darryl Dr.
- Los Gatos: 600 N. Santa Cruz Ave.
- Mountain View: 595 Showers Dr.
- San Jose: 111 West Alma Ave.
- San Jose (south): 180 Martinvale Ln.
- Santa Clara: 3665 Flora Vista Ave.
- Gilroy: 8200 Church St.

Driver's License

To obtain a driver's license, you must be 16 years old, pass a state-certified Driver's Education (classroom) and Driver's Training (behind-the-wheel) course, and at Department of Motor Vehicles a vision test and written and driving tests.

Once you pass the test, your license is usually renewed by mail. Retesting is rare, unless your driving record is poor. High schools used to offer free driving courses but these have all but disappeared due to state budget cuts. Private driving schools have moved in to fill the gap, at a cost of $200 to $250.

Teenagers older than 15 1/2 years who have completed driver's training can be issued a permit. New law restricts driving hours for young teens to daylight hours and, unless supervised, forbids them for six months to drive other teens. Law also requires more parental training and extends time of provisional license. Purpose is to reduce accidents.

If no driver's education program has been completed, you must be at least 18 years old to apply for a driver's license. Out-of-state applicants must supply proof of "legal presence," which could be a certified copy of a birth certificate. Foreign applicants must supply other documents. Law is aimed at illegal immigrants. If going for a driver's license, ask to have the booklet mailed to you or pick it up. Study it. All the questions will be taken from the booklet.

Turning Rules. If signs don't say no, you can turn right on a red light (after making a full stop) and make a U-turn at an intersection.

Stop for pedestrians. Stop for discharging school buses, even if on opposite side of road. Must have insurance to drive and to register vehicle.

- Out-of-state applicants must supply proof of "legal presence," which could be a certified copy of a birth certificate. Foreign applicants must supply other documents. Law is aimed at illegal immigrants.

Earthquakes

They're fun and great topics of conversation, until you get caught in a big one. Then they are not so funny. At the beginning of your phone book is some advice about what to do before, during and after a temblor. It's worth reading.

Garbage Service

The garbage fellows come once a week. Rates vary by city and lately a lot of competition has been coming into this business. Figure $15-$20 a month for one-can-a-week service. Besides the cans, almost every home will receive recycling bins for plastics, glass and cans.

Pickup weekly, usually the same day as garbage. Some garbage companies are switching to wheeled carts that can be picked up by mechanical arms attached to truck.

Don't burn your garbage in the fireplace or outside. Don't burn leaves. Against the law. To get rid of car batteries, motor oils and water-soluble paints, call your local garbage firm and ask about disposal sites. Or call city hall.

Property Taxes

The average property tax rate in California is 1.25 percent. If you buy a $250,000 home this year, your property tax will be $3,125. Once the basic tax is established, it goes up about 2 percent annually in following years.

"Average" needs to be emphasized. Some jurisdictions have tacked costs on to the property tax; some have not. Some school districts, in recent years, have won approval of annual parcel taxes.

Property taxes are paid in two installments, due by April 10 and December 10. They are generally collected automatically through impound accounts set up when you purchase a home, but check your sale documents carefully. Sometimes homeowners are billed directly.

Some cities, to fund parks and lights and other amenities in new subdivisions, have installed what is called the Mello-Roos tax. Realtors are required to give you complete information on all taxes.

Sales Tax

Varies by county. In Santa Clara County, it is 8.25 percent. If you buy something for $1 you will pay $1.08 and if the item costs $100, you will pay $108.25. Food, except when sold in restaurants, is exempted.

State Income Taxes

State income taxes range from 1% to 9.3%. A single person earning between $26,045 and $32,916 would pay $899.56 plus 8% of amount over $26,045. A married couple filing jointly with an income of $65,832 would pay $2,898 plus 9.3% of the amount over $65,832 .

Disclosure Laws

California requires Realtors to give detailed reports on every home sold, including information about earthquake faults. Megan's law applies: for home

Grocery Prices

Item	High	Low	Average
Apple Juice, 64 oz. bottled	$2.39	$1.99	$2.19
Apple Pie, Mrs. Smith's, 37 oz.	$4.49	$2.99	$3.74
Apples, Red Delicious, 1 lb.	$.0.99	$0.59	$0.79
Aspirin, cheapest, 250 ct.	$3.69	$2.29	$2.99
Bacon, 1 lb. Farmer John Sliced	$3.09	$1.99	$2.54
Bananas, 3 lbs.	$1.65	$1.17	$1.41
Bayer's Children's Aspirin, 36 count	$2.49	$2.49	$2.49
Beef, top round rump roast, 1 lb.	$2.99	$1.69	$2.34
Beef, ground round, 1 lb.	$1.79	$1.69	$1.74
Beer, Budweiser, 6-pack, cans	$4.59	$4.59	$4.59
Beer, Coors, 6-pack, cans	$4.59	$4.59	$4.59
Bisquick, 2# 8 oz.	$2.49	$2.33	$2.41
Bleach, Clorox, 1 gal.	$1.95	$1.79	$1.87
Bread, sourdough, Colombo, 1 lb.	$2.49	$2.39	$2.44
Bread, white, cheapest, 1 lb.	$1.59	$0.99	$1.29
Broccoli, bunch	$0.99	$0.99	$0.99
Butter, Challenge, 1 lb.	$4.49	$4.29	$4.39
Cabbage, 1 lb.	$0.39	$0.35	$0.37
Cantaloupe, 1 lb.	$0.39	$0.39	$0.39
Carrots, fresh, 1 lb.	$0.39	$0.25	$0.32
Cat Food, store brand, small can	$0.33	$0.25	$0.29
Charcoal, Kingsford, 10 lbs.	$4.69	$4.49	$4.59
Cheese, mild Cheddar, 1 lb.	$3.79	$0.88	$2.34
Chicken, breasts, boneless skinless 1 lb.	$5.79	$4.29	$5.10
Chili, Stagg, with beans,15 oz. can	$1.69	$1.53	$1.61
Cigarettes, Marlboro Lights, carton	$32.42	$37.34	$34.88
Coca Cola, 12-pack, 12 oz. cans	$4.49	$2.99	$3.74
Coffee, Folgers, 13 oz.	$3.79	$3.39	$3.59
Cookies, Oreo, 20 oz. pkg.	$3.59	$2.99	$3.29
Wheaties, Kellogg, 18 oz.	$4.09	$3.89	$3.99
Diapers, Huggies, 64 count	$13.99	$10.70	$12.35
Dishwasher Soap, Ajax, 22 oz.	$3.69	$3.65	$3.67
Dishwashing Liquid, Dawn, 28 oz.	$3.39	$3.29	$3.34
Dog Food, Friskies, 13.2 oz. can	$0.83	$0.75	$0.79
Eggs, large, Grade AA, doz.	$2.08	$1.99	$2.04
Flour, Gold Medal, 5 lbs.	$1.95	$0.69	$1.32
Frozen Yogurt, Dreyers, half gal.	$4.99	$4.99	$4.99
Gerber's Baby Food, Fruit, 4 oz.	$0.47	$0.47	$0.47
Gerber's Baby Food, Vegetables, 4 oz.	$0.47	$0.47	$0.47
Gerber's Baby Food, Meat, 2.5 oz.	$0.73	$0.73	$0.73
Gerber's Baby Food, Cereal, 26 oz.	$3.18	$2.59	$2.89
Gerber's Baby Food, Turkey, 2.5 oz.	$0.73	$0.73	$0.73
Gin, Gilbeys, 1.75 Liter	$17.29	$16.99	$17.14
Grapes, Thompson Seedless, 1 lb.	$1.99	$1.49	$1.74
Grapefruit, 1 lb.	$0.79	$0.59	$0.69
Grapenuts, Post, 24 oz.	$3.49	$3.43	$3.46
Ham, Armour, 1.5 lb. canned	$12.99	$11.69	$12.34
Ice Cream, Dreyers, vanilla half gal.	$4.99	$4.99	$4.99
Jam, Mary Ellen, 18 oz.	$2.69	$1.99	$2.34
Ketchup, Del Monte, 28 oz.	$1.89	$1.85	$1.87
Kleenex, 175 count box	$1.69	$0.99	$1.34

Grocery Prices

Item	High	Low	Average
Laundry Detergent, Tide, 92 oz.	$8.49	$8.49	$8.49
Lettuce, Iceberg, head	$0.89	$0.69	$0.79
Margarine, Can't Believe It's Not Butter, 1-lb. Tub	$1.69	$1.55	$1.62
Mayonnaise, Best Foods, 1 qt.	$3.39	$2.29	$2.84
Milk, Reduced Fat (2%), half gal.	$1.96	$1.89	$1.93
Mixed Vegetables, frozen, 10 oz.	$0.89	$0.69	$0.79
Mushrooms, sliced, 8 oz.	$1.59	$1.49	$1.54
Olive Oil, cheapest, 17 oz.	$4.99	$3.49	$4.24
Onions, yellow, 1 lb.	$0.33	$0.25	$0.29
Orange Juice, Tropicana, 64 oz.	$3.69	$2.59	$3.14
Oranges, Valencias, fresh, 2 lb.	$1.18	$1.18	$1.18
Paper Towels, single pack	$0.95	$0.93	$0.94
Peanuts, cocktail, Planter's, 16 oz. jar	$3.29	$3.19	$3.24
Peas, frozen, 10 oz.	$0.89	$0.79	$0.84
Pork, chops, center cut, 1 lb.	$3.99	$3.49	$3.74
Potato Chips, Lays, 14 oz.	$2.99	$1.99	$2.49
Potatoes, 2 lbs.	$0.98	$0.89	$0.94
Raisins, bulk, 24 oz.	$3.29	$2.99	$3.14
Red Snapper, fresh, 1 lb.	$5.99	$4.99	$5.49
Rice, cheapest, 5 lbs.	$2.59	$1.99	$2.29
Seven-Up, 6-pack, cans	$2.59	$2.59	$2.59
Soap, bar, Zest, 3-pack, 5-oz.	$2.45	$2.33	$2.39
Soup, Campbell, Chicken Noodle, 10.5 oz. Can	$0.75	$0.49	$0.62
Soy Milk, boxed, 1 qt.	$2.49	$2.39	$2.44
Soy Sauce, Kikkoman, 20 oz.	$2.79	$1.93	$2.36
Spaghetti, cheapest, 1 lb.	$0.89	$0.85	$0.87
Sugar, cheapest, 5 lbs.	$1.89	$1.89	$1.89
Tea, Lipton's, 48 bag box	$2.59	$2.29	$2.44
Toilet Tissue, 4-roll pack, cheapest	$0.99	$0.89	$0.90
Tomatoes, extra large, 1 lb.	$1.89	$1.89	$1.89
Toothpaste, Colgate, 8.2 oz.	$3.29	$3.09	$3.19
Tortillas, cheapest, 12 count pack	$1.69	$1.59	$1.64
Tuna, Starkist, 6 oz.	$1.99	$1.95	$1.97
Turkey, breast, 1 lb.	$4.99	$2.89	$3.94
Turkey, ground, 1 lb.	$3.99	$2.99	$3.49
Vegetable Oil, store brand, 64 oz.	$3.49	$2.62	$3.06
Vinegar, store brand, 1 pint	$0.69	$0.59	$0.64
Whiskey, Seagrams 7 Crown,1.75 Liter	$16.99	$16.79	$16.89
Wine, White Zinfandel, 750 ml.	$4.99	$4.99	$4.99
Merlot, Kendall Jackson 1996, 750ml	$15.89	$15.89	$15.89
Merlot, Clos du Bois 1996, 750ml	$16.59	$16.59	$16.59

Other Prices

Item	High	Low	Avg
Baby Shampoo, Johnsons, 15 fluid oz.	$3.79	$3.69	$3.74
Babysitting (per hour)	$6.00	$5.00	$5.50
Parental Stress Reliever (qt. Haagen Daz ice cream)	$4.99	$4.99	$4.99
Latte/Mocha at coffee shop	$2.30	$2.05	$2.18
Diaper Service, 1 mo., 80 diapers/wk	$13.50	$13.25	$13.38
Mu Shu Pork	$7.25	$7.25	$7.25
MovieTickets	$4.75/7.50	$4.50/7.25	$4.63/7.38
School Backpack	$49.99	$34.99	$42.49

sales and rentals, sales agent must tell you where you can get names and addresses of registered sex offenders. Usually, this will be the local police department.

Cigarette-Tobacco Tax

Passed in 1998, took effect on Jan. 1, 1999. Adds 50 cents to a pack of cigarettes. Tax opponents predict that many Californians will load up on cigarettes in Nevada or Mexico or order over Internet.

Gas and Electricity

Most homes are heated with natural gas. No one, or almost no one, uses heating oil. Pacific Gas and Electric reports that gas bills, year round, average about $30 a month, and electric bills $60 a month.

Almost never between May and September, and rarely between April and October, will you need to heat your home. Winter days are often balmy; no heating required.

Air conditioners are used throughout the summer but on many days they're not needed. PG&E, the utility, will give you advice on insulating your home.

Cable TV Service

Almost all East Bay homes are served by cable. Rates vary according to channels accessed but a basic rate plus one tier is $30 a month. Installation is extra. For clear FM radio reception, often a cable connection is required.

Bottled Water

If the direct source for your town's water is the Sierra, then you may not need bottled water. If the source is wells, many people take the bottled.

Tipping

It's not done in the Bay Area as much as it is done in other parts of the country. Tip the newspaper delivery person, cab or limo drivers, waiters and waitresses and, at the holidays, people who perform regular personal services: yard maintenance, child care, housekeeping.

Don't tip the supermarket employee who carries bags to your car. Don't tip telephone or cable TV installers. Your garbage collector will usually be a Teamster. No beer. No money. Maybe a little cake or box of candy at Christmas. If a garbage collector gets nailed for drunk driving, it will probably cost him his job. Some people give the mail carrier a little holiday gift; many don't. Let your conscience be your guide: The coffee shops. Many are sprouting "tip" cups at the counter.

Smoking

In public places, increasingly frowned upon and in the workplace forbidden. In 1998 a state law took effect forbidding smoking in saloons, one of the last bastions of smoking. Bars in restaurants generally comply. Saloons sporadically enforce but many people refrain from smoking and those that do, often hide the cigarette under the table. In San Francisco, people routinely smoke in bars (but a crackdown is supposedly underway.)

If visiting socially, you are generally expected to light up outside.

Love and Society

San Francisco often flaunts its sexuality, hetero and homo. Except in rare instances, the suburbs don't but the cosmopolitan virtues apply. In the Bay Area, consenting adults, in sexual matters, are generally free to do what they want as long as it doesn't harm others.

In professional society in Santa Clara County and the Bay Area, same-sex couples attend office parties and social events, and no subterfuge is put up to disguise the relationship but what is accepted in San Francisco will often cock eyebrows in the suburbs. If you slobber over your loved one, no matter what the sexual orientation, you won't be stoned but you might be shunned.

If you want the society of men or the society of women or both, numerous groups exist to help to make connections.

Ages

You must be 18 to vote and smoke and 21 to drink alcohol. Watch the booze. California has a drunk-driving law so stringent that even a drink or two can put you in violation. Clerks are supposed to ask you for ID if you look under 27 for smokes and under 30 for booze.

Dress

Casual from the clerk to the CEOs making millions. But not universal. An older boss may dress more traditionally than a young.

If your job requires you to meet the public or to make a good impression, suits or sports coats are donned.

For almost all social occasions, even, in some circles, weddings and funerals, the dress is casual. The person who wears a tie to a restaurant on Friday or Saturday often stands out (depends a little on the town). San Jose and several towns throw Black-and-White balls to raise money for charity or schools. Break or rent out the tux; cut loose for that fabulous gown. These are the social events of the year.

Dress formal for dinner in San Francisco and the theater or opera (but even here, many men go in sports coats, no tie; women in slacks).

For the coast and San Francisco in the summer, bring a jacket or sweater. It's often chilly, even during the day.

Chapter 9

SANTA CLARA COUNTY
Rental Housing

AFTER SEVERAL YEARS OF SHARP INCREASES, rents in 1998 began to level off, more so at the upper end than at the low or middle, newspapers reported.

As to what you will pay, here is an approximate idea from one local source: for a two-bedroom apartment, Gilroy, $960 per month, Morgan Hill, $1,400, Santa Clara, $1,300, Los Altos, $1,550, Cupertino, $1,700, San Jose, $1,190. See also Bay Rentals chart in this chapter.

For those new to the region and shopping for homes, a hotel might do the trick — short term. The major chains have built large and small hotels in the suburbs, many of them near freeway exits and a few smack in the middle of residential neighborhoods. Prices range from below $60 to well over $100 a night, the higher amount buying more of the extras: pools, game rooms, etc.

Residency hotels offer a slightly different experience. They combine the conveniences of a hotel — maid service, continental breakfast, airport shuttle — with the pleasures of home: a fully-equipped kitchen and a laundry room (coin-operated). They may also have a pool, a spa, a sportscourt, a workout room. Some offer free grocery shopping and on evenings a social hour.

Residency hotels welcome families. Typically, guests remain at least five days and often much longer. At a certain stage, a discount will kick in.

In the Bay Area, apartments come in all sizes and settings. If you're strapped for funds, you can find single bedrooms and studios for under $600 a month. No pool, no spa, no extras. What goes for $1,400 in Palo Alto may rent for $1,100 in San Jose. If the neighborhood is safe and nice, if the apartment complex is close to light rail, you will probably pay extra.

Renters pay for cable service, electricity or gas and phone (in some instances, deposits may be required to start service.)

You will be asked for a security deposit and for the first month's rent up front. State law limits deposits to a maximum two months rent for an unfurnished apartment and three months for a furnished (this includes the last month's rent.) If you agree to a lease, you might get an extra month free. If you

Average Rents

City	1 bdrm. apt.	2 bdrm. apt.	2 bdrm. hse/condo townhouse	3 bdrm. hse/condo townhouse
Campbell	$940	$1,100	$1,495	$1,915
Cupertino	$1,080	$1,408	$1,632	$1,997
Los Altos	$1,070	$1,768	$2,083	$2,458
Los Altos Hills	$1,713	N.A.	N.A.	N.A.
Los Gatos	$1,190	$1,463	$1,753	$2,313
Milpitas	$875	$1,307	$1,308	$1,465
Mountain View	$1,132	$1,327	$1,588	$2,003
Saratoga	$1,125	N.A.	N.A.	$2,619
Santa Clara	$865	$1,182	$1,366	$1,768
San Jose	$866	$1,120	$1,313	$1,654
Sunnyvale	$978	$1,180	$1,521	$1,977

Key: Average rents of listed units available in late 1998. **Source:** Bay Rentals of San Jose, (408) 244-4900.

move out before the lease is up, you pay a penalty.

Some apartments forbid pets, some will accept only cats, some cats and small dogs. Many will ask for a pet deposit (to cover possible damage.)

To protect themselves, landlords will ask you to fill out a credit report and to list references. In one instance that made the newspapers an apartment complex asked the prospective tenant for her parents' tax returns. With the shortage of apartments, the manager could afford to be choosy. The shortage has made apartment hunting more of an adventure than it should be. If you want help or are striking out with the classified ads, you might try a rental agency. Some complexes supposedly are renting only through agencies.

The Fair Housing laws will apply: no discrimination based on race, sex, family status and so on. But some complexes will be designed to welcome one or several kinds of renters.

A complex that wants families, for example, might include a tot lot. One that prefers singles or childless couples might throw Friday night parties or feature a large pool and a workout room but no kiddie facilities.

Some large complexes will offer furnished and unfurnished apartments or corporate setups, a variation of the residency hotel.

If hotels or apartments are not your cup of tea, you might take a look at renting a home or townhouse. See classified ads or Real Estate Rentals in Yellow Pages. Many owners turn the maintenance and renting over to a professional property manager.

In older towns, many of the cottages and smaller homes in the older sections will often be rentals. If you see a "For Sale" sign in front of a home that interests you, inquire whether the place is for rent.

What about rates? They will vary by town but in a middle-class town you often can rent a three-bedroom home for $1,000 to $1,500 a month. Older, smaller homes in some suburbs will go for about $900 a month but you might have to drive quite a way to job centers. In upscale towns, home rents are much higher.

Finally, there are shared rentals. Typically, they are most popular around colleges and universities. Berkeley, San Francisco, Palo Alto, San Jose, Hayward — where major universities are located — all possess a thriving market in shared rentals. For information, consult the campus housing office.

Some universities run housing departments that try to line up homes and apartments for single students, married students and staff and faculty. The larger universities have dorms.

Community colleges will sometimes support, just off campus, a small shared-rental neighborhood.

Newspapers routinely carry ads from people looking to share a rental. Preferences are stated: no smokers, women only, no pets, etc. If you really want to save the bucks and possibly pick up a friend or two, a shared rental might be just the thing.

A word on furniture. If you don't want to buy it, you can rent it. Check the Yellow Pages under furniture rental. For cheap furniture, check out the garage sales. They are usually advertised on weekends in the local newspapers.

When you're out scouting for a rental, check out the neighborhood, do a little research, and think about what you really value and enjoy.

If you want the convenient commute without the hassle of a car, pick a place near a light rail-line or bus stop. If it's the active life, scout out the parks, trails and such things as bars and restaurants and community colleges. Say the first thing you want to do when you arrive home is take a long run. Before you rent, get a map of local trails. City recreation departments will usually be able to give you information.

For parents, your address will usually determine what public school your child will attend. If you want a high-scoring school, see the scores in this book before making a decision. Always call the school before making a renting decision. Because of crowding, some schools are changing attendance zones. You may not be able to get your child into the "neighborhood" school. Ask also whether the school is year round. See the chapter on how public schools work. The same advice applies to day care. Make sure that it is available nearby before signing a lease.

Many of the larger apartment complexes offer some kind of security: parking lot lights, gates, guards. Happy hunting!

Rent Sampler from Classified Ads

Almaden Valley (San Jose)
Townhouse, 2 BR/2BA, A/C/, fireplace, W/D, $1,500.
Home, 4 BR/2.5BA, family room, fireplace, gas stove, $1,500.

Berryessa (San Jose)
Home, 3 BR/2.5BA, all appliances, covered patio, yard, $2,250.
Home, 4 BR/2.5BA, $2,100.

Blossom Valley (San Jose)
Townhome, 2 BR/1BA, 1-car garage, pool, laundry, $1,100.
Home, 3 BR/2.5BA, 2-story, living/family/dining rooms, $1,850.

Cambrian (San Jose)
Townhouse, 2 BR/1BA, $1,100.
Home 4 BR/2BA, 2-car garage, hardwood floors, $1,700.

Campbell
Apt., 1 BR, garden setting, pool/spa/tennis, $1,025.
Townhouse, 2 BR/2BA, fireplace, W/D, pool/spa, $1,600.

Cupertino
Studio cottage, $750.
Townhouse, 2 BR/2BA, fireplace, 2-car garage, pool/spa, $1,950.

East Valley (San Jose)
Apt., 1 BR, poolside living, $925.
Studio, 1 BR, utilities inc., $800.

Evergreen (San Jose)
Townhouse, 1 BR, condo, W/D, gym, pool, $1,095.
Home, 4 BR/2BA, lg. yards, $1,875.

Gilroy
Home, 5 BR/3BA, 3-car gar., $1,950.
Home, 3 BR/2BA, pet OK, $1,300.

Los Altos
Apt., 2 BR/2BA, new inside, extra large, A/C, dishwasher, $1,895.
Apt., 2 BR/2BA, fireplace, private deck/patio, garden, pool, $1,900.

Los Altos Hills
Cottage, garden, den, new appliances, $1,850.
Home, 3 BR/2BA, family room office, gated estate, $,5750.

Los Gatos
Apt., 1 BR, A/C, pool, courtyard, covered parking, $950.

Apt., 2 BR/1BA, penthouse, downtown, $2,600.

Milpitas
Cottage, 1 BR/1BA, living & dining rooms, kitchen, hill views, $1,100.
Home, 3 BR/2BA, 2-car garage, fireplace, $1,600.

Morgan Hill
Apt., 1 BR, garden setting, A/C/, $895.
Apt., 2 BR/1BA, senior complex, $825.

Mountain View
Studio, heated pool, next to park, $920.
Apt., 1 BR, quiet setting, $1,025.

North Valley (San Jose)
Apt., 2 BR/1BA, all elec. kit., $1,025
Apt. 2 BR/21BA, remodeled, new refrigerator, garage, $1,300.

Palo Alto
Apt., 1 BR, pool, picnics/BBQ areas, near downtown, $1,090.
Apt., 1 BR, upstairs, private patio, pool, laundry, covered parking, $1,150.

Rose Garden (San Jose)
Apt., 1 BR, remodeled, $950.

San Jose (Downtown)
Apt., 1 BR/1BA, $850.
Cottage, 1 BR, $1,000.

San Jose (Central)
Studio, yard, deck, $625.
Apt., 1 BR, newly refurbished, $910.

San Jose (South)
Apt. 1 BR, downstairs, carport, $825.

San Jose (West)
Apt. 1 BR, pool, patio, $965.
Apt., 1 BT/1BA, remodeled upstairs, $950.

Santa Clara
Apt., 1 BR/1BA, courtyard, pool, $1,185.
Apt., 2 BR/2BA, $2,350.

Saratoga
Apt., cozy, near town, 1-car, $925.
Apt., 1 BR, all utilities/garbage paid, nonsmoking, $1,700.

Sunnyvale
Apt., 1 BR/2BA, pool/spa/fitness center, near park, $1,095.
Apt., 2 BR/1BA, near freeway/shopping/schools, pool, exercise room, $1,295.

Chapter 10

SANTA CLARA COUNTY

City & Town Profiles

COMMUNITIES HERE COME in all sizes, shapes and life-styles - rich and poor, rural and urban. Where do you want to live? What can you afford? What are the choices? The following profiles of Santa Clara County cities and towns may help.

INDEX TO PROFILES

CAMPBELL	142	MORGAN HILL	160
CUPERTINO	144	MOUNTAIN VIEW	163
GILROY	146	PALO ALTO	166
LOS ALTOS	148	SAN JOSE	170
LOS ALTOS HILLS	152	SANTA CLARA	176
LOS GATOS	154	SARATOGA	179
MILPITAS	157	SUNNYVALE	182
MONTE SERENO	159		

SANTA CLARA CITY & TOWN PROFILES

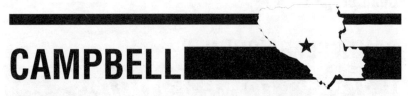

CAMPBELL

ROUNDED COMMUNITY, mix of bedroom, high-tech and the charms of modern suburban life, bookstores, restaurants, shops and parks.

Close to the Silicon Valley job centers, which makes Campbell a good commute. Bisected by two freeways and one expressway and close to another expressway.

One of the older suburbs. Has done a nice job of restoring and preserving its downtown.

School scores generally high and much attention paid to schools. In recent years, voters approved bonds for school improvements and to open another elementary school. Served by Moreland and Campbell elementary districts and Campbell High School District, which also educate kids in other towns.

Some Moreland parents are trying to disconnect Campbell High School from its district and attach it to the Moreland district. They contend that this would improve planning between the elementary schools and the high school. No action yet; matter at arguing-political stage.

Crime rate low suburban average. FBI reported zero homicides in 1997, 1996, 1995, 1994 and 1993, one each in 1992 and 1991, zero in 1990 and 1989, one in 1988, and zero in 1987.

Increased its population by 33 percent in the 1980s, rising to 39,720 residents in 1998. Regional planners predict that in about 20 years Campbell will have 41,000 residents, a modest increase by county standards. The town is almost surrounded by San Jose.

Campbell, in times past, was famous for its prunes. The name "Sunsweet" was first used in reference to a local plant that processed dried fruit. Orchards all went in the building boom that started in the 1940s. Campbell remembers its past in diverse ways, among them The PruneYard, a picturesque shopping mall, remodeled in 1996, and an annual Prune Festival.

Residential units in 1998 numbered 16,111 of which 6,774 were single homes, 1,908 single attached, 7,032 multiples, 397 mobile homes.

Campbell's housing boom started in the 1940s when the town built about

1,200 residential units. In the 1950s, Campbell erected about 3,100 homes and apartments, in the 1960s about 4,100 units, and in the 1980s about 2,600 units. So far in the 1990s, the city has built about 800 units, an indication that Campbell now will slowly fill out.

The town was built for the middle class. Among owner-occupied units, two- and three-bedroom homes account for 77 percent of the total, with four-bedroom homes making up another 16 percent. In design, Campbell falls into the category of typical suburban but the neighborhoods differ. The homes east of Bascom Avenue are slightly older and more upscale and have more trees and foliage than the homes west of Bascom. Well-cared-for town. Residents mow the lawns, apply the paint and generally do a good job of keeping up appearances. Many of the apartments are located along Campbell Avenue, one of the main thoroughfares.

Campbell has upgraded its downtown, using that tax-capture plan that California cities love: redevelopment. The results are nice: buildings restored, streets spruced up, many small shops, restaurants, theater, and coffee houses, Barnes and Noble, Trader Joe's, brew pubs. City Hall is trying to position Campbell as a small-town schmoozer with (or close to) big-city ornaments (downtown San Jose, about 7 miles to east).

Campbell streets get a lot of traffic from adjoining towns. City Hall has upgraded lights to keep cars and trucks moving. Campbell was the first city in California to use photo radar to nab speeders. In 1998, police department killed the project. Chief said many judges tossed out the radar-tickets.

Light-rail is supposed to pull into town in five or six years. Tall office buildings near the downtown and a few high-tech businesses make the commute easy for some residents.

Many service clubs. High school, a 30-acre site, was converted into a community center (gyms, auditorium, track, tennis). John F. Kennedy University. Year-round pool. Fifteen parks. Old mansion was converted into a city museum. Bike trail along creek. You can pedal to Los Gatos or, if your job is close by, to work. One park features giant plastic tubes with water spigots. When the kiddies enter, the spigots kick into action, administering a good soaking. Many activities for kids and seniors. Exercise courses. Summer day camps. Scottish Highland games, Prune Festival (more wine than prunes), Easter Egg Hunt, Christmas Crafts Faire, Oktoberfest. Many restaurants (The PruneYard itself has over a dozen.) Many shops. Among newer stores: Staples, Home Depot.

Campbell is a mature suburb that has had the time to build a comfortable community life with much to do. It is an intimate town with many long-time residents who know each other. The politicians know what the residents will take in the way of development and work to build consensus for anything major. Chamber of Commerce: (408) 378-6252.

SANTA CLARA CITY & TOWN PROFILES

CUPERTINO

SILICON VALLEY town famous for the quality of its schools, particularly computer education. Passed bond, $71 million, in 1995 to improve elementary schools and rewire them for high tech. Much of the work has been completed.

Being almost in the heart of Silicon Valley, many Cupertino residents have a short but often sluggish commute. Town is served by Highway 85, Interstate 289, Foothill Expressway and on the east side by the Lawrence Expressway. Local streets also lead to the job centers. Shuttle bus to CalTrain, which travels up the Peninsula to San Francisco. Buses from Santa Clara Valley Transportation Authority.

Heart of the town is De Anza Community College, lovely campus that includes a planetarium and the Flint Center for Performing Arts, which presents top talents — from San Francisco Symphony to Henry Kissinger to Beijing Acrobats and Mikhail Gorbachev. In 1994 the college opened an Advanced Technology Center to train students in math, physics, computers, programming. In 1995, the Flint Center was renovated.

Served mainly by Cupertino School District and Fremont High School District. The latter in 1998 won voter approval of a $144 million bond for more renovations and for equipment and lab and facilities improvements.

Schools score very high. Many schools have won state and national recognition for academic excellence. Homestead High was honored in ceremony at White House. In last round of SAT, Monta Vista High School in math came in second in the state.

Cupertino elementary district runs three "alternate" schools, each with a different approach to education: loose structure, traditional structure, mandatory parent. In the last school, parents agree to work in schools and take a seven-week prep course. Of the remaining schools, some accept children from any address in the district, some restrict to immediate neighborhood. Admission to some schools is determined by lottery.

Cupertino is the headquarters city for Tandem and Apple, and has about 50 high-tech firms. Many businesses have gotten behind the schools and work with the kids to make them computer sharp.

Town is jammed with high-tech parents and the local newspaper reports that the town is famous in the Far East for the excellence of its schools. The school districts have introduced language classes for the kids, employed translators to prepare materials for parents, and worked into the curriculum more information on Asian cultures. If a Realtor is selling a home in Cupertino, the first thing he or she will mention is school quality.

Local community-business foundation raises $300,000 annually for schools, a nice shot in arm. De Anza College offers "College for Kids" in summer and runs a high-school program during the regular school year. NASA, the space agency, is located in nearby at Moffett Field. Its scientists occasionally pitch in on projects with the school kids. Bond passed in 1994 allowed library to stay open seven days a week and expand its book and CD collection.

Crime rate is low-average for suburban cities. Zero homicides in 1997, 1996, 1995, 1994. Counts for previous years are 1, 0, 3, 0, 0, 1, 2, 1.

In 1998 the state tallied 17,069 housing units: single homes 9,787, single attached 2,145, multiples 5,130, mobile homes 7. As of 1998, the population was 46,682.

A farm village for most of its life, Cupertino started 1950 with fewer than 500 homes, and then was swept up in the great suburban boom. About three of every four homes and apartments were built between 1950 and 1980, census data shows.

Although Cupertino has its mansions, the city was built almost entirely for the middle class. The last census noted that three-bedroom homes were the most popular style, followed closely by four-bedroom homes.

In the 1980s Cupertino constructed 2,134 residential units, a sharp drop from previous decades, and, typical for upper-income towns running out of space, found itself becoming more concerned over what should be built on the remaining land. For the older homes, drive the neighborhoods east of DeAnza Boulevard. For the newer, cruise Phar Lap Drive and other neighborhoods west of DeAnza.

Cupertino rises from flatlands to hills. Hill homes command higher prices. Pleasant-looking town in suburban way. Many trees. Well-kept lawns. Vallco Fashion Park, 180 shops and restaurants. Anchored by Sears, Penney's.

Baseball, gymnastics, girls softball. Over 200 activities, from painting to karate. Soccer draws over 1,000 kids. After-school music program. Shakespeare for the Kids. Thirteen parks, nature preserve, a winery, a racquet club. Loads of classes, events at De Anza, which has an art gallery. Two golf courses, seniors center, movies , community center, sports center, bowling alley, ice skating rink, YMCA, city museum, arts and wine festival, De Anza Days, Heritage parade, Oktoberfest, Dickens Faire, Cherry Blossom Festival. Chamber of commerce (408) 252-7054.

SANTA CLARA CITY & TOWN PROFILES

GILROY

SOUTHERN-MOST TOWN in Santa Clara County. Moving from rural to suburban. Has an old downtown that's picking up antique stores and one of the most successful outlet malls in the South Bay. Famous for its Garlic Festival.

In percentages, one of the fastest-growing cities in Santa Clara County. Added 9,846 residents in last decade, a rise of 46 percent. Lots of playmates for the kiddies. In the 1990 census, 33 percent of the residents came in under age 18, unusually high. Countywide, the percentage was 24. State estimates population in 1998 to be 37,455.

Despite this, Gilroy has a lot of "country" in the farms that start on its outskirts and the hills and mountains to the east and west. City favors gradual growth and limits the number of homes that can be built. As the newcomers settled in, shops, supermarkets and stores opened to meet their needs. The Gilroy outlet mall draws about 4 million shoppers annually. Gilroy also has a Wal-Mart. All this raises revenue for the city and helps fund city programs.

Split by freeway, Highway 101. A long haul to Silicon Valley and job centers in north but Gilroy, with plenty of open land, would like to woo high-tech south. Neat streets, many tree-lined. Many sections plain old nice suburban, three- and four-bedroom homes, lawns mowed, shrubs trimmed.

Housing units in 1998 numbered 11,084 — 6,921 single homes, 629 single attached, 3,165 multiples, 369 mobiles. Tract homes for commuters make up the great majority of the housing but you can find turn-of-the-century and early 1900s homes near the downtown and some nice custom homes. For tight budgets, modest homes east of the freeway. The new homes can generally be found west of the freeway, on the outskirts of the town. In 1994, a sewage treatment plant for Morgan Hill and Gilroy was opened. South County Hospital. Kaiser office-clinic offers outpatient services.

Traffic a problem as commuters have to crawl up Highway 101 to reach Silicon Valley. But there is an alternative: CalTrain, which runs up to San Jose, takes a left, and finishes in downtown San Francisco. Runs have been added and schedules changed to attract commuters. More trains are being added. Historic train depot has been restored.

Bookstore, historical museum, golf course, kid sports, youth center, swimming, softball, bingo, dancing, roller-skating, athletic clubs, bowling, 10 parks, regional parks nearby, ice cream and yogurt parlors, poker parlor, movies, community theater, delis, restaurants — for a small town, Gilroy does all right in amusements. New county park, four miles west of town. Honors and calls attention to culture of Ohlone Indians.

To open in 1999, a golf course. To open in 2001, a horticultural theme park, 167 acres, expected to attract 1 million visitors. Trees, picnic benches and rides. Family oriented. County government, for parks and open space, in 1996 purchased 6,187 acres in east hills between Gilroy and Morgan Hill. In 1998, in the same area, another 9,234 acres were purchased for open space.

Annual Garlic Festival (last full weekend in July) draws about 130,000 who consume about 5,000 pounds of garlic. Gilroy also throws a Hispanic Cultural Festival, dancing, singing, cultural events, eating (food booths). Mexican Independence Day in September. Antique and Micro-Breweries Fest. Farmers market, called El Mercado, good for fresh vegetables. In the spring, flowers, grown commercially, light up the countryside. Voters in 1994 approved tax to extend library hours and buy books.

Gavilan Community College is located at the south end of town. Pretty place and a plus for Gilroy, many classes, activities.

Gilroy is trying to tap the tourist trade. Wineries and redwoods a short distance off. Picturesque city hall, damaged in 1989 earthquake, was reopened as a sort of arts center. About 16 antique stores in downtown.

Crime rate in suburban range. Three homicides in 1997, one in 1996, two in 1995, zero in 1994, two in 1993, one each in 1992, 1991 and 1990, two in 1989, two in 1988, none the three preceding years, reports FBI. Stepped-up efforts against graffiti. Dress code at high school to discourage gang colors and activity. No hats. High school forbids students from leaving during school hours and has installed security measures.

Schools score low to middling, a few high. Portable classrooms. Year-round education at some schools. In 1994, school district spent $4 million to renovate elementary schools and junior highs, the money coming from a bond passed in 1993. Several schools have been built in recent years. Another elementary school is to open in year 2000. School district may introduce middle schools. In talk stage, two bonds, one for new schools and renovation, one to repair streets and sidewalks.

School district uses magnet schools to blend kids by ethnicity. Magnet schools use special, attractive programs to draw kids away from their neighborhoods, thereby breaking down segregation based on housing patterns. One Gilroy junior high school stresses science, another humanities. Other schools stress bilingual instruction, math, classes for high achievers. "Block" method being used at high school — 90-minute classes.

Visitors bureau-chamber of commerce: (408) 842-6436.

SANTA CLARA CITY & TOWN PROFILES

LOS ALTOS

PRESTIGE TOWN. Quaint downtown. Streets lined with tall redwoods, pines and various other trees. Police station and civic center hide behind apricot trees. School rankings quite high. One of the lowest crime ratings in the state. Only drawback: traffic congests on commercial streets.

Los Altos started 1998 with 28,415 residents. By the year 2010, predict regional planners, it should have 29,100 — essentially built out. Home to managers, administrators and professionals, and, increasingly, retirees. About 31 percent of the residents are over age 55. About 21 percent are under age 18, reported 1990 census.

Seven shopping centers. Downtown has attracted first-class restaurants, bakeries, coffee shops, sidewalk cafes, boutiques and art galleries. Statues spotted here and there. At the corner of Main and State streets is a spic-and-span plaza decorated with bricks and stones and a large four-faced clock that looks like it stepped out of London. Town started as a summer vacation spot. When railroad arrived, Los Altos took off as second home of San Francisco wealthy, then as home for upper-middle class.

Single homes account for 89 percent of housing stock. Great majority built on about quarter-acre lots. In 1998 state counted 10,592 residential units — 9,381 single homes, 338 single-family attached, 870 multiples, 3 mobile homes. Many of the streets go without sidewalks, part of the country atmosphere that residents seem to love. Despite the name, Los Altos has few hills but it does slope gently toward the Bay.

Schools scores among highest in state. All six elementary schools have been designated "distinguished," meaning the state thinks they are well-run. Junior high and high schools received similar honors. Day care at elementary schools. Voters in 1989 passed a parcel tax to restore school programs and fix buildings and in 1993 renewed the tax, and in 1997 renewed it again with an increase to $264. Another tax measure for the elementary schools was passed in 1998. Los Altos High in 1993 added classrooms, new library. A $58 million bond to improve schools in the Mountain View-Los Altos High School District passed on the third try in 1995. The money was used to remodel and add classrooms, repair heating and plumbing, and add security lighting. Tax passed in 1994 to keep libraries in Los Altos and Los Altos Hills open longer.

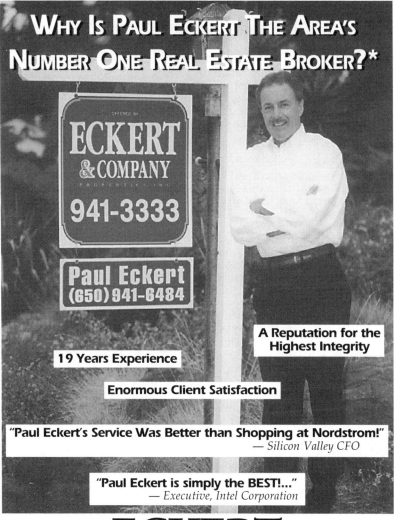

WHY IS PAUL ECKERT THE AREA'S NUMBER ONE REAL ESTATE BROKER?*

ECKERT
& COMPANY
PROPERTIES INC.
941-3333

Paul Eckert
(650) 941-6484

19 Years Experience

A Reputation for the Highest Integrity

Enormous Client Satisfaction

"Paul Eckert's Service Was Better than Shopping at Nordstrom!"
— *Silicon Valley CFO*

"Paul Eckert is simply the BEST!..."
— *Executive, Intel Corporation*

ECKERT
PROPERTIES INC.
RELOCATION DIVISION

100 University Ave., Los Altos, CA 94022

Call Paul Eckert at the office or at home anytime!

Office: (650) 941-3333 • Home: (650) 941-6484 • Toll Free: 1-800-655-2954

e-mail:paul@eckertinc.com   www.eckertinc.com

**Last year and this year, Paul Eckert has represented more
Buyers and Sellers in Los Altos and Los Altos Hills than anyone else!*

Home Price Sampler from Classified Ads

Almaden Valley (San Jose)
4 BR/2.5BA, $349,950.

5 BR/2.5BA, hardwood floors, 50-year roof, pool, sauna, $555,000.

Berryessa (San Jose)
2 BR/1BA, townhouse, $137,000.

Blossom Valley (San Jose)
3 BR/2BA, new paint, carpet, stove, $270,000.

3 BR/2BA, culde-sac, near foothills, rock fireplace, spa, $339,950.

Cambrian (San Jose)
4 BR/2.5BA, 2,280 sq. ft., 4 years old, 3-car garage, $571,950.

3 BR/2BA, cul-de-sac, new carpet, paint, huge family room, $375,000.

Campbell
3 BR/1.5BA, starter home, $305,000.

4 BR/2.5BA, 2 fireplaces, oak floors, Dry Creek area, $685,000.

Cupertino
3 BR/2BA, 1,248 sq. ft., remodeled baths, hardwood floors, $429,000.

3 BR/2BA, 2,534 sq. ft., overlooks golf course, $859,000.

East Valley (San Jose)
2 BR/1BA, corner lot, new kitchen & bath, $195,500.

4 BR/2BA, remod. kitchen , $269,950.

Evergreen (San Jose)
3 BR/2.5BA, 1,900 sq. ft., solar pool & spa, $329,500.

4 BR/4 BA, 3,685 sq. ft., 2 family rooms, dining, spa, den, $844,950.

Gilroy
3 BR/1.5BA, 1,200 sq. ft., new kitchen,

2-car garage, fireplace, $195,000.

5 BR/3BA, deluxe 2nd master or guest retreat, $359,900.

Los Altos
3 BR/2BA, almost 1/3 acre, Los Altos schools, $675,000.

4 BR/2BA, den, pool, Los Altos schools, $899,000.

Los Altos Hills
3 BR/2BA, family room, 2 fireplaces, spa, , $675,000.

4 BR/3.5BA, 2,900 sq. ft., pool, cul-de-sac, $1,425,000.

Los Gatos
3 BR/2BA, family room, 2 fireplaces, spa, $675,000.

5 B R/3BA, 4,000 sq. ft., pool, formal dining rooms, $1,425,000.

Milpitas
4 BR/3BA, 1,886 sq. ft., hardwood floors, large back yard, $390,000.

4 BR/3BA, 1 story on 1 acre, pool, city views, $1,095,000.

Monte Sereno
4 BR/2.5BA, on 2/3 acre, cul-de-sac, vaulted ceilings, large family room, $1,195,000.

4 BR/2.5BA, $1.550,000.

Morgan Hill
3 BR/2BA, spool & spa, quiet court, $265,500.

4 BR/4BA, 6 level acres, hardwood floors, $849,500.

Mountain View
2 BR/1BA, cottage, living rm, dining w/fireplace, hardwd flrs, $289,950.

Parents raise $100,000 annually for physical ed, science, music classes.

Montclair Elementary is located in Los Altos but served by Cupertino School District, which in 1995 passed a renovation bond. About eight private schools are located either in Los Altos Hills or Los Altos.

Crime rate among the lowest in California. Zero homicides in 1997, 1996, 1995, 1994 and 1993, one in 1992, three in 1991, zero in 1990 and in 1989.

Commute pretty good. Foothill Expressway runs through town. Highways 280 and 101 are close by. Other freeways, Silicon Valley industries, within a short drive.

Home Price Sampler from Classified Ads

3 BR/3BA, 2-car garage, half basement, $529,000.

North Valley (San Jose)
4 BR/3BA, 1,700+ sq. ft., 2 master suites, $272,500.

3 BR/2.5Ba, on 6 acres, hilltop retreat, $875,000.

Palo Alto
2 BR/2.5BA, 10-year-old townhouse, 2-car garage, $399,000.

5 BR/4BA, gated Mediterranean estate on .6 acre, $2,800,000.

Rose Garden (San Jose)
3 BR + den, 2,400+ sq. ft., 2-story California bungalow, $399,000.

4 BR/3BA, on 1/2 acre, pool, patio, game room, $1.675,000.

San Jose (Downtown)
Duplex, tree-lined street, $315,000.

San Jose (Central)
2 BR/1BA bungalow, deep lot, $249,000.

3 BR/1BA, Victorian, country kitchen, parlor, bay windows, $269,500.

San Jose (South)
4 BR/2BA, 1,610 sq. ft., living/family/ dining rms, new carpet, $249,000.

3 BR/2BA, corner lot, $268,500.

San Jose (West)
4 BR/2BA, quiet street, Moreland Schools, $359,950.

4 BR Colonial, 2,800 aq. ft., + 4810 sq ft. guest quarters, $649,999.

Santa Teresa (San Jose)
3 BR/2.5BA, tile roof, central air, $318,000.

4 BR/2BA, 2,671 sq. ft., former model, french doors, A/C/, $369,950.

Santa Clara
4 BR/2BA, family room, hardwood floors, new sod, $410,100.

4 BR/2.5BA, high ceilings, gourmet kitch, 3 yrs. old, $659,000.

Saratoga
3 BR/2BA, 1,720 sq. ft., portion rebuilt 5 years ago, $595,000.

5 BR/3BA, 2,950 sq. ft., gour. kitchen, bay windows, skylights, $869,000.

Sunnyvale
3 BR/1BA, new paint in & out, updated kitchen, $315,000.

3 BR/2BA, cul-de-sac, 2,367 sq. ft., $649,000.

Willow Glen (San Jose)
4 BR/3BA, 1,800+ sq. ft., large basement, 2-car garage, $379,000.

4 BR/2.5BA, kitchen w/cherry cabinets, tile floor, new appliances/ carpet, $615,000.

The problems: so many people shop the local stores and restaurants that traffic often creeps along the business streets — many traffic lights, delays.

Community Center, skateboard playground, 10 parks, including one with a redwood grove, adult education and recreation programs at the schools. Little theater. Art and wine festival, antique fairs, a lot to do in a small-town way. Baseball, soccer, drama, dance, many clubs. Seniors center. Youth center. Library recently expanded. Farmers market. Festival of Lights Parade draws 20,000-30,000. Annual pet parade, big hit with kids. In 1996, for a future park, the city purchased 5.5 acres, the site of a closed school.

Los Altos Morning Forum secures pundits and celebrities for its talks. Nearby Foothill College attracts big-name speakers at its forums: George Bush, Jimmy Carter, Colin Powell and Gregory Peck, to name a few. Los Altos borders Palo Alto. For many people, a drive of 10 minutes brings them all that Palo Alto and Stanford offer. Arguments over quality of life. No gas-powered leaf blowers; only battery and electric. Chamber of commerce (650) 948-1455.

SANTA CLARA CITY & TOWN PROFILES

LOS ALTOS HILLS

MOST PRESTIGIOUS CITY in Santa Clara County. Home to many of Silicon Valley's bosses and bigwigs. Small and essentially built-out. Located in hills and valleys above Silicon Valley. School scores very high. One of the lowest crime rates in state. Many mansions and custom homes. No business, no commercial. The Poor Clares, an order of nuns, run a cloistered monastery.

Minimum one-acre lots. Valley views. Trees overhang roads, creating tunnels of leaves and branches. Mansions hide behind walls and shrubs. Population increased by 93 in last decade; as of 1998 stands at 8,168. Large unincorporated neighborhood to south of town. Also upscale. Managed by residents through homeowner association.

Zoning and building codes are described by city as "elaborate." City has issued handbook spelling out what Los Altos Hills would like to see in way of housing — homes that fit in, heed neighbors' wishes, etc. Housing units in 1998 numbered 2,794, of which 2,735 were single homes, 24 single attached, 31 multiples, 4 mobile. Many homes go for well over a million. Tiny city hall.

Many homes have pools and tennis courts, some have horses grazing out back. Paths wander throughout town. Many dead-end streets. Ride-a-thons to save open space on ridges. Law protects redwoods, oaks, large trees. Fremont Hills Country Club: pool, 10 tennis courts, riding facility, golf. Two other golf courses nearby. Town started off as a place for wealthy San Franciscans to escape summer fog. Incorporated in 1956 to get control of developers.

Foothill Community College adds life to cultural scenes and runs a speakers program, attracting top names, George Bush, Colin Powell, Jimmy Carter, Palo Alto borders Los Altos Hills. Short drive to movies, plays, delights of Stanford. Interstate 280 soothes the nerves, scenic freeway.

Schools score very high. Santa Rita and Bullis-Purissima have received national blue ribbons for academic excellence. Served by Los Altos district. Strong support from residents, parents, Several bonds passed for school. See Los Altos profile for more information. Two private schools.

Zero homicides for 1997, 1996, 1995 and 1994. Stable, intimate. Residents know one another. One of lowest divorce rates in county, 4 percent of residents vs. 10 percent for county (1990 census). No chamber of commerce.

WHY IS PAUL ECKERT THE AREA'S NUMBER ONE REAL ESTATE BROKER?*

ECKERT & COMPANY PROPERTIES INC.

941-3333

Paul Eckert
(650) 941-6484

A Reputation for the Highest Integrity

19 Years Experience

Enormous Client Satisfaction

"Paul Eckert's Service Was Better than Shopping at Nordstrom!"
— *Silicon Valley CFO*

"Paul Eckert is simply the BEST!..."
— *Executive, Intel Corporation*

ECKERT
PROPERTIES INC.
RELOCATION DIVISION

100 University Ave., Los Altos, CA 94022
Call Paul Eckert at the office or at home anytime!
Office: (650) 941-3333 • Home: (650) 941-6484 • Toll Free: 1-800-655-2954
e-mail:paul@eckertinc.com   www.eckertinc.com

**Last year and this year, Paul Eckert has represented more
Buyers and Sellers in Los Altos and Los Altos Hills than anyone else!*

SANTA CLARA CITY & TOWN PROFILES

LOS GATOS

TRANSLATION, THE CATS but in fact, one of the nicer, more prestigious towns of Santa Clara County. School scores high, crime low. Voters in 1994 renewed a tax to sustain schools.

Many nice homes. Flat lands rising to wooded hills and open hills. Jesuit Novitiate covers 340 hillside acres. Many trees. Good views. Historic downtown. First city in county to adopt ordinance preserving historic buildings.

Between 1980 and 1990, Los Gatos added 451 residents and about 830 residential units, about three-fourths of them single homes or single attached. Many of the new homes jump up the scale but a good deal of the housing runs to well-done suburban with a high level of maintenance. Town is essentially built out. ABAG, the regional planning agency, expects the population to increase by only 1,400 over the next 15 years. State estimated population in 1998 at 30,122.

Housing units in 1998 numbered 12,373, of which 7,059 were single homes, 1,722 single-family attached, 3,442 multiples, 150 mobile homes. Rentals in the downtown, which also has the older homes.

Small is not a dirty word here and the city government is famous — or notorious, depending on your point of view — for discouraging growth and fine-tuning style of life.

The commute, historically awful, got much better in late 1994 with the opening of Highway 85 to Cupertino and Saratoga and other Silicon Valley cities. One of these years light rail might connect Los Gatos to San Jose.

Los Gatos suffered major damage in 1989 quake, mostly to old structures, although chimneys and walls were cracked in newer homes. No one killed but many emotionally shaken.

Building codes were revised to make reconstructed buildings better able to withstand earthquakes. Other safety measures taken. Town recovered quickly.

One homicide in 1997, zero in 1996, one in 1995, zero in 1994, 1993, 1992 and 1991, one in 1990, two in 1989, zero in 1988, two in 1987, and one in 1986. In 1996, elementary district adopted DARE program to discourage

RANDY J. WALDEN
REALTOR

- *Serving Silicon Valley Since 1979*
- *Specializing in the Cities of Los Gatos, Campbell, Cambrian Park & Almaden* (Homes accessible to the newly constructed California Highway 85)
- *1992 Masters Hall of Fame Inductee*
- *Over 500 Homes Sold*
- *Ten Time Centurion Winner*
- *Voted "M.V.P." by Our Los Gatos Agents Last Year*

Call us today if commitment, integrity, professionalism and great service are important to you in your real estate matters.

408 • 559 • 9440 Direct
408 • 354 • 2295 Business
e-mail: rjwalden@aol.com

Resume and References Available on Request

PHH
Home
Equity
Reloca-
tion

kids from trying drugs.

Schools among the tops in the state. One study showed 85 percent of high school seniors going on to college. Los Gatos High in 1991 received national honors for its programs. Fisher School received a similar award. White House ceremony.

Computer labs, music, art at elementary. Foreign languages at junior high. Teen center next to high school.

Los Gatos Union School District voters in 1990 approved a $180-a-year parcel tax. Money is used to keep class sizes down, services up, to repair buildings and buy books and supplies. The tax was to have expired in 1994 but residents voted to renew it. Parents also fund elementary school programs through a foundation formed in 1982; have raised $1 million in about 15 years. Computer training emphasized. Steve Wozniak, a.k.a. "the Woz," co-founder of Apple, is a Los Gatos resident. He helped set up computer lab-arcade at Fisher school and trained many of the teachers. Also chipped in for a math lab at high school.

High school district, which also serves Monte Sereno and Saratoga, is talking about asking voters to approve a renovation tax.

Oak Meadows-Vasona Park, one of the nicest in the county (reservoir, miniature trains, playgrounds), is full on weekends with parents cooing over kiddies. Fifteen parks total, eight playgrounds, over 400 acres of open space, miles of trails for hiking and biking. Golf course on the northwest side of town.

Tennis, softball, soccer, rowing club, baseball, activities, classes. Concerts. Movie house. YMCA. Jewish Community Center with pool. High school pool used to teach young children and adults how to swim. Racquet and swim club. Banquet hall. Creek trail. Fitness clubs. Farmers market year-round. Latest addition: bocce courts.

Summer concerts. Two historical museums. Library open seven days a week. Art galleries. Fiesta de Artes. Cats Festival. Quaint Old Town Shopping Plaza. More parking added recently. Carriage rides in downtown. Top-notch and diverse restaurants. Community Foundation throws parties to raise money for parks, service groups and such endeavors as the high school band.

Many small towns can't or won't support a local newspaper. Los Gatos is an exception.

Among those who call or have called Los Gatos home: Peggy Fleming, Olympic ice skater; writer John Steinbeck; and Yehudi Menuhin, violinist.

A nice town to stroll. At Christmas, residents gather in old town for tree lighting and caroling and kids' parade. Stores go all out for holidays with lights and displays. Chamber of commerce (408) 354-9300.

SANTA CLARA CITY & TOWN PROFILES

MILPITAS

FAMILY TOWN. Average to above-average schools. Low crime rate. Good commute. Dynamic, changing town that in 1994 opened one of the largest and most unusual shopping centers in the Bay Area.

Milpitas started out as an industrial community, home to the giant Ford auto plant, but switched gears in the 1980s. Wooed electronic high-tech firms and moved within the elastic boundaries of "Silicon Valley." Business parks scattered throughout the flatlands.

High-tech jobs and relatively low home prices attracted many professionals to Milpitas. The city added over 31,000 residents since the electronics boom. The state put the 1998 population at 61,588.

Housing in Milpitas has expanded to meet the demands of a growing population. Much of Milpitas is new or fairly new. The south and much of the middle of Milpitas are a mix of single homes (some upscale — two stories, three-car garages), townhouses and a few apartments. More apartments can be found east of Interstate 680, along with new tracts. Sound walls buffer the newer subdivisions from traffic noise. Arterial traffic is shunted around many neighborhoods and this makes the residential streets safer. City has established "urban boundary limit" to discourage housing in hills.

As you drive north, you encounter the old neighborhood, generally small single homes, somewhat faded, but many showing signs of care and attention. Here and there new tracts will be found. Further north, more new tracts. In the northeast hills, a gated golf course subdivision. In the winter rains of 1998, some new homes on Dixon Landing Road flooded.

Good housing mix, 16,956 residential units — 11,001 single homes, 2,051 single attached, 3,332 multiples, 572 mobile homes (1998 count). In the 1980s, Milpitas added about 3,600 residential units, increasing its housing stock by over 30 percent. Fast-growing towns generally mean many kids. The 1990 census found 27 percent of residents under age 18, only 11 percent above 55.

Overall academic rankings, compared to other schools in the state, land in the 60th to 90th percentiles. Indicates good support for education. DARE program to discourage kids from using drugs, drinking booze. School district runs morning and evening care programs for kids. New middle school.

For a middle-class suburban city, the overall crime rate is low. Two homicides in 1997, 1996 and 1995, three in 1994, zero in 1993, one each in 1992 and 1991, zero in 1990, one in 1989, three in 1988, two in 1987.

Lots of family activities in Milpitas. Twenty-one parks, 11 playgrounds. New community center and library. New aquatics center (four pools). Soccer, tennis, baseball, Little League, racquetball, waterslides, two golf courses in foothills, basketball, softball, volleyball, hang gliding, day camp, movies, bowling, roller skating, billiard parlor. On the unusual side: a string orchestra for children, a teen choir, and kid's theater. Many fast-food and middling restaurants. Art and Wine Festival.

Milpitas has a solid commercial base to support its above-average amenities. Besides the high-tech industries located throughout the city, retail centers contribute much to the city coffers.

The old Ford assembly plant, which closed in 1983, was converted 10 years later into "The Great Mall of the Bay Area," one of the largest outlet malls in California. If plans pan out, it will hold nine to eleven "anchor" stores and 240 smaller stores. A big plus for Milpitas: providing not only tax revenues, but many entry-level and part-time jobs for local residents. Milpitas has also landed a Wal-Mart, located in another shopping complex. Great Mall to add a movie-plex, 20 screens.

The old downtown, lost in the shuffle, is tucked in near the train tracks but a new downtown — called Town Center — has risen to take its place. Anchored by civic complex, it's located off Calaveras and North Milpitas.

Few South Bay cities have great commutes but Milpitas has better than most. The town is divided north-south by Interstates 880 and 680 and east-west by Highway 237. The Interstates are usually a mess at peak hours, but the commute into downtown San Jose is only 7 to 10 miles. I-880 was recently widened and improved. Highway 237, also improved, shoots into the heart of Silicon Valley, 10 to 15 miles to the west. Short drive to Fremont and its jobs and relatively short haul across Dumbarton Bridge to Palo Alto and other Silicon Valley jobs. But even with road and freeway improvements, traffic often congests during peak hours, exasperating drivers.

BART (commute rail) station located in nearby Fremont and one of these years, money permitting, either BART will be extended south from Fremont or the light rail north from San Jose.

Overall Milpitas is a middle-class town that delivers on many of the important aspects of suburban life. Chamber of commerce (408) 262-2613.

Dog days: Dude and Argose, Milpitas neighbors and dogs, got into a fight and were labeled by the city as "dangerous," which meant the owners were required to post warning signs on gates and muzzle Dude and Argose. City agreed to drop the label if the owners built a dog run and hired a trainer and put a fence between the yards. City council is keeping an eye on the situation.

SANTA CLARA CITY & TOWN PROFILES

MONTE SERENO

SMALL CITY beteen Los Gatos and Saratoga, famous in a minor way for saying no to growth. Many custom homes on large lots. Built over gentle hills. Country feeling. Considered a prestigious address.

One of two Santa Clara cities in the last decade to lose population. It dropped 147 people. Population 3,416 (state count 1998).

When development galloped toward Monte Sereno in the 1950s, the town's leaders said, hell, no. They incorporated the hamlet as a city to keep planning under the control of the locals (through the city council), and since then have pretty much kept new construction down.

State tally (1998) showed 1,250 residences, of which 1,217 were single homes (many of them custom jobs), 25 single attached, 7 apartments, 1 mobile home.

Monte Sereno wines and dines in Los Gatos. Many kids attend Los Gatos schools. Scores very high. See Los Gatos profile. Los Gatos Police Department is paid to patrol the town, the assessment $100 to $125 per parcel. Crime low. Zero homicides in 1997 and 1996.

Commute improved in 1994 with the opening of Highway 85, which runs from South San Jose up to Mountain View (Silicon Valley).

City manager prepares budget, does planning and a host of other jobs. Every once in a while someone throws a snit over housing and appearances. In 1996, voters decided that city hall was butting in too much when residents wanted to make cosmetic repairs to homes. Elections ushered in a new mayor.

Golf course to north of city. Community college (many classes-activities) in adjoining Saratoga along with concerts and other events. Many parks and trails in region. Residents big on recycling; Monte Sereno a leader in this endeavor.

John Steinbeck, while living at Monte Sereno, wrote "Of Mice and Men."

Local paper calls town "Monte Snoreno," but residents want it that way, quiet and peaceful.

SANTA CLARA CITY & TOWN PROFILES

MORGAN HILL

IF SAN JOSE EPITOMIZED the building spirit of 50 years ago, its neighbor to the south captures the different mood of modern Santa Clara County.

San Jose said, "let 'er rip," and cheered as developers marched their tracts down the Santa Clara Valley.

A half century later, Santa Clara County is booming again. Silicon Valley, short of housing, is drawing its employees from bedroom communities as far east as Tracy, and Morgan Hill, surrounded by miles of open land, is saying, let's take it nice and slow — with a big exception: If you've got a high-tech firm and are shopping for a site, Morgan Hill would love to hear from you.

The result: a pretty town, a mix of country, farm and suburbia, population 30,786, a town that vows not to repeat the mistakes of yore but a town also in search of the right blend of elements to buy and sustain the amenities of modern life.

The town takes its name not from a local hill but from Hiram Morgan Hill who married into a pioneer family. But there is a striking hill to the west of town, called El Toro. Stately oaks grace a few lawns and trees planted around the city soften the housing lines. Hills to east and west. Most of town built on valley floor.

Served by Morgan Hill Unified School District, which has one major high school, Live Oak. School rankings generally follow demographics. These scores place Morgan Hill in the category of middle-class, which in the big picture is accurate but details are important.

Morgan Hill schools educate rural, low-income children and children from middle- and high-income neighborhoods. Scores will vary from school to school depending upon the demographics of the attendance zones.

Renovation bond was passed in 1991. Another high school will be opened in a few years. Several private schools. Bond effort failed in 1998; needed two-thirds approval, got 63 percent.

Overall crime rate low. One homicide in 1997, zero in 1996 and 1995, the FBI reports. The counts for the previous years are one, one, one, zero, zero, zero, one, one, zero.

Commuting: to south and central San Jose, on many days not bad. Both are a straight shot down Highway 101. CalTrain runs commute trains to both destinations and to other Silicon Valley cities, finishing up in San Francisco. Expanded parking at the train station.

For residents who have to travel by car to other towns in Silicon Valley the

Santa Clara County Single-Family Home Prices

City	Sales	Lowest	Highest	Median	Average
Campbell	106	$68,500	$750,000	$342,500	$341,347
Cupertino	138	$60,000	$1,387,500	$550,000	$560,342
Gilroy	134	$82,000	$787,500	$290,000	$309,651
Los Altos	124	$219,000	$2,675,000	$875,000	$980,768
Los Gatos	159	$73,000	$3,100,000	$640,000	$699,008
Milpitas	183	$50,000	$1,020,000	$280,000	$288,464
Morgan Hill	135	$75,000	$980,000	$370,000	$402,154
Mountain View	100	$69,000	$1,250,000	$432,500	$443,381
Palo Alto	90	$54,545	$2,750,000	$580,000	$658,816
San Jose	2,392	$50,000	$1,657,500	$295,000	$315,329
San Martin	10	$180,000	$864,500	$601,500	$547,950
Santa Clara	199	$50,000	$690,000	$312,000	$313,658
Saratoga	106	$118,509	$2,400,000	$800,000	$864,819
Sunnyvale	255	$82,000	$1,085,000	$412,500	$396,904

Source: Data Quick Information Systems, LaJolla: Single Family residence sales from Sept. 1 to Nov. 31, 1998. Median means halfway. In 100 homes, the 50th is the median.

commute will often be an ordeal. More trains are being added to CalTrain line. Funding has been lined up to widen Highway 101 to three lanes, to and from San Jose.

Recreation offerings are plentiful but fragmented. About five years ago, Morgan Hill ran into money woes and scrapped its recreation department (but public works maintains the parks). Parents groups, the school district, the YMCA and other groups either stepped into the breech or had their own programs in place. Soccer, football, the typical kids' sports, swimming — all there but it has to be said that many other cities do a better job on recreation.

Large regional park and lake (reservoir) to east of town. Boating on lake.

To listen to many people, what San Jose did in the 1950s was a horror. It allowed (gasp!) developers to run free.

So did thousands of cities across the country. America was coming out of a world war and the Depression. Mobility had been stifled for almost 20 years.

Freeways were built, the car came into full flower and the great exodus was on, from city to suburbs, aided by developers but also enjoying great public support. A home in the suburbs — the American dream. Governments imposed few controls not only because they wanted the growth but because they didn't know what controls to impose.

This gave developers "free rein" but in reality they had to build to the discipline of the market. Still, corners were cut and stupid things done.

Morgan Hill missed this era. Until the 1980s, it was a hick hamlet in the middle of fields and orchards.

When its time came to develop, planners were in place, they had a much better idea of what worked and what didn't, the public was aware of environmental concerns, protecting open space was accepted — a different ball game.

If you buy into Morgan Hill, you are very much buying into a planned, controlled-growth community — which many people consider a plus.

And a community moving up the scale. The 1980s housing coincided with a period of prosperity in the South Bay. The same holds for the housing going up now.

In appearance, Morgan Hill traces the fortunes of Santa Clara County: small and modest, bungalows and cottages, in the old town. Three-bedroom, two-car-garage homes in the next ring and on the outer ring, two-story, four- to six-bedroom homes built in the modern style, creamy stucco and red-tile roofs, plenty of light, California Mediterranean. In the east hills, many of the homes were custom built along tract designs and positioned to command views of the valley or Lake Anderson.

The state in 1998 counted 9,951 residential units, of which 6,324 were single detached homes, 1,286 single attached, 1,489 multiple units and 869 mobile homes.

To pay for civic amenities and to shorten some commutes, city hall is wooing clean, high-tech firms. Several have been landed — Abbott Labs, Cidco, Anritsu and a number of smaller firms.

For information about opening a business, call the city's economic development office at (408) 779-7271.

San Jose is holding up development on its south side to figure out what to do. Conceivably, a lot of land around Morgan Hill could remain in farming. The county has purchased 6,187 acres to the southeast for open space. In 1998, another 9,234 acres were secured.

• Morgan Hill honors the mushroom with a festival. The town also has at least four wineries. The winter holidays are welcomed with a crafts fair, caroling and the lighting of a Christmas tree.

• In the early 1980s, city hall for some reason turned down a Mervyn's, to the displeasure of residents, who wanted closer shopping. Voices were raised, picket signs paraded, decisions reconsidered. Mervyn's got the nod. In local lore, incident is known as the Mervyn's Revolt.

Among recent shopping additions: One of the largest supermarkets in the county.

Downtown Morgan Hill, spruced up with trees and brick sidewalks and crosswalks, is attracting coffee shops, brew pubs and restaurants. Chamber of commerce (408) 779-9444.

SANTA CLARA CITY & TOWN PROFILES

MOUNTAIN VIEW

THE ONLY CITY in Santa Clara County where apartments outnumber single homes. Attracts many of the young and newcomers to the county. One of best night life cities of county.

Crime suburban average on the low side. School rankings fairly high. Voters have approved higher taxes to rebuild schools. Commute good and soon to get better. Light rail is coming to Mountain View.

Key player in Silicon Valley. Home to over 200 manufacturing and high-tech firms. About 70,000 jobs in town. Among the big guys: Silicon Graphics and Alza, a pharmaceutical firm, Netscape. More coming: Microsoft is consolidating its Silicon Valley operations in Mountain View. Alza and Silicon Graphics are expanding.

A city that's doing a lot of handwringing over what could be one of the region's biggest assets: Moffett Field, which borders Mountain View on land controlled by the county government. The Navy in 1994 said goodbye to its base in Moffett, a landmark because of its tall hangars that used to house dirigibles. NASA Ames Research Center took over Moffett, about 2,000 choice acres. NASA is researching computer systems for 21st century space exploration and hopes to find private partners for its projects.

In an advisory vote in 1996, Mountain View voters said no to opening Moffett to air cargo flights but many power people in Silicon Valley would like to keep this option open. The county's two other airports, San Jose and Reid-Hillview, are crowded, and many business leaders see air cargo from Moffett as quite important to the county's continued prosperity. In the planning fund-raising stage for Moffett Field: An Air and Space Center that would feature cutting-edge technology, and a Computer History Museum. Stanford University, to house some of its faculty and graduate students, is negotiating with Moffett to rent 300 residential units formerly used by the military.

Apartments outnumber single homes two to one. Total housing units 32,806: single homes 9,054; 3,942 single attached; 18,621 multiple units; 1,189 mobile homes (state figures, 1998).

Apartments are not everyone's cup of tea but for the many people starting out in the computer business, they are quite acceptable.

A place for singles. Census in 1990 revealed that over half of Mountain View (55%) has never married or is either divorced, widowed or separated.

Most of the single homes can be found west of El Camino Real; most of the apartments, east of El Camino Real but this section also has many single homes. New homes and townhouses are going up on Whisman Road, near the Central Expressway and light-rail line. Innovative designs.

Many Mountain View homes sell in some instances well over $100,000 above what you would pay for similar homes in other parts of the Bay Area. Silicon Valley housing is hot. Signs of the times: BMWs, Volvos, SUVs and at one place a Lincoln town car parked in front of quite modest homes.

Many were built in the Fifties and Sixties and in size and design reflect what people wanted in those decades, generally three-bedroom units. In other Bay Area cities, older neighborhoods serve as way stations for people going up the scale or just marking time. Some homes are well-kept, some neglected.

In Mountain View (and Silicon Valley), home prices are so high and land so scarce that the old neighborhoods have increased their value, adding to stability and beauty. Lawns are well-tended, bungalows freshly painted and often remodeled, streets lined with trees. Older, smaller (two-bedroom) homes can be found south of City Hall.

City council has before it a proposal to build two 10-story apartment buildings on El Camino Real. Some opposition. Project may get green light but with fewer units.

In the 1980s, Mountain View added 8,805 residents and 2,800 residential units. Population now 74,730 (1998 estimate). About 18 percent of residents are under age 18, which is low for Santa Clara County, but still amounts to 12,000 children and teenagers (1990 census).

Some of the recent arrivals are immigrants and Mountain View is trying to ease them into community life. Church group has opened a workers center to lessen complaints about men clustering on some street corners waiting for people to offer work.

Downtown overhauled: brick sidewalks, kiosks, pedestrian lighting, more trees. Choice of 50 restaurants (Asian cuisine popular). Nice place to stroll. Bookstore, free parking, monthly festivals, art. Ballet school. New city hall and Performing Arts Center (plays, musicals, dance, recitals) opened in 1991. Annual art and wine festival draws 200,000. City hall encourages public art. New library opened in 1997, pride of the city, holds up to 300,000 books. Large night club-restaurant, called Rio Grand, holds 700, recently opened, country-western food, music and dancing. Also disco.

Many activities. Tennis, swimming, boating, movies, theater, art and wine festival, sports — the typical offerings of well-managed town with some money in its pocket. City school districts have gone partners on playgrounds used by kids and community.

Big park on shore with golf course. Swim Center. Movie complex. Palo Alto and Stanford, and all they offer, are just up the road. Large shopping center off of El Camino Real on north side of town.

Shoreline Theater, managed by Bill Graham organization, draws top performers in U.S.

Crime rate about suburban average. One homicide in 1997, zero in 1996, one in 1995, five in 1994, two in 1993 and 1992, zero in 1991, four in 1990, three in 1989 and 1988, one in 1987 and 1986. Cops, through DARE program, work with schools to discourage drugs. Graffiti ordinance puts the burden of cleanup on property owner.

Academic rankings, in statewide comparisons, land mostly in the 70th to 90th percentile, which reflects well on parents and schools. Mountain View High School has been pronounced "distinguished," national award for good management, academic excellence. State "distinguished" awards to several elementary schools.

In 1995, a $58 million bond measure passed; money to be used to remodel high-school classrooms in the Mountain View-Los Altos High School District, repair heating and plumbing and add security lights.

Whisman elementary district, which serves part of Mountain View, in 1996 passed a $34 million bond to replace portable buildings with permanent and upgrade wiring, plumbing and heating. Mountain View Elementary District in 1998 won a $36 million bond to renovate all schools. Some people would like the two elementary districts to merge.

St. Francis High, a private school, was awarded a Blue Ribbon in 1991, a national honor, signifying that it's one of the best in country.

Freeways crisscross town. In 1994, Highway 85 was opened, another connection with San Jose.

Being in the heart of Silicon Valley, Mountain View does much better in the commuting department than many other cities in the county. CalTrain to the City and down to Sunnyvale, Santa Clara and San Jose.

In 2000, a light-rail line that starts in South San Jose will be extended into Mountain View. Job is well under way. Line will end near downtown, where new transit center is being built.

Chamber of commerce: (650) 968-8378.

SANTA CLARA CITY & TOWN PROFILES

PALO ALTO

ONE OF THE MOST DESIRABLE ADDRESSES in the nation. Cultural center of Silicon Valley. Prestigious. Sophisticated. A financial powerhouse. What Wall Street is to New York, Sand Hill Road (which Palo Alto shares with Menlo Park) is to venture capital in computer projects.

"Home" of Stanford University, birthplace of Silicon Valley. In 1995, passed one the largest school-renovation bonds in the history of California, a great boost for local schools.

Well-to-do, highly educated, cosmopolitan, built out. Added only 675 residents in last decade, increase of 1 percent. Population 60,492 (state figures 1998).

Every year, the town's two high schools in the math SAT score among the highest in the state.

In 1988 and 1991, the San Francisco Chronicle ranked Bay Area towns on such measures as crime, school quality, restaurants, commuting distances, cultural ornaments and more. In both rankings, Palo Alto was pronounced the best place to live in the Bay Area.

Invariably tied to Stanford University, located just outside city limits.

Tree-lined streets. Walls of ivy. Lovely campus. Excellent restaurants and coffee shops. Bookstores. First-run and foreign films near campus. Many cultural events on campus, theater, classical to rock music. Big-time college football and basketball. In 1998, the Stanford men's basketball team made it to the final four in the NCAA. Bay Area was rooting for team.

One of every four acres in parks, 4,233 acres total, 30 parks in all, including one, 1,400 acres in the Santa Cruz Mountains solely for Palo Alto residents.

Swimming, libraries, community centers, farmers' market, playgrounds, bike and pedestrian trails, Barbie Doll Hall of Fame, first children's theater in U.S., junior museum and zoo, teen center, ice-skating rink, skateboard bowl, golf, soccer, baseball, many fitness and seniors classes. Summer concerts. Recently added a Bloomingdale's, a big deal among those who measure ooo-la-laah.

Some samplings from the city recreation program: T'ai Chi, Strollerrobics (usually moms and babies), lawn bowling, table tennis, chess, circuit training, drawing and painting (about dozen classes), bead making, photography, ceramics.

Also, indoor soccer, gym for boys and girls, rock climbing, skateboarding (several levels), Tae Kwon Do, tennis, tumbling, dance (including preschool ballet) and piano for kids, library readings, kinder science, children's theater.

Dance including classes in clog, country, folk, lindy, line, tap, salsa, swing and jitterbug, ballet, belly, Brazilian, Carribean, flamenco, jazz and tango.

Other groups run soccer, baseball, football and basketball leagues.

Annual ball draws thousands in tuxes and gowns and raises money for community recreation. Local firms donate food, wine, delicacies and other goodies for the ball, one of the big social events of the town.

Stanford has a huge stadium and in the past has hosted a Super Bowl and World Cup soccer games.

Children's hospital opened in 1991. State-of-the-art. $100 million. Named for Lucille Salter Packard, late philanthropist.

Many arguments between libs and conservatives over policies of university and life in general. Stanford produces Supreme Court justices and rebels but overall the town has a healthy respect for the buck. Pro-choice, pro-gays in military, anti-discrimination.

Housing units number 25,671 — 15,458 single homes, 1,008 single-family attached, 9,092 multiples, 113 mobile homes (1998 state figures). This does not include housing in the immediate vicinity of the campus. Stanford is leasing about 300 units of former military housing at Moffet Field near Mountain View. The units are for graduate students and young faculty.

A fair number of older, modest homes — the postwar housing — but you pay for the Palo Alto address. Many expensive homes but also many Eichlers, homes built just after World War II. Open design, many windows; light.

Restrictions on building big homes on small lots, a practice of the late 1980s when real estate was booming. Height limits in some neighborhoods.

When it comes to beauty and housing, Palo Alto, like many well-to-do towns, is picky, picky. If you want to do anything on a major scale, you're in for arguments. But in 1995 voters trounced a measure that would have sharply limited commercial development and the city council's zoning powers.

A lot of shaking during the 1989 quake but almost no damage to the town. The university, however, took a bad hit: damage well over $100 million. Cuts and bruises, no major injuries.

Crime rate low suburban average. More thefts than violence. Having shopping plazas and many stores, Palo Alto attracts the light-fingered. One homicide in 1997, one in 1996, zero in 1995, one in 1994, zero in 1993, one in 1992 and 1991, zero in 1990 and 1989, one in 1988, zero in 1987, two in 1986, reports FBI. Like several other cities, Palo Alto in 1994 enacted a curfew. In 1997, a NASA scientist, a young man with a family, was murdered on a downtown street, robbery the motive. Suspects captured. In 1998, at least three deaths: father, who may have been upset about financial losses, is believed to have killed self, wife and son.

School district in 1995 passed a $143 million bond to renovate schools and equip them for high-tech instruction. Another middle school to be built on Charleston Road. Will include a technology center and science labs.

School scores range from high to very high, what's expected of a university town. Lot of students taking advanced classes. Excellent placement rate with colleges. Palo Alto High won Excellence in Education Award, honored at White House.

Schools offer instruction in French, German, Spanish, Latin and Japanese.

Commute generally good, because of location. Two freeways to other Silicon Valley towns, several wide arterials, CalTrain up to San Francisco or down to San Jose, with stops along the way. Not too far from San Francisco International Airport. Express buses to East Bay.

A sizeable portion of Silicon Valley is located in Palo Alto — Hewlett-Packard, Varian, Syntex, Ford Aerospace. Historic tour shows the garage where Bill Hewlett and David Packard started out.

Supposedly the only city in California to own all its utilities, Palo Alto, thanks to clever decisions, enjoys unusually low power rates.

Miscellaneous:

• Another — ho-hum — Stanford Nobel in 1998. Congratulations, Robert Laughlin, physics.

• On some occasions having to do with cloud cover, the music from the Shoreline Theater in Mountain View bounces into Palo Alto. Some complaints but Mountain View City Council in 1996 indicated it would take no action.

• Sand Hill project. Proposed by Stanford University, it entails expanding the shopping center and adding two four-story garages, and building 630 apartments in one complex and 388 in a senior housing and health-care center. To be located north of the shopping center, the project has run into opposition from some residents and from neighboring Menlo Park, which doesn't like the extra traffic the expansion will bring. The job would connect Sand Hill Road with El Camino Real and this might smooth traffic flow. Palo Alto voters in 1997 endorsed the project. Work is expected to proceed.

Chamber of commerce: (650) 324-3121.

SANTA CLARA CITY & TOWN PROFILES

SAN JOSE

LARGEST CITY IN SANTA CLARA COUNTY. One of the high-tech giants. Suburban in nature, dynamic in action, especially in rejuvenating its downtown.

In Money Magazine's annual rankings of most livable cities, San Jose usually lands in the top 10. In 1998, Money placed it ninth among major cities. San Jose often picks up awards like this. Its secret: Unlike many major cities, San Jose has retained its middle class. It has its poor and its rich but it is not a town of great extremes. The great majority of residents land in the middle and practice the traditional middle-class habits of keeping appearances up, the kids under supervision and the schools focused on basics.

The middle-class character shows itself especially in the crime figures. One recent study gave the city the lowest crime rate of any metropolis (400,000 or more residents) in the country.

This is not to say San Jose doesn't have its problems. Like other cities it has trouble with gangs and works to keep gang activity to a minimum. In 1995, the city implemented a 10 p.m-5 a.m. curfew for juveniles 15 and under; older juveniles have to be in by 11:30 p.m. If caught after hours, kids are dropped off at neighborhood centers and parents are called. Other measures: school gyms and swimming pools are being kept open longer, teen centers have been opened, after-school programs were expanded. The FBI reported 43 homicides in 1997, 40 in 1996, 38 homicides in 1995, 33 in 1994, 41 in 1993, 43 in 1992, 53 in 1991, 35 in 1990, 39 in 1989, 37 in 1988, 24 in 1987, and 39 in 1986.

In appearance, suburban nice although critics call the town bland. San Jose has hills but much of the city is built on flat land. Outside of the downtown, very few buildings rise over three stories.

San Jose is not an "old" city with cosmopolitan traditions. Well into the 20th century, it was no more than the largest town in an agricultural region. The city's population in 1950 was only 95,000. When it grew, it grew rapidly, adding subdivision after subdivision, annexing almost everything in its path. Added 152,806 residents in the last decade, an increase of 24 percent, and still growing. The state's 1998 estimate placed the population at 893,969. Ethnically diverse.

School rankings bounce all over the map in San Jose, but many are fairly high. School situation is confusing because San Jose is served by 19 separate school districts. The city grew up around established school districts, some of which serve other communities besides San Jose. Some districts are crowded, some are opening new schools, which forces changes in attendance boundaries.

If you have children, check with the local district to find out where your child will be attending school. Ask about hours and times of attendance. Some schools will offer buses, some will start later than others, some have year-round schedules with vacations in October.

In recent years, many bonds have been passed to improve schools. Some bond or tax winners: Fremont High School district, East Side Union district, Alum Rock district, Oak Grove, Union and Evergreen. In 1997, the largest district, San Jose Unified, passed a renovation-building bond for $165 million. Local firms are "adopting" schools and getting more involved in civic causes.

Among homes, the tract look dominates — hence the accusation of bland. Many people put their creative energies into landscaping and gardening and interior decorating. And the bland label, which doesn't seem to bother residents in the least, is misleading. In cultural events, restaurants and quality of metropolitan life, the city has made great strides over the past 25 years.

The San Jose Arena opened in 1993, part of an effort that started 20 years ago to equip San Jose with the trappings of a big-time city. The Arena came with a professional hockey team, the Sharks, who have caught San Jose's fancy and support. The town is now a frequent stop when big-name singers, rock bands and opera stars tour the country.

Since 1982, well over $1.5 billion has been spent to make the downtown the great heart of the city. The jobs included a light-rail system (now being extended to Mountain View), a convention center, the Fairmont Hotel, the Children's Discovery Museum, a retail mall, a highway and the arena. An international airport, located near the downtown, has been expanded. In 1998, San Jose opened a Tech Museum of Innovation.

The downtown also offers the cultural and recreational ornaments of metropolitan life: a symphony, an opera, light opera, ballet. Repertory theater opened in 1997. The opera company regularly visits elementary schools and sings for the students. San Jose State University, one of the largest in the state, is located in the downtown. Besides the state university, San Jose City College and Evergreen Valley College enhance the educational offerings of the town. Other additions: ice-skating rink; a carousel with 33 animals, including a panda, an eagle and a rabbit; and self-cleaning public toilets (25 cents).

Although such cities as Sunnyvale have more high-tech firms than San Jose, the larger city is becoming to be viewed by many as true capital of the Silicon Valley. It is trying to provide the leadership to make the region prosper. And it has a fair amount of industry, especially on its north side, miles of sleek plants. Plus the airport. Good employment base.

Many commute into other areas of the Silicon Valley, a tortuous daily trek. In recent years, the opening of two freeway stretches —Highways 85 and 87— has greatly improved matters. Some neighborhoods are located next to the Silicon Valley employment centers; an easy commute. With additional light-rail transit, freeway widenings and additions, things might get better. But don't hold breath. All of Silicon Valley suffers from traffic congestion. Buy a map.

San Jose offers many activities. A good town for families. Little League, soccer, youth service organizations, libraries thrive. Museums, rose garden, many nice parks, water slide. Cinco de Mayo parade draws 100,000.

The real strength of the city is in its neighborhoods, all sustained by their own shops, movies, restaurants, video outlets, churches, and social organizations, and activities, many of them organized around schools. The great majority of residents take their pleasures in the back yard or local park. City council members are elected by district, which gives the neighborhoods more clout in local politics.

Good choice of housing; a lot of the new, the great majority of it suburban tract, although some streets seem straight out of New England or the midwest.

San Jose in the 1980s added about 42,500 residential units, far more than any other city in the Bay Area. Prices bounce all over. Although the housing falls into the category of suburban tract, variety is plentiful, housing styles having changed frequently over the past 50 years. Residential units in 1998 numbered 278,403, of which 158,558 were single homes, 25,487 single-family attached, 82,689 multiples, 11,669 mobile homes.

San Jose's Neighborhoods

San Jose is spread over 175 square miles of Santa Clara Valley floor and hillside. In some instances, the neighborhoods are distinct: they might contain housing from a certain era, or have a "look" that sets them apart from others, or contain many members of a particular ethnic group.

But in many places market forces have placed new subdivisions next to old. Much has been jumbled. The following should be used as a rough guide.

The distance of each from the city of Santa Clara, near the heart of Silicon Valley, is given as a point of reference (see map on Page 173 for zones).

• Santa Teresa. Zone 2. South section of the city. About 25 years ago farm country. Now divided into housing, industrial complex (IBM), schools and stores. Borders large county park with golf course. Some homes built in '50s and '60s. Most homes built in the '70s. Well-maintained. Stucco and wood shingles. Many two-story homes. From 10-14 miles to Santa Clara.

End of the line for the light-rail system to downtown San Jose and Silicon Valley. Parking lot at station.

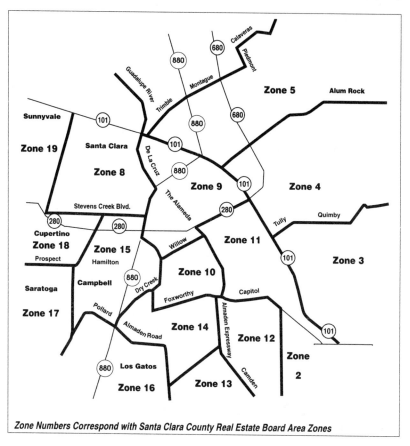

Zone Numbers Correspond with Santa Clara County Real Estate Board Area Zones

For about 15 years, an old, large closed building, formerly Fairchild Semiconductor, on Bernal Road, offended the eyes of local residents. It's coming down, to be replaced by a shopping center.

• Evergreen. Zone 3. Southeast San Jose, slightly above and to the east of Santa Teresa neighborhood. Rolling hills. Subdivisions, three-bedroom, built over 12-20 years ago and earlier. Newer subs feature four bedrooms. Many new homes going up in this section. Country club subdivision just south of Evergreen Community College. Apartments. Evergreen Elementary District is to use its bond money to build new schools, renovate and improve others. Local schools have won national blue ribbons for meeting high academic standards. From 10-14 miles to Santa Clara.

• East Valley. Zone 4. Also known as "Eastside." Above Evergreen. Typical home is over 20 years old but many new homes mixed in. Diverse cultures and choices among restaurants. Many apartments. Some custom homes in hills. From 10-14 miles to Santa Clara. Note Reid-Hillview Airport, near Eastridge Mall. Every once in a while a plane crashes taking off or landing. Some want to close airport but it has its supporters and will probably be around for a long time.

• North Valley. Zone 5. Also known as Berryessa. Above East Valley and unincorporated (governed by county) neighborhood of East San Jose. Middle to upper income. Many four-bedroom, two-story homes. Also townhouses and condos. Some apartments. Bedroom community. Berryessa Art and Wine Festival, an annual event. Ruskin Elementary in 1997 opened a science-technology lab. Section includes San Jose Flea Market, large and popular. Alum Rock and Penitencia Creek Parks, large. From 8-12 miles to Santa Clara. Split by Interstate 680, a fast shot to downtown San Jose.

East San Jose is building a Mexican Cultural Heritage Center and Plaza. Facility to include theater, art gallery, rooms for workshops and receptions. To open in 1999.

• Alviso. North of Highway 237. Small, low-income neighborhood, just east of Santa Clara. Used to be seaport. History of flooding. Little housing turnover but homes are less costly than elsewhere. Small marina. In 1997 the light rail was extended to Tasman Drive, making the commute easier. Many high tech firms just south of Alviso. City is trying to preserve portion of old neighborhood and limit new housing to 200 units.

• Central San Jose. Zone 9. Offices, government buildings, hotels, restaurants — and a lot of housing. Great variety, from apartments to bungalows to mansions. Queen Annes, Tudors. Condos coming in strong. San Jose State University generates much foot traffic. Rose Garden adds nice touch to its neighborhood. Light rail. Well-kept neighborhoods. Note the location of San Jose International Airport; possible noise problems for some sections. Close to many ornaments of city life: restaurants, arena, museums, night life. Farmers' market. From 2-5 miles to Santa Clara.

• Willow Glen. Zone 10. Located south and slightly west of downtown. Older neighborhood. Many streets worthy of the adjective "lovely." Well-kept, leafy, quaint. Many custom homes built in '30s, basements, hardwood floors, brick, large gardens. Midwest-New England look, charming, expensive. Large child-care center near light-rail station.

Close to Highways 17 and 280 but close enough to downtown San Jose to drive by street. Many residents are within walking distance of light-rail station. From 7-11 miles to Santa Clara.

• South San Jose. Zone 11. South of downtown, east of Willow Glen. Housing tracts from '50s mixed in with newer housing. Older homes mean lower prices. Light rail accessible. Highway 87 extension opened in 1993; improved commute. Many apartments, mobile homes. From 8-12 miles to Santa Clara.

• Blossom Valley. Zone 12. South of South San Jose, north of Santa Teresa. Identifying street: Blossom Hill Road.

Didn't start developing until '60s. Typical home is three-bedroom, two-bath, 1,400 sq. feet. Condos. Got its name from blossoming fruit trees. Middle America.

Light-rail. Highway 82. Straight ride to downtown San Jose. From 10-14 miles to Santa Clara.

• Almaden Valley. Zone 13. West of Blossom Valley. Mix of housing, some very old, some from '60s, many new, custom, upscale. Scenic views from hill homes. Country feeling. Almaden Quicksilver Park. Almaden Country Club. Light-rail end of line. From 12-16 miles to Santa Clara.

• Cambrian. Zone 14. Borders Los Gatos and Campbell. Tract homes, many ranch style, built over last 10 to 30 years. Big trees. Stable. Many original owners. Some remodelings. Some townhouses, condos, duplexes.

Commute made easier with the opening of Highway 85. Short drive to light-rail station. From 9-13 miles to Santa Clara.

San Jose Chamber of Commerce (408) 291-5250. Convention and Visitors Bureau (408) 295-9600. Miscellaneous:

• Altamont Commuter Express in 1998 started rail service between San Jose and San Joaquin Valley, with stops in Santa Clara, Fremont, Pleasanton, Livermore, Tracy, Manteca and Stockton.

• Free shuttle bus around downtown, between parking lots.

• City government has targeted run-down sections for small parks, recreation equipment, better traffic lights, more improvements.

• In the works, more improvements for the airport, especially access roads.

• Downtown and airport areas drawing several more hotels.

• Town and Country Village, 1960s mall on Stevens Creek Boulevard, is to be demolished and replaced with another mall (with twice the square footage), 1,200 housing units, two hotels, movie plex.

• Decades ago, the people at the Lick Observatory on top of Mt. Hamilton were worried that San Jose lights would interfere with their telescopes. They appealed to the city, and the San Jose turned down its lights and encouraged the dim. In 1998, the observatory said thanks by naming a newly discovered asteroid "San Jose." Nice but some locals, including night golfers, are asking the city to turn up the lights.

• New mayor, Ron Gonzales.

• City and San Jose State University are funding large library at downtown campus. Will be open to community.

SANTA CLARA CITY & TOWN PROFILES

SANTA CLARA ★

THIRD MOST POPULOUS city in the county. One of the high-tech heavy-weights: many industries. An unusual mix of fun, commerce and education.

Big news for 1999. Sun Microsystems is scheduled to begin work on a large complex located on one of sites that housed part of Agnews State Hospital. When completed, the complex will employ 4,000.

The Agnews Project, when rounded out, will also include 2,600 residential units, a park, a library and a school.

School district in 1997 passed $145 million renovation bond.

Home to Santa Clara University, Jesuit institution. A pretty campus and the site of Mission Santa Clara De Asis. Also Mission College, a campus of West Valley Community College.

Triton Museum of Art is located in Santa Clara. The 49ers train in Santa Clara. Convention center, a testament to Santa Clara's importance in the Silicon Valley.

Great America. Major amusement park serving the Bay Area. Loads of diversions for kids and adults. When owners threatened to close Great America years ago, the city bought them out, then later sold the park to a private outfit, which is running it now. City retained ownership of property.

Added 5,876 people in 1980s. Population now 101,877 (state estimate 1998). Census in 1989 showed 19 percent of the residents were under 18 years and 18 percent were over 55 — graying a bit at the temples.

Industry to the north, homes to the south, San Jose Airport to the east, with runways headed over the industrial sector.

Almost all cities say they want business, but few aggressively pursue it. Santa Clara is an exception. It went after and got a lot of high tech, and made itself into one of the silicon cities. Its industries include: Intel, Applied Materials, 3-Com and Synoptics.

The payoff comes in parks and recreation, and in ability to fill potholes, field cops, keep up appearances and perform dozens of jobs cities are supposed to do but often don't. When you look at a map of Santa Clara, you see parks

BEFORE YOU MOVE... BUY

McCormack's GUIDES

The GUIDES have the information to make your move to a new location easier.

Feel comfortable about the change because you have the facts about city profiles, school rankings, SAT scores, private school directories, medical care, commuting, recreation, crime ratings, area weather, and much more!

McCormack's Guides are published for these counties:

**ALAMEDA · CONTRA COSTA-SOLANO
SANTA CLARA · SAN FRANCISCO-SAN MATEO
SAN DIEGO · LOS ANGELES · ORANGE COUNTY
MARIN-NAPA-SONOMA · GREATER SACRAMENTO
RIVERSIDE-SAN BERNARDINO
SANTA BARBARA-VENTURA**

1-800-222-3602

$13⁹⁵ SINGLE COPY

VISA & MASTERCARD ACCEPTED

DISCOUNTS FOR BULK BUYERS. SEE LAST PAGE

spotted all around town. Many other cities don't have this "look."

Thirty-one parks and playgrounds. One city-owned golf course, plus private course. Tennis, baseball, basketball, adult classes, community theater and ballet, loads of activities. Santa Clara International Swim Center is famous for turning out Olympic winners. Restaurants, major hotels, bowling greens, seniors center, college basketball, movie complex, youth center, ample shopping and on and on.

Nice looking town in suburban way: lawns mowed, houses painted, streets clean, apartment complexes maintained.

A great commute if you have local job or a job in a nearby town. A difficult one if you have to travel some distance. The industries attract a lot of traffic.

Overall, however, Santa Clara has to be rated fairly good in commuting because of its central location. Freeways or parkways traverse the city. CalTrain up the shore to San Francisco with stops on the way or down to San Jose. Light rail starts at Great America, goes down to South San Jose and in 2000 will be extended to Mountain View.

Close to San Jose International Airport. Take-offs and landings are away from Santa Clara's residential sections but check out noise for yourself. San Jose is planning to improve the access roads to the airport.

Crime rate about suburban average. One homicide in 1997, zero in 1996, three in 1995, two in 1994, three in 1993, four in 1992, three in 1991, nine in 1990, six in 1989, five in 1988, and three in 1987 and 1986.

School scores from low-middle to quite high. School district includes diverse neighborhoods. Parents chip in to support arts programs.

Eisenhower Elementary is located in high-scoring Cupertino school district, which in 1995 passed a bond to renovate schools.

Good mix of housing — 38,950 residential units, of which 17,263 are single homes, 3,096 single attached, 18,470 multiples, 121 mobile homes (1998 state tally).

Many of the homes were built in Fifties and Sixties, and Santa Clara, in parts, has a dated suburban look, which is a little deceiving. Location, school rankings and amenities have made the city a desirable address, in a middle-class way. In other towns, the housing might be allowed to deteriorate. In Santa Clara, a lot of money has gone into renovations and remodelings. For pre-World War II housing, drive "old quad" neighborhood near university.

Chamber of commerce (408) 244-8244.

SANTA CLARA CITY & TOWN PROFILES

SARATOGA

LOCATED ON THE EDGE of a valley that dotes on computer hardware and software and measures speed in nanoseconds, this city of 30,591 values the contrary intangibles of quiet and repose, grace and beauty.

Its school rankings are high, its crime low, its old town charming, its setting delightful, flatlands ascending into the foothills of the Santa Cruz Mountains.

On the downside, Saratoga is struggling to fund city services but, please, no tears. If the shoe really starts pinching, residents have ample resources to relieve the pain. The average annual income for Saratoga, according to the Association of Bay Area Governments, is about $177,000. City is home to judges, doctors, computer chiefs, plus many middle and upper managers.

Served by six school districts, among which the most popular are Saratoga Elementary and the high school district including Saratoga High. Overall rankings for Saratoga High and the Saratoga elementary schools are in the high 90s, among the tops in the state. In the 1996 math SAT, Saratoga High scored fourth highest in California; in 1997 it tied for third highest, in 1998, it tied for fifth highest. Three private schools, located in or near the town: Harker, St. Andrew's, Sacred Heart.

Saratoga Elementary district in 1997 passed a $40 million bond to renovate schools. High school district passed one for $79 million in June 1998 for upgrades and modernization.

Overall crime, as tracked by the FBI, is low. Between 1985 and 1997, the most recent year reported by the state, Saratoga had zero homicides.

Compared to other Silicon Valley cities, the Saratoga commute falls into the range of "not that bad." The city borders or is close to the job centers of Cupertino, Sunnyvale, San Jose and Santa Clara. In 1996, Highway 85, which bites off a corner of Saratoga, was completed. This ties the town into the freeway network serving Santa Clara County. Walls muffle sounds from Highway 85 but some residents say the noise is still irritating. Buses from Santa Clara Valley Transportation Authority. CalTrain to downtown San Francisco or San Jose can be picked up in Santa Clara.

Lovely town, one reason why its homes cost so much. Hill homes overlook the Santa Clara Valley. Much attention to preserving and old town. Streets clean. Homes well-maintained. Many have custom landscaping. City codes restrict repairing cars in driveway or street, allowing junk to accumulate in yards, leaving cars parked on public street for more than three days.

Recreation, cultural ornaments, unusually bountiful. Concerts, art exhibits at Villa Montalvo, a mansion that was turned into an artists' residence. Jazz and pop concerts at the Mountain Winery. City hall runs recreation programs for kids and adults. About nine parks. Community theater. Hakone Gardens, created by a gardener who worked for the Emperor of Japan. Shakespeare festival.

In the middle of town sits West Valley, a community college, a cornucopia of facilities and activities, cheaply priced (average class $36), all open to local residents. West Valley has a library, a theater, a gym and workout rooms, a track and playing fields, plus many classes on arts, literature, computers and business subjects. Saratoga has a town band. To join, you sign up for a certain band class at the community college, an instance of a town shaping another institution to meet its interests. First-class restaurants in the downtown. Golf course-country club on the west side.

First a lumber town, Saratoga in last century evolved into a resort-farming community that attracted people of money who liked the mild climate, the mountain setting and possibly the mineral springs in the hills. In one version of how Saratoga got its name, civic leaders lifted it from Saratoga, New York, a wealthy town that also has mineral springs.

Among the early residents was James Phelan, a U.S. senator who built a palatial home (Villa Montalvo) in the Mediterranean style. Phelan was a patron of the arts and helped set the artistic tone of the town. The home was later deeded to the county for the benefit of artists. By 1940, the census counted about 350 homes. The war decade, when Santa Clara County developed its electronic muscles, saw the number of Saratoga homes more than double and in the 1950s, home construction boomed, 2,884 units. In 1956, Saratoga incorporated as a legal city. This took planning and zoning away from the county government, which was strongly pro-growth, and placed them in the hands of local residents. In the 1960s, Saratoga built 3,189 units, in the next decade, 2,264 units and in the 1980s, 908 units.

So far this decade, the town has built about 500 residential units. The town is not built out but its boom days are over. The state in 1998 counted 10,718 units, of which 9,602 were single-detached homes, 483 single attached, 628 multiples and 5 mobile homes. About one-third of the single homes have three bedrooms, about 40 percent have four bedrooms and 16 percent have five or more bedrooms (1990 census). If a tally were taken today, it would probably show more four-bedroom and five-plus-bedroom homes. In recent years, the trend has been to build larger homes. For the most part, the four-bedroom homes run to mid-manager-space engineer upscale: two-story structures built along enticing tract designs. The custom homes, many opulent, can be found west of city hall, around Villa Montalvo and in the hills off of Big Basin Way. If you have ever wondered where the wealth of Silicon Valley was invested, take a spin up Pierce Road.

Although considered part of Silicon Valley, Saratoga is not home to computer industries. The town has five small business sections and little else in way of stores that produce tax revenue. Proposals to add more stores (or parking) almost always run into town's wish to remain low-key and rustic. City restricts use of portable signs, streamers, banners, balloons in commercial district.

Saratoga has a formal government, the city council, and an informal one, the Good Government Group, a sort of watchdog, particularly sensitive to growth and aesthetics. If you like to argue about art, beauty and quality of life, this is the burg for you.

Local lasses who made good: the daughters of Lilian Fontaine, who under the umbrella of Adult Education ran a theater workshop and staged plays. Her daughters: Joan Fontaine ("The Women") and Olivia de Haviland ("Gone with the Wind"). Chamber of commerce (408) 867-0753.

SANTA CLARA CITY & TOWN PROFILES

SUNNYVALE

HIGH-TECH BEDROOM CITY located smack-dab in the middle of the original Silicon Valley. Bordered by Mountain View, Cupertino and Santa Clara, and on north side, San Francisco Bay and a wildlife refuge of marshes and salt ponds and trails.

For many residents great commute because the jobs are so close. Second most populous city in Santa Clara County, 131,127 residents, and still adding homes and apartments. Although some housing can be found the north side, most residents live south of Highway 101.

Housing units in 1998 totaled 53,608 and included 21,021 single homes, 3,919 single attached, 24,447 multiples and 4,221 mobile homes.

From 1950 to 1960, Sunnyvale built 11,347 residential units; the following decade, 14,939; the next decade, 12,759. In the 1980s, construction dropped to 6,558. Sunnyvale in the 1990s will probably construct about 10,000 homes and apartments.

When Sunnyvale building boomed, the three-bedroom home was the rage. For owner-occupied homes, the 1990 census reported that 42 percent were three-bedroom, 25 percent two-bedroom, and 22 percent four-bedroom. Five or more bedrooms came in at 5 percent.

Sunnyvale offers a lot of choice in housing, across the price spectrum. With the exception of San Jose, it has the most mobile homes in the county, the great majority of them located in parks on the east side, north of Highway 101.

Homes, landscaping, generally well maintained. Nice-looking city in suburban way. As with many other Santa Clara cities in the last two decades, more diverse but still Middle America. Many homes have been remodeled or renovated in some way, a common practice in Silicon Valley. Home prices are so high that many owners can draw from their equity to make improvements.

Sunnyvale is home to hundreds of high-tech firms — semiconductors, software, telecommunications, global positioning equipment — and in recent years has been pushing into bio-tech, which now fields about 30 firms. Also new: space satellites, a Lockheed Martin specialty. The firm in 1996 opened a giant clean-room manufacturing facility. Lockheed Martin is the city's largest

employer.

Military presence in town is changing. The Navy in 1994 left Moffett Air Field, located on county unincorporated land between Sunnyvale and Mountain View. As a result fewer planes fly over Sunnyvale enroute to the landing site.

Onizuka, formerly a secret Air Force base in Sunnyvale, was up for closing but now appears to have escaped the post-Cold War knife and may emerge as an Air Force-private venture to track satellites.

The National Aeronautics and Aerospace Administration (NASA) took over Moffett Field from the Navy and is looking to attract private partners for its ventures. With so many scientists and so much technical knowledge, Sunnyvale, Mountain View and a few other towns hope to establish the region as a space center.

Stanford University, for its faculty and grad students, is renting 300 units of former military housing at Moffett. See Mountain View profile for more on Moffett.

For a fairly large city, Sunnyvale has a low crime rate. Homicides totaled zero in 1997 and 1996, three in 1995, two in 1994, three in 1993, two in 1992, three in 1991, two in 1990 and 1989, ten in 1988, five in 1987, and four in 1986. In 1988, a man went on a rampage, killed seven.

In summer, cops patrol parks on bicycles. Graffiti Hotline; city tries to remove graffiti within three days of notice. Cops work with schools and counselors to keep kids straight. Neighborhood watches to discourage crime.

Served by Sunnyvale and Santa Clara School districts and, at high school, by Santa Clara and Fremont School districts, for the latter, mainly Homestead and Fremont High schools. Rankings on a statewide comparison for all come in well above the 50th percentile, some in the 80s and 90s, an indication of high parental interest in education. In recent years, distinguished school awards were given to Bishop, Cherry Chase, Columbia Community, and Cumberland elementary schools.

Voters in Sunnyvale Elementary District in 1996 passed a renovation bond. In mid-1998, Fremont Union High School District passed a renovation-construction bond for $144 million. Fremont High School recently opened a science center.

Some Sunnyvale neighborhoods are in the Cupertino School District, which in 1995 passed a renovation bond.

Seventeen parks, tennis center with 13 courts, another 55 courts at other locations, two theater groups, 200-seat theater, dance company. Community center. Senior center. City has contracted with school district to make school facilities open to public: gyms, swimming pools, playing fields. Baseball, soccer, two golf courses (9 and 18 holes), Twin Creeks Softball Complex, 10 fields. Bowling alley, lawn bowling. Youth Family Center at Columbia Middle School. Gymnastic center.

Baylands Park, 70 acres, opened in 1993. Trails to Bay, picnic grounds, playground, next to a 100-acre wildlife preserve.

Several shopping centers. Great variety of restaurants. Penney's in 1992 opened store in TownCenter Mall, joining Ward's and Macy's. Old Del Monte building was gutted and rebuilt as bank-shopping complex. Other recent addition: a Home Depot. Night life showing some sizzle on Murphy Street. Palace night club popular. City for years has been working to revive downtown.

Four freeways, two expressways. Highway 237 at north end had its traffic lights removed, which speeded up traffic. Other improvements made. CalTrain up the shore to San Francisco or down to San Jose. Buses. San Jose Airport is within a drive of 10-15 minutes, when traffic is moving.

Light-rail line being laid on north side. When finished in year 2000, it will tie Sunnyvale to Mountain View and downtown San Jose.

Sunnyvale has been singled out by Bill Clinton and Al Gore and ABC News as the city that knows how to make things work. Its officials are supposedly very efficient. Goals are set and met. Jobs priced out to the penny. Managers rewarded or penalized by how well they perform. Projects are completed ahead of schedule. Cops and firefighters are one and the same, public safety officers.

The payoff for residents: more services at less cost. Tax dollars that work harder.

City hall, to encourage entrepreneurs, runs a patent office-library located in what is called the Sunnyvale Center for Innovation, Invention and Ideas. Folks using the system can tap into the main patent database in Washington, D.C.

In the early Thirties, when Sunnyvale was orchard country, an employee of Libby, McNeil & Libby, the canner, scooped up leftover chunks of pears, pineapples, peaches and cherries to bring home to his children. Presto! The first fruit cocktail. Water tank at company was painted to resemble a fruit cocktail can. When the company closed the plant, the tank was retained and declared an historic monument.

Another Sunnyvale first: Rooster T. Feathers, a comedy club, was the first place to install a video game — 1972. Chamber of commerce (408) 736-4971.

Chapter 11

SANTA CLARA COUNTY
Fun & Games

SANTA CLARA COUNTY is bulging with places to visit and things to do but with some exceptions it is not oriented toward tourists.

No battle monuments summon visitors simply because there were no battles. Only the Indians suffered catastrophe and they went quietly and quickly, mostly through disease, leaving little behind. The Spanish built a mission at Santa Clara, later destroyed and rebuilt — well worth a visit but little else of great interest remains from the ranchero era.

For most of its "American" history, the county has been run by farmers and shopkeepers — people who for the most part doted on grapes, raisins and prunes, welcomed settlers but saw little need to encourage tourism. Indeed, some of their actions — the cutting of great redwood groves — later worked against the tourist trade.

In recent decades the county has built a few museums and amusements that attract outsiders. And such places as downtown San Jose and Palo Alto have put together clubs, galleries, restaurants and cultural events that have made the county much more palatable to the business visitor.

For its own residents, however, the county, in parks, culture, recreation and amusements, the county and its cities have done very well. Where there have been gaps, the county has inventively filled them. Of note are the celebrations of the stomach, the food festivals which flow nicely out of the county's history.

Here is some advice about making the most of local activities.

City Recreation Departments

Most cities have recreation departments that sponsor their own activities and coordinate or assist private groups. Chambers of commerce are excellent sources for club and activity lists. School districts occasionally run after-school programs and other activities. Adult schools and community colleges are loaded with recreational, exercise and cultural classes and activities.

Softball, possibly the most popular adult sport, thrives in many communities, complete with umpires, schedules, playoffs and trophies. Many teams are organized through jobs. Some live wire will recruit fellow employees and field a team. There are men's and women's leagues and mixed teams.

Private Classes and Clubs

What the public sector lacks, the private sector provides — racquetball, golf, bowling, tennis, movies, special-activity classes. Also shopping, an unsung, often maligned pursuit but one that brings pleasure to thousands. Santa Clara County has some delightful malls and shopping centers.

Club life is varied and, as might be expected, computer clubs abound, great fun for the many enthusiasts. There are also model sailboat, powerboat, airplane and rocketry groups, water skiing, sailboating, powerboat racing, hiking, horseback and hunting trails, trap, skeet, pistol and rifle ranges, car clubs, even hang-gliding and hot-air balloon groups.

Church and Home

A number of people organize their lives around church activities.

Watching television is by far the most popular pastime in the county — or, for that matter, any other California county. Thanks to cable reception and satellite dishes, the stations are many and the diversity of choices great, from schlock to Stravinsky. Video recorders have spawned many video rental stores, another great source of entertainment. Libraries are plentiful, if not as popular as television.

City Parks, Sports, the Arts

Regional parks tend to get most of the attention, but city parks can be counted in the dozens and draw many people. Bicycle and jogging trails wind their way throughout the county.

Of the many children's activities, soccer is probably the most popular, attracting kids by the thousands, and a good deal of parental interest and screams. Little League, Pop Warner football, basketball, swimming — almost every town will have a league or several leagues. Girls participate in all these sports. Some sports — gymnastics — may attract more girls than boys.

Art guilds and galleries, dance schools, bands, a symphony, choral groups, college football and basketball, little theater — Santa Clara County has them.

And if the local offerings are not to your liking, San Francisco and Monterey are within an hour's drive and the Sierra Nevada (skiing, hiking and gambling) a few hours off.

Sorting It All Out

Sometimes hard to know just what to do. Here are suggestions to help with the sorting out.

• Find out who is organizing activities in your town and in nearby towns.

Usually this can be accomplished by calling or visiting the chambers of commerce, the city recreation departments and the school districts. Some activities take more digging than others.

Soccer and baseball leagues are occasionally put together by parents' groups with no connection to City Hall. A phone call to the city recreation department will usually turn up a phone number that will lead to another phone number that will pan out.

• Get on mailing lists. Adult schools and recreation departments change their classes about every three months. Theaters and orchestras issue calendars every season.

• Find out the rules. Some cities provide minimal support for certain activities. You may have to sign up players on your softball team and collect the fees and meet application deadlines. Baseball and soccer leagues usually guarantee the younger children, no matter what their skill, two innings or two quarters of play. But other sports (football) often go by skill. Ask about playing time.

• Ignore city boundaries. If you live in Campbell and want to take a class in San Jose, go ahead. A person with a Mountain View job might want to tackle an aerobics class in that city before hitting the freeway.

• Do a little investigation and spadework before making choices. This sounds obvious, but many people, to their unhappiness, do not.

If you are new to the county and wish to make friends, almost assuredly you will mingle with people if you attend movies, art shows and concerts. But the opportunities for conversation may be few.

The trick is to put yourself in a situation where you can meet and talk to people who share your interests or might in other ways make good friends. For a mother, this could be something as close as the PTA. For a person who delights in politics, it might be the local Democrat or Republican clubs.

• Subscribe to a local newspaper, of which there are many. Almost all will have calendars of events, lists of local attractions and hours of operation.

• Visit or call the San Jose Visitors and Convention Bureau, 333 West San Carlos St., San Jose. Phone (408) 295-9600. Maps and other information.

Places to Visit, Things to Do

Please phone ahead to find out hours of operation. Many of these places charge for admission.

Barbie Hall of Fame. Barbie dolls from around the world, along with friends: Skipper, Todd, Tootie, Ken, Midge, and more. 433 Waverly St., Palo Alto. Phone (650) 326-5841.

Children's Discovery Museum. Hands-on exhibits with themes of "community, connection and creativity," with technology, science, humanities and the arts interwoven. Third-largest such museum in the nation, largest in the west.

Purple building. 180 Woz Way, San Jose. (408) 298-5437.

Great America. Located in city of Santa Clara, off Great America Parkway. First-class amusement park. Over 100 attractions, many of spine-tingling, stomach-churning variety.

Great place for kids. Enjoyable for adults. Entertaining musical reviews. When the kids poop out, take them inside for a show. (408) 988-1776.

Intel Museum. Located at Intel complex in the Robert Noyce Building at 2200 Mission College Blvd., Santa Clara. How computer chips are constructed and used and other aspects of high tech. Changing exhibits. Phone (408) 765-0503.

Lick Observatory. Atop Mt. Hamilton, southeast of San Jose, one of the most powerful observatories in the world, although in modern times its effectiveness has diminished because of background light from San Jose.

The history of Santa Clara County has been blessed by two benevolent screwballs, Sarah Winchester and James Lick. An adventurer and land speculator, Lick purchased a good deal of downtown San Francisco at the time of the gold rush and, as a consequence, became one of the richest men in the state.

Withdrawn, inclined to lawsuits and shabby dress, Lick was also an admirer of Tom Paine and determined to do good, particularly by encouraging education. Someone suggested a great telescope to study the heavens, to which Lick replied with the 19th century equivalent of "right on" and advanced the money to build the observatory, which was bequeathed to the University of California.

Scenic but slow and winding ride to the top. Tours. For schedules, phone (408) 274-5061.

Mission Santa Clara de Asis. Located on Santa Clara University campus, at 500 El Camino Real, Santa Clara. Old California, a good introduction to the Franciscan padres and what they tried to accomplish in pioneer days. Fires and other calamities destroyed early buildings. In 1929, Mission Santa Clara was rebuilt. While there, tour the university, a pretty campus. (408) 554-4023.

Raging Waters. Your typical wild and wet water-slide and swimming park. Picnic areas, video arcade, shops, entertainment. Open May to September, exact dates depending on weather. In Lake Cunningham Park, San Jose, on the east side, at Tully Road and Capitol Expressway. (408) 654-5450.

Rose Garden. Naglee and Dana avenues, in San Jose. Park planted with 5,000 rose bushes in 150 varieties.

Rosicrucian Museum. Park and Naglee avenues, San Jose. The

Rosicrucians are a fraternal order of men and women who encourage the study of ancient learning. At their world headquarters in San Jose, the Rosicrucians built a striking museum that houses a large collection of ancient Egyptian artifacts. Highlights include a mummy gallery, a full-sized rock tomb, and exhibits on the Assyrians and the Babylonians.

The planetarium, one of the first in the U.S., explores the universe and pays particular attention to the mythologies and star lore of the ancients. Phone (408) 947-3636.

San Jose Flea Market. 12000 Berryessa Rd., between Highway 101 and Interstate 680, San Jose. One of the great bazaars of the West Coast. Open Wednesdays through Sundays. Draws 50,000 to 75,000 on weekends. Also includes farmers' markets and kiddie amusements. (408) 453-1110.

San Jose Historical Museum. 635 Phelan St., San Jose. Old Santa Clara County recreated at Kelley Park — an Indian acorn granary, the Pacific Hotel, a candy store, an electric tower, a 1920s gas station, a dental building, stables and more. Much memorabilia from the old days, also exhibits on Costanoan Indians, the rancheros, high-wheeler bicycles. Well worth a visit, especially with kids. Petting zoo nearby. Also nearby, the Japanese Friendship Park, six acres of waterfalls, stone bridges, bonsai plants — peaceful, restful, inviting. Phone 408-287-2290.

San Jose Museum of Art. Market and San Fernando streets. 20th century and contemporary art. Photography, paintings, sculpture, drawings. Many classes in art for children and adults. Taught by working artists. (408) 294-2787.

San Jose Sharks. Professional ice-hockey team. San Jose Arena. For information on events and sports schedules, phone (800) 755-5050. Sharks tickets are sold at the arena and through BASS (408) 998-2277.

Stanford University. Palo Alto. A beautiful campus, a delight to tour. Spanish architecture. Hoover Tower (good view). Rodin Sculpture Garden, museums, galleries. Daily walking tours. For information on campus and group tours, and Hoover Tower, call (650) 723-2560. Palo Alto is also a good shopping town, lots to choose from.

Tech Museum of Innovation. San Jose, helped by Silicon Valley firms, opened a new tech museum. The museum features 250 exhibits divided into the following galleries, "Life Tech; The Human Machine"; "Innovation: Silicon Valley and Beyond"; "Communication: Global Connections"; "Exploration: New Frontiers." Located at 201 S. Market St., San Jose. For more info (408) 279-7150.

Triton Museum, 1505 Warburton Ave., Santa Clara. Folk, contemporary, classic art. Pastoral scenes and wildlife of the early valley. Phone (408) 247-9340.

Villa Montalvo. Located just outside Saratoga on Saratoga-Los Gatos Road. Italian Renaissance villa built by politician with an artistic soul. James Phelan, a three-term mayor of San Francisco and a U.S. senator, was a patron of the arts. He left his beloved Villa Montalvo as a retreat for artists, writers and musicians. Many shows and programs on cultural subjects. The grounds, 175 acres, are maintained as a public arboretum. For information about programs, call (408) 741-3421.

Winchester Mystery House. 525 S. Winchester Blvd., San Jose. Sarah Winchester, heiress of the shooting Winchesters, pumped about $5 million into this four-story, 160-room house.

A reclusive, whimsical eccentric with a perverse eye for beauty, Mrs. Winchester ordered carpenters to build doors that opened to walls, staircases that lead nowhere and a window that peered out of a floor. Excellent rifle collection. Beautiful garden. Cafe. Banquet facilities. Tours. (408) 247-2101.

Musical and Cultural Events

Music and culture buffs should get on mailing lists of four "must" places:

• Flint Center, De Anza College, 21250 Stevens Creek Blvd., Cupertino. (408) 864-8816.

• San Jose Center for the Performing Arts. Almaden Boulevard and Park Avenue. (408) 277-3900.

• Shoreline Amphitheater at Mountain View, (650) 967-3000.

• Stanford University, Palo Alto. Musical and cultural events, (650) 725-ARTS; athletic events, (650) 723-1021.

Regional Parks

• **Alum Rock Park.** Old favorite of San Jose. In east hills, via Penitencia Creek Road. Dappled sycamores. Hiking, bike trails, picnicking, falls and springs. A spa, now long gone, used to attract people to Alum Rock for the cure.

• **Anderson Lake County Park**. East of Morgan Hill, off East Dunne Avenue or Coyote Road. About 2,000 acres of park around north and east sides of Anderson Reservoir, which is occasionally drained. Views. Picnic tables.

• **Coe State Park.** A big one, 68,000 acres, east of Morgan Hill. Take East Dunne Avenue. Hiking, backpacking, about 100 miles of trails. Nature center.

• **Grant County Park.** 9,522 acres on the road to Mt. Hamilton, east of San Jose. Hiking, horseback riding trails. Many natural history exhibits. Four lakes.

• **Mount Madonna County Park.** West of Gilroy. Take Highway 152. Redwoods and bay, oak and large madrone trees among 3,093 acres of hilly land. Rewarding but strenuous trails.

Chapter 12

SANTA CLARA COUNTY
Job Training & Colleges

IF YOU ARE LOOKING for a job but need training or additional education, local colleges, public adult schools and private institutions have put together a variety of programs, ranging from word processing to MBA degrees.

Many institutions have devised programs for working adults or parents who must attend the duties of school and child rearing.

In many instances jobs and careers are mixed in with personal enrichment. At some colleges, you can take word processing, economics and music.

This chapter lists the major local educational and training institutes. All will send you literature (some may charge a small fee), all welcome inquiries.

Adult Schools

Although rarely in the headlines, adult schools serve thousands of Santa Clara County residents. Upholstery, microwave cooking, ballroom dancing, computers, cardiopulmonary resuscitation, aerobics, investing in stocks, art, music, Quicken, how to raise children — all these and more are offered in the adult schools.

These schools and programs are run by school districts and by cities. Many schools also run adult sports programs, basketball, volleyball, tennis. Call your local school or city for a catalog.

Older Students

As the public's needs have changed, so have the colleges. The traditional college audience — high school seniors — is still thriving but increasingly colleges are attracting older students and working people.

Many colleges now offer evening and weekend programs, especially in business degrees and business-related subjects. Some programs — an MBA — can take years, some classes only a day. The Bay Area is loaded with educational opportunities. Here is a partial list of local colleges. As with any venture, the student should investigate before enrolling or paying a fee.

Universities and Colleges

• San Jose State University. At 25,000 plus students, the largest university in Santa Clara County and one of the largest in the Bay Region. Located in downtown San Jose. Bachelor's and master's degrees. Schools of Business, Education, Engineering, Applied Arts and Sciences, Science, Humanities and the Arts, Social Work, Social Science.

Regular program generally accepts high school students that score in top 35 percent. State universities are very popular with community college students: Two years at community college, last two years at state university. San Jose State offers day and evening classes, room and board.

What is the difference between the University of California schools and the state university schools? Both award bachelor's and master's degrees but only the UC schools award doctorates. Also, the UC schools have higher admission standards; e.g. the top 13 percent of high school students. UC schools also admit many community college grads.

The UC schools have the edge in prestige but there is much argument over which is academically superior. Critics charge that the UC schools do a better job on research than on undergraduate instruction.

State universities also run extension schools — one-shot classes or short programs generally aimed at building business skills but many cultural offerings are mixed in. These are cheap, often quite helpful classes for busy people.

For admissions information, call (408) 283-7500.

For a schedule of extension classes, call (408) 924-2630 or (408) 985-7578.

• Santa Clara University. Located in city of Santa Clara. Enrollment about 7,500, half undergrads. Run by Jesuits. Founded in 1851. One of the oldest

Santa Clara County Jobless Rate — % Unemployed

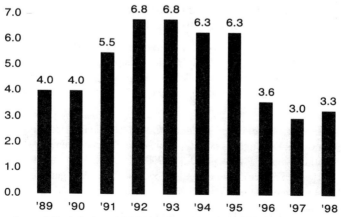

Source: California Employment Development Dept. 1998 percent is for November.

colleges in the state. Site of mission, which has been rebuilt. Pretty campus. Good scholastic reputation. Traditional university, bachelor to doctorate degrees. Undergraduate programs include engineering, business and arts and sciences.

Like many private colleges and universities, Santa Clara is tapping the market in education for mature adults, particularly for the strivers who want to stick an MBA in their resumes. Other graduate programs popular with the over-25 age group: Engineering, Counseling, Psychology, Education, Law, Catechetics-Liturgy-Spirituality. Phone (408) 554-4000 for information.

• Stanford. Located in Palo Alto. One of the great universities of the planet. About 13,500 students are enrolled in seven schools: Earth Sciences, Education, Engineering, Graduate School of Business, Humanities and Sciences, Law, Medicine. Continuing studies, (650) 725-2650. Well worth a visit even if you or yours don't stand a ghost of a chance of attending.

• University of California Extension. UC Extension in Santa Clara County is run by the University of California at Santa Cruz. Professional development classes are taken by about 30,000 adults each year at the Extension's facility at 3120 De La Cruz Blvd. in the city of Santa Clara (Trimble Road at Hwy. 101).

Courses offered in computer science, engineering, business and management, environmental sciences, arts and humanities, English language, teacher education, and behavioral sciences. Over 1,000 seminars annually. Also, courses and seminars leading to certificates in 25 professional programs. For schedule of courses, call (800) 660-4991.

• University of San Francisco. Jesuit University, based in San Francisco, but offers bachelor's and master's programs at its South Bay Center in Cupertino at 7337 Bollinger Rd. Aimed at working adults.

Bachelor's degrees in Applied Economics, Information Systems Management, Organizational Behavior. Master's in Human Resources, Organization Management. Classes are also offered in Sunnyvale, Palo Alto, South San Jose and San Jose. For information call (408) 255-1701.

• Golden Gate University. Based in Los Altos. Phone (650) 961-3000. For working adults. Bachelor's degrees in Human Relations, Management, Telecommunications. Master's in Banking and Finance, Management, Human Resources Management, Information Systems, International Management, Marketing, Taxation, Telecommunications.

• St. Mary's College. Based in Contra Costa County but offers programs in Santa Clara County through its facility in San Jose. Degree programs scheduled for working adults. Phone 1-800-538-9999. Bachelor's and master's degrees in Health Services Administration, bachelor's in Management, master's in Procurement and Contract Management.

• National Hispanic University, 14271 Story Rd., San Jose, 95127. Phone

(408) 254-6900. Associate and Bachelor's degrees in arts. Master's in education and business administration. English as second language.

Community Colleges

Three community college districts with campuses located throughout the county: San Jose-Evergreen, Foothill-De Anza and West Valley-Mission community college districts. Academic and vocational subjects, day and evening classes. Many students attend community colleges for first two years of college then transfer as juniors to four-year colleges.

• San Jose City College, 2100 Moorpark Ave., San Jose, 95125. Phone (408) 298-2181.

• Evergreen Valley College, 3095 Yerba Buena Rd., San Jose, 95135. Phone (408) 274-7900.

• De Anza College, 21250 Stevens Creek Blvd., Cupertino, 95014. Phone (408) 864-5678.

• Foothill College, 12345 El Monte Rd., Los Altos Hills, 94022. Phone (650) 949-7777.

• West Valley College, 14000 Fruitvale Ave., Saratoga, 95070. Phone (408) 867-2200.

• Mission College, 3000 Mission College Blvd., Santa Clara, 95054. Phone (408) 988-2200.

Tidbits

• With the boom in jobs, local universities have added classes to train students in high tech. San Jose State University in 1997 reported a 30 percent increase in enrollment in computer sciences.

Chapter 13

SANTA CLARA COUNTY
New Housing

SHOPPING FOR A new home? This chapter gives an overview of new housing under way in Santa Clara and nearby counties. Smaller projects are generally ignored. If you know where you want to live, drive that town or ask the local planning department, what's new in housing.

Prices change. Incidentals such as landscaping fees may not be included. In the 1980s, to pay for services, cities increased fees on home construction. Usually, these fees are included in the home prices but in what is known as Mello-Roos districts, the fees are often assessed like tax payments (in addition to house payments).

Nothing secret. By law, developers are required to disclose all fees and, in fact, California has some of the toughest disclosure laws in the country. But the prices listed below may not include some fees.

After rocketing in the 1980s, home prices, new and resale, stabilized and in many instances dropped. Some developers, particularly in towns with many new units, have gotten very competitive in pricing — a break for buyers. But in the last year or so, as employment has boomed, home prices and sales have increased. A lot depends on how far you are willing to commute.

This information covers what's available at time of publication. For latest information, call the developers for brochures.

If you have never shopped for a new home, you probably will enjoy the experience. In the larger developments, the builders will decorate models showing the housing styles and sizes offered. You enter through one home, pick up the sales literature, then move to the other homes or condos. Every room is usually tastefully and imaginatively decorated — and enticing.

An agent or agents will be on hand to answer questions or discuss financing or other aspects you're interested in. Generally, all this is done low-key. On Saturdays and Sundays, thousands of people can be found visiting developments around the Bay Area and Northern California. Developers call attention to their models by flags. When you pass what appears to be a new development and flags are flying, it generally means that units are available for sale.

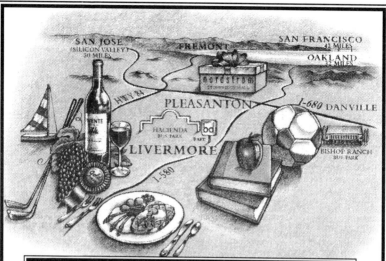

A TRADITION OF GREAT HOMES IN A GREAT PLACE TO LIVE.

Home-town pride. Scenic vineyards and wineries. Highly-ranked schools, regional shopping, great restaurants, recreation and entertainment. The Tri-Valley area is unsurpassed for its quality of life. Throughout the region, you'll find new home neighborhoods of extraordinary quality by Signature Properties. Every Signature neighborhood features homes that are carefully designed, classically styled and meticulously constructed for years of comfort. It's easy to see why Signature Properties has one of the highest homeowner satisfaction ratings in the entire Bay Area! Whatever your price range, look to Signature Properties for a great place to live. For information on our neighborhoods in Pleasanton, Livermore, Brentwood and Hayward, call (800) 300-4123 or visit our web site at www.sigprop.com.

SIGNATURE PROPERTIES

A Tradition in Homebuilding

BROKER CO-OP INVITED

EQUAL HOUSING OPPORTUNITY

SANTA CLARA COUNTY

Cupertino

Oak Valley, O'Brien Group, 28505 Oak Valley Rd., (650) 988-2555, single-family homes, 4-5 bedrooms, from high $900,000s.

Gilroy

Casa Blanca, L. J. W. Enterprises, Longmeadow Road, (408) 847-5757, single-family detached, 3-5 bedrooms, from $290,000s.

Lions Creek, Arcadia Development Co., Longmeadow Road, (408) 848-1744, single-family detached, 3-6 bedrooms, from $300,000.

Oakbrook, Kaufman & Broad, Thomas Road, (408) 846-0050, single-family detached, 3-6 bedrooms, from $280,000.

Los Gatos

Bella Vista Village, (408) 356-8919, townhouses, 3-4 bedrooms, from $490,000.

Morgan Hill

Coyote Ranch, east of Hwy. 101 off Cochran Road, (408) 782-1458, single-family detached, 3-5 bedrooms, from $200,000s.

Mountain View

California Station, Kaufman & Broad, off Whisman Road, (415) 966-8329, condominiums & single-family detached, 2-4 bedrooms, from high $300,000s.

San Jose

Blossom Cove, Braddock & Logan, Berryessa neighborhood near Four Oaks Road, (408) 578-0893, single-family detached, 4-5 bedrooms, from mid-$300,000.

California Fairways, Kaufman & Broad, near Hwy. 101 & Alum Rock Road, (408) 259-1553, single-family detached, 3-4 bedrooms, from $200,000+.

California Gateway, Kaufman & Broad, Berryessa neighborhood on Wayne Avenue, (408) 573-0638, single-family detached, 3-6 bedrooms, from $370,000.

Chandler Woods, Standard Pacific, Evergreen neighborhood, Fowler Road east of San Felipe Road, (408) 270-2882, single-family detached, 4-5 bedrooms, from mid-$400,000s.

Country View, Shapell, in Almaden Valley near Glenview, (408) 927-0415, townhouses, 3-4 bedrooms, from mid-$300,000s.

Greystone Estates, Greystone Homes, Inc., (408) 532-8294. Neiman off of Yerba Buena in Evergreen neighborhood. Single family detached homes, high $400,000s.

Hillside II, Greenbriar Bel Aire Co., near Silver Creek Valley Road, (408) 238-8909, estate homes on 1/2 acre+ lots, from $500,000s.

Serenade at Basking Ridge, Shea Homes, (408) 224-3890, single-family detached, 3-5 bedrooms, from $300,000s.

Shadow Ridge, Greystone Homes, Inc., (800) 794-1926. Story Lane off Clayton Road. Single family attached homes, 4-5 bedrooms, from low $500,000s.

Silver Creek Valley Country Club, multiple developers, Silver Creek Valley Road east of Hwy. 101, (408) 239-5700, custom estates & condominiums, $350,000 to $1.5 million.

San Martin

San Martin Estates, Barnes & Co., 670 W. San Martin Ave., (408) 237-3314, custom homes, $975,000 & up.

Santa Clara

Mission Park, Citation Homes, near Lafayette Street south of Hwy. 237, (408) 927-0415, single-family detached, 3-5 bedrooms, from mid-$300,00s.

ALAMEDA COUNTY

Alameda

California Heritage Bay, Kaufman & Broad, (510) 864-0653, single-family detached, 3-4 bedrooms, from mid-$280,000s.

Ponderosa homeowner Mila and daughter Kendall

At Ponderosa, we design homes to hold a lifetime of memories.

There's nothing quite like the feeling you get when you open the door to your new home for the very first time. At Ponderosa, we take great care to make sure that feeling lasts year after year. We design our homes with the perfect balance of tradition and flexibility to make sure it accommodates your family as it grows—and grows up. Construction is meticulous, with some of the toughest internal quality inspections in the industry. So the pride you feel in your home on your daughter's first day of school will last well beyond her high school graduation. Visit a Ponderosa neighborhood today, and see why, to families all over the Bay Area, Ponderosa means home.

Ponderosa Heights at Scott Creek *in Fremont* (510) 226-9090	**Gossamer Cove** *in Redwood City* (650) 631-9732	**Ponderosa Country** *in Antioch* (925) 778-5533	**Ponderosa Orchard & Ponderosa Ridge** *in San Jose* (408) 223-8230

House shown is The Hills at Bent Creek.
Prices effective as of publication deadline.

http://www.baynet.com/ponderosa

PONDEROSA HOMES

Alameda (Continued)

The Headlands at Harbor Bay Isle, Shea Homes, (510) 523-0533, single-family detached, 3-6 bedrooms, from high $400,000s.

Albany

Bayside, (510) 528-2200, condominiums, 2 bedrooms, 2 baths, from $149,000.

Castro Valley

Five Canyons, Centex Homes, (510) 886-7745, single-family detached, 3-6 bedrooms, from low $200,000s.

Palomares Hills, Shapell, 20438 Summerglen Pl., 1-800-SHAPELL, single-family detached, 3-4 bedrooms,

The Views, (510) 247-0777, single-family detached, 3-5 bedrooms, from high $200,000s.

Wildwood, Centex, 3730 North Canyon Ct., (510) 886-5201, townhomes, 2 & 4 bedrooms, attached garages, from mid-$150,000s.

Dublin

Hansen Hill, Silvergate Road, (510) 556-9612, single-family detached, up to 5 bedrooms, 2,400-3,347 sq. ft., from low $400,000s.

SummerGlen, SummerHill Homes, (800) 585-0085. End of Hacienda Drive, East Dublin. Three new neighborhoods in master planned area. 3-4-5 bedroom homes. New school. Park. Pool.

Fremont

Arbor Court, Shea Homes, (510) 742-1352, single-family detached, from mid-$200,000s.

Castro Ranch, Greystone Homes, Inc., (800) 794-1926. Castro Lane off Mission Boulevard. Single family attached homes, 3-4-5 bedrooms, from high $500,000s.

Glenmoor Village, SummerHill Homes, (800) 585-0085. Eggers Drive. Single homes in Glenmoor District. From low $400,000 to low $500,000.

Liberty Commons, Shapell, (510) 353-9052, Liberty Street, townhomes, from mid-$200,000s.

Niles Glen, Greystone Homes, Inc., (800) 794-1926. Single family detached homes, 3-4-5 bedrooms, mid $300,000s.

Reserve at Scott Creek, Brookfield Homes, off Scott Creek Road, (510) 353-9680, single-family detached, 4-5 bedrooms, 2,322-3,058 sq. ft., from low $400,000s.

Livermore

Coventry, Signature Properties, 5720 Arlene Way, (510) 447-1314, single-family detached, 3-5 bedrooms, in Stratford Park, from low $300,000s.

Mill Creek, north of I-580 east of Vasco Road, (510) 371-0233, single-family detached, 3-5 bedrooms, from mid-$200,000s.

Montrose, Warmington Homes, Highland Avenue, (510) 371-6001, single-family detached, up to 6 bedrooms, 2,140-3,123 sq. ft., from high $300,000s.

Portola Collection, (510) 371-3040, single-family detached, 3-4 bedrooms, up to 1,920 sq. ft., from low $200,000s.

Portola Meadows Townhomes, Davidon Homes, 1801 Calle Del Sueno, (510) 371-8377, single-family detached, 3-4 bedrooms, 1,752-1,964 sq. ft., $226,990-$243,990.

Tapestry by Shea Homes, Shea Homes, (510) 449-4694, single-family detached, up to 4 bedrooms, from low $400,000s.

Oakland

Lark Bellevue Tower, 510) 433-1900, condominiums, 1-3 bedrooms, on Lake Merritt, pool, fitness center, clubroom, door & parking security, from $130,000 to $500,000s.

Parkwoods, (510) 848-4663, condominiums, gated community, from $123,900.

Pleasanton

Avila, Signature Properties, 5102 Angelico Ct., (510) 734-9569, single-family detached,

We've Got The Bay Area Covered... Standard Pacific

Everywhere, in all the best locations, Standard Pacific is building great neighborhoods of quality homes. You'll discover that every Standard Pacific home has not only a special address, but architectural excellence and many luxury features.

For buyers who know the best investment they can make in their family's future is a home with a terrific location, head for your choice of these truly outstanding Bay Area Standard Pacific communities.

San Ramon
Crown Ridge
From Upper $400's
925/829-1873

San Ramon
Four Oaks
From Upper $400's
925/833-0890

Danville
Autumn Creek
From Upper $500's
925/833-0890

Pleasanton
Stoneridge Place
From Mid $300's
925/462-2711

Hayward
Highlands at Clearbrook
From Low $400's
510/583-9542

Hayward
Twin Bridges
From Mid $300's
Links:
510/475-0367
Champions:
510/475-5585
Masters:
510/487-0500

Union City
Seabreeze
From Mid $300's
Villas:
510/489-9331
Classics:
510/489-9300

Neighborhoods also in:
San Benito County
Monterey County

New Neighborhoods
Coming Soon To:
Dublin
Gilroy
Livermore
Pleasanton
San Jose
Tracy

*For More Information
Call Toll Free*
1- (877) STNDPAC
(786-3722) or visit
us at our website:
www.stndpac.com

HOME BUILDERS ASSOCIATION / EQUAL HOUSING OPPORTUNITY

Prices, terms and specifications subject to change without prior notice

STANDARD PACIFIC
The Standard of Enduring Quality

Pleasanton (Continued)
2-4 bedrooms, European style w/courtyards, from mid-$200,000s.

Ascona at Ruby Hill, Signature Properties, (510) 417-5808, single-family detached, 4-5 bedrooms, gated golf club community, from mid-$500,000s.

Carriage Hills, just east of I-680 at Arlington Drive, (510) 426-8119, custom homes on 1/2 ac. sites, 3,000-4,200 sq. ft., from low $700,000s.

Oak Tree Farms Estate Lots, (510) 462-3740, home estate sites from $297,000.

Siena, Signature Properties, 4252 Lucero Ct., (510) 227-1817, townhomes, 2-3 bedrooms, from $180,000s.

SummerHill Homes, (800) 585-0085. Executive single-family homes, country environment. Coming in spring 1999. In the $600,000s.

The Preserve, Presley Homes, near Vineyard Avenue in south hills, 510) 737-0223, single-family detached, 3,424-4,345 sq. ft. on 17,000 sq. ft. homesites, au pair & guest cottages, from high $600,000s.

Valencia II, Signature Homes, 3868 Appian St., (510) 227-1819, single-family detached, 3-5 bedrooms, from low $300,000s.

San Leandro
Bay Walk, Robert's Landing, Inc., near Lewelling Boulevard at the waterfront, (510) 351-1179, single-family detached, 3-4 bedrooms, 1,321-1,651 sq. ft., from under $200,000.

Seaport, Robert's Landing, Inc., west end of Lewelling Boulevard on the water, (510) 895-9614, single-family detached, 3-5 bedrooms, 1,545-2,246 sq. ft., from $242,950.

Stillwater Cove at Heron Bay, Greystone Homes, Inc., (800) 794-1926. Single-family detached homes, 4 bedrooms, from low $300,000s.

Union City
California Rosecrest, Kaufman & Broad, (510) 489-7597, single-family detached, 3-7 bedrooms, from $280,000s.

New Valencia, Ponderosa Homes, 32345 Derby St., (510) 471-7869, single-family detached, 3-car garages, from $300,000s.

The Village/The Bay, Ponderosa Homes, 31417 Marlin Ct., (510) 471-2140, single-family detached, 3-5 bedrooms, from mid-$300,000s.

CONTRA COSTA COUNTY
Alamo
Alamo Orchards, Orchard Drive off Danville Boulevard, (925) 820-4160, single-family detached, 4-5 bedrooms, from $519,000.

Stonebridge Estates, Greenbriar Homes, 1512 Serafix Rd., (925) 947-0395, single-family detached, from 5 bedrooms, from $638,950.

Antioch
Almond Ridge North, McBail Company, 2817 Nogal Ct., (925) 609-8181, single-family detached, 3-4 bedrooms, from $126,500.

Autumn Brook, Kaufman & Broad, 5129 Trailridge Way, (925) 778-9380, single-family detached, 3-4 bedrooms, from $172,990.

California Countrybrook, Kaufman & Broad, 1328 Rock Springs Rd., (925) 778-6630, single-family detached, 3-4 bedrooms, from $126,990.

California Southbrook, Kaufman & Broad, 5105 Springcrest Ct., (925) 778-6630, single-family detached, 3-4 bedrooms, from $168,900.

Castellana at Black Diamond Knolls, Richland Development, 1958 Badger Pass, (925) 706-8855, single-family detached, 3-5 bedrooms, from $206,000.

Daybreak, The Hofmann Company, 4125 Jarosite Ct., (925) 756-7782, single-family detached, 3-5 bedrooms, from $166,990.

Deer Valley Estates, Porter Homes, 5012 Apache Ct., (925) 777-1895, single-family detached, 3-5 bedrooms, from $177,990.

SUMMERHILL HOMES
COMMUNITIES OF DISTINCTION

THE BAY AREA'S AWARD-WINNING BUILDER
IS PLEASED TO ANNOUNCE
THE FOLLOWING NEW COMMUNITIES

P E N I N S U L A / W E S T   B A Y
FOSTER CITY
From the low-$300,000s

Spacious, single level condominium homes in a prime peninsula location. Walking distance to saltwater lagoons and shopping. Models open corner of Edgewater & East Hillsdale Boulevards.

Meridian Bay is Now Selling! ▼ Call 1-650-638-1100

SOUTH SAN FRANCISCO
From the mid-$300,000s

Traditional style homes adjacent to the city's "crown jewel" park.

ParcPlace Coming Spring 1999 ▼ Call 1-800-585-0085

E A S T   B A Y
DUBLIN
From the low-$400,000s

A new neighborhood in a master-planned community. Brand new elementary school. Brand new park. Brand new pool. Models open at the corner of SummerGlen and Aspen Drives.

SummerGlen at Emerald Park ▼ Call 1-925-829-9630

FREMONT
From the mid-$400,000s

Americana style homes in the desirable Glenmoor district. Models open at the corner of Eggers and Glenmoor Drives.

Glenmoor Village ▼ Call 1-510-574-0826

HAYWARD
From the high-$200,000s

Traditional style homes in the heart of the Bay Area.

Coming Spring 1999 ▼ Call 1-800-585-0085

Antioch (Continued)

Diablo Hills Terrace, Pacwest Development, 5107 Sundance Ct., (925) 754-1788, single-family detached, 3-5 bedrooms, from $129,950.

Discovery at Black Diamond Canyon, Pulte Homes, 5104 Tehachapi Way, (925) 779-1116, single-family detached, 3-5 bedrooms, from $169,500.

Generations at Black Diamond Canyon, Richland Development, 4909 Union Mine Ct., (925) 706-8883, single-family detached, 4-5 bedrooms, from $242,900.

K&B New Homes Center, Kaufman & Broad, Dallas Ranch Road off Lone Tree Way, (925) 778-9380, single-family detached, 3-6 bedrooms, from $170,000.

Lone Tree Glen, Davidon Homes, 1825 Vender Ct., (925) 706-1986, attached 2-story homes, 3-4 bedrooms, from $138,990.

Lone Tree Estates-Masters Collection, Davidon Homes, 2105 Bamboo Way, (925) 778-3092, single-family detached, 3-6 bedrooms, from $207,990.

Ponderosa Country, Ponderosa Homes, 4513 Country Hills Dr., (925) 668-5533, single-family detached, from 5 bedrooms, from $180,000.

Ponderosa Glen, Ponderosa Homes, 4518 Country Hills Dr., (925) 778-5533, single-family detached, 3-4 bedrooms, from $144,000.

The Colony at Deer Valley, Pacific Valley Housing Corp., 2300 Crystal Ct., (925) 779-1477, single-family detached, from $171,500.

The Estates at Dallas Ranch, Suncrest Homes, 5401 Amberdale Way, (925) 706-8436, single-family detached, 5-6 bedrooms, from $257,900s.

The Estates II at Dallas Ranch, Suncrest Homes, 5401 Amberdale Way, (925) 706-8436, single-family detached, 5-6 bedrooms, from $278,900s.

Tourelle, Richland, Golf Course Road off Lone Tree Way, (925) 706-8883, single-family detached, 4-6 bedrooms, high $200,000s.

Bay Point

California Tradewinds II, Kaufman & Broad, 367 Powell Dr., (925) 458-6100, single-family detached, 3-4 bedrooms, from $164,900.

Blackhawk

Shadow Creek Manor, Damé, Trailer/Green Meadow, (925) 736-7369, single-family detached, from 5 bedrooms, from $454,000.

Brentwood

Creekside at Brentwood, Pulte Homes, 1310 Crescent Dr., (925) 516-1893, single-family detached, 3 bedrooms, from $165,900s.

Garin Ranch/Signature, Signature Properties, 581 Orange Ct., (925) 513-1057, single-family detached, 3-5 bedrooms, from $251,500.

Garin Ranch/Morrison, Morrison Homes, 793 Redhaven St., (925) 516-9784, single-family detached, 4-5 bedrooms, from $226,990.

Inspirations II, Seeno, 970 Orchid Dr. (925) 634-2020, single-family detached, 3-5 bedrooms from $169,950.

Madison Greens, Kiper Homes, 701 Apple Hill Dr., (925) 634-9669, single-family detached, 4-6 bedrooms, from $198,950.

Summerset I, Blackhawk-Nunn, 1675 Crispin Dr., (925) 516-7600, single-family detached, 2 bedrooms, from $119,900.

Summerset II, Blackhawk-Nunn, 190 Summerset Dr., (925) 516-7600, single-family detached, 2 bedrooms, from $133,900.

Sunrise, Greystone Homes, 1751 Diamond Springs Ln., (925) 513-0452, single-family detached, 3-4 bedrooms, from $144,950.

The Foothills at Brentwood Lakes, Lee Hancock Construction, 2258 Putter Ct., (925) 634-0770, single-family detached, 4-6 bedrooms, from $211,950.

Towne Square, Greystone Homes, 1061 Mill Creek Way, (925) 513-0905, single-family detached, 4-7 bedrooms, from $176,950.

Clayton

Falcon Ridge, Presley Homes, 707 Acorn Dr., (925) 672-0504, single-family detached,

O'BRIEN GROUP

Four Seasons at Silverado Creek, Napa
3 and 4 bedroom traditional homes
Priced from the mid $200,000's
(707) 253-8566

South Gate at Hamilton, Novato
3 to 6 bedroom traditional homes
Priced from the high $300,000's
(415) 382-9399

Oak Valley, Cupertino
4 and 5 bedroom classic homes
Priced from the high $900,000's
(650) 988-2555

www.obriengroup.com
650-377-0300

prices effective as of date of publication

3% broker cooperation

Clayton (Continued)
3-5 bedrooms, from $345,450..

Peacock Creek/Legacy, Legacy Homes, Rolling Woods Way, (925) 687-3522, single-family detached, from 5 bedrooms, from $436,950.

Peacock Creek/Presley, Presley Homes, 1105 Peacock Creek Dr., (925) 672-3673, single-family detached, from 5 bedrooms, from $416,500.

Ironwood at Oakhurst, Kaufman & Broad, 4004 Hummingbird Way, (925) 672-3660, single-family detached, from 3 bedrooms, from $312,990.

Concord
Crystal Ranch, Legacy Homes, 5313 Oak Point Ct., (925) 687-3522, single-family detached, 4-5 bedrooms, from upper $363,950.

Estate Collection, Pulte Homes, 5304 Woodgrove Ct., (925) 672-8985, single-family detached, 4-5 bedrooms, from $384,900.

Ygnacio Woods Estates, Zocchi Company, Treat Boulevard at San Miguel Drive, (925) 685-9070, single-family detached, 3-5 bedrooms, from $355,990.

Kestrel Ridge Estates, Myrtle Road off Ygnacio Valley Road, (925) 246-0310, single-family detached, 4-6 bedrooms, from low $400,000s.

Danville
California Meadows, Kaufman & Broad, 43 Lily Ct., (925) 736-8327, single-family detached, 3-6 bedrooms, from $393,900s.

Campbell Place, Pacific Union Homes, Glascow Drive off Sycamore Valley Road, (925) 743-0238, single-family detached, from $700,000s.

Lawrence Estates, Pulte Homes, 19 Shelterwood Pl., (925) 648-9346, single-family detached, 3-5 bedrooms, from $260,900.

Magee Ranch, Broadmoor Development Co, 100 Magee Ranch Rd., (925) 837-8900, single-family detached, from 4 bedrooms, from $529,000.

Tassajara Ridge, Pinn Brothers Construction, 20 Camino Tassajara, (925) 648-9589, single-family detached, from 5 bedrooms, from $298,950.

Discovery Bay
Miramar, Hofman Co., 2079 Newport Dr., (925) 634-0500, single-family detached, single-family detached, 2-3 bedrooms, from $286,990.

Country Meadows, Marsh Creek and Bixler roads, (925) 634-6874, single-family detached, 3-4 bedrooms, from $170,000s.

Country Lane, Centex Homes, 4016 Regatta Dr., (925) 634-6874, single-family detached, 3-5 bedrooms, from $165,990.

El Sobrante
Appian Knoll Mansion, Broker I Marketing, 890 Appian Knoll Ct., (510) 669-9718, condominiums, 3 bedrooms, from $149,950.

Hillcrest, Laurelwood Homes, 822 Bridgeway Cir., (510) 758-8888, single-family detached, 3-5 bedrooms, from $299,900.

Lafayette
Olde Creek Place, Lenox Homes, Old Tunnel Road off Pleasant Hill Road, (925) 284-0415, single-family detached, 3-5 bedrooms, from $490,000s.

Reliez Valley Highlands, Davidon Homes, 921 Dana Highlands Ct., (925) 370-2272, single-family detached, 3-6 bedrooms, from $518,990.

Martinez
California Manors at Westaire, Kaufman & Broad, 344 Westaire Blvd., (925) 370-8893, single-family detached, 3-5 bedrooms, from $237,990s.

California Vistas, Kaufman & Broad, 137 Loire Ct., (925) 370-8893, single-family detached, 3-5 bedrooms, from $298,990.

Creekside, Lamonde Katzakian Company, Williamson Court, (707) 747-2880, single-family detached, 3-5 bedrooms, from $194,500.

Glen View, south of Highway 4 west of I-680, (925) 356-2265, single-family detached, 3-4 bedrooms, from high $200,000s.

Chapter 14

SANTA CLARA COUNTY
Commuting

ALMOST EVERY YEAR, Santa Clara County does something that improves the commute or lays the groundwork for improvements but often the number of new vehicles on the road overwhelms whatever steps are taken — with exceptions.

Many people live close to their jobs. One survey released in 1998 showed that about 46 percent of Bay Area commuters travel fewer than 10 miles to work. If you are one of these lucky stiffs, your commute at times will be irritating but it will also be endurable.

Proximity to the job is one the mantras of reformers these days, and in fact "Silicon Valley," partly because of the commute but also because land was cheaper elsewhere, leaped over its original borders years ago. Many high-tech jobs can be found in Fremont, Milpitas, San Ramon, Dublin, Livermore, Pleasanton, and cities of San Mateo, notably Menlo Park and South San Francisco (bio tech).

But many firms still want to settle in the original Silicon Valley. Several large complexes are under construction or about to begin construction. These included Microsoft and Silicon Graphics in Mountain View and Sun in Santa Clara.

In the 1980's, Santa Clara County added about 202,000 residents and since 1990, it's taken on about 152,000 more. And studies show that more people are driving solo.

Alternatives out are there: bus, light rail, commute train, car-pooling. If you are going nuts with driving, you might think about other ways of commuting.

Time-saving Strategies
• Buy a good map book and keep it in the car. The editors favor Thomas Guides, which are updated annually. Sooner than later you will find yourself jammed on the freeway and in desperate need of an alternate route. They're out there.

• Listen to traffic reports on the radio. Helicopters and planes give immediate news of jams. Avoid trouble before you get on the road.

• Buy bridge ticket books and, for buses and light rail, flash passes (good for a month) or ticket books. All will save you time and money.

• Join a car pool. RIDES, 1-800-755-7665, will help you find a car pool in your town — no charge. In the typical arrangement, passengers meet at one or two spots and are dropped off in one or two destinations. The pools go all over. All that's needed are passengers and a driver.

If you want to set up your own pool, RIDES will help you find passengers and finance the lease of a van. Passengers split the cost, which is based on the type of van, mileage and operating expenses. The driver gets a free commute and use of the van.

• Avoid peak hours. If you can leave for work — it gets earlier every year — about 6:30 a.m. and hit the freeway home before 4 p.m., your kids might not greet you, "Hey, stranger."

• Take public transportation. Yes, the car is flexible, so handy, so private. But if other, easier, cheaper ways of commuting are at hand, why ignore them?

Buses

Run by the Santa Clara Valley Transportation Authority. They go all over the county: Gilroy, Milpitas, Palo Alto, San Jose, Los Gatos.

During morning commute hours, express buses travel from Gilroy and Santa Cruz to destinations in Silicon Valley.

Wheelchair access. Stops at Park & Ride lots, CalTrain stations, shopping malls, hospitals, San Jose State University and other colleges, city halls, parks, airports, Fremont BART station. Connections to AC Transit (Alameda County) and SamTrans (San Mateo County) buses.

Dial-A-Ride — bus pickup at door — in south county.

Historic trolleys circle the downtown transit mall, 1.5-mile route. 9 a.m. to 5 p.m. Weekends and holidays.

The transportation authority puts out a handy map. To obtain one and for more information, phone (408) 321-2300; from south county, (408) 683-4151; Los Gatos, (408) 370-9191; from Palo Alto, (800) 894-9908.

Light Rail

From South San Jose (and other neighborhoods) to downtown San Jose to Great America and the city of Santa Clara. A sleek ride. Work is now underway to extend the line up to Mountain View, which is spending about $6 million to build a transit center in its downtown. Scheduled opening is the year 2000.

For the present, about 33 stations. Bus connections at each. The line also provides service to the San Jose neighborhoods of Blossom Valley (Santa Teresa Boulevard and San Ignacio Avenue) and to Almaden (Winfield and

Coleman).

Run by Santa Clara Valley Transportation Authority. All tickets sold from machines, none on board. Day passes can be used for bus and light rail. For information, (408) 321-2300. Ask for light-rail brochure.

CalTrain

The old Southern Pacific route, now employed for commute service by the Peninsula Corridor Joint Powers Board, an agency with representatives from San Francisco, San Mateo and Santa Clara counties.

Trains from Gilroy to San Francisco. Stops at Morgan Hill, San Jose, Santa Clara, Sunnyvale, Mountain View, Palo Alto, Menlo Park, Redwood City, San Carlos, Belmont, San Mateo, Burlingame, Millbrae, San Bruno, South San Francisco, San Francisco. Transfers are available for buses from SamTrans, Santa Clara County Transportation Agency and Muni. More trains are being added. For schedules and more information, call (800) 660-4287.

AMTRAK

Amtrak is used more for excursions, especially during ski season, than commuting but for some people it can work as a commute train. Service nationwide and for locals throughout the East and South Bay. Stations in San Jose and Santa Clara. Nice ride. Check the schedule. (800) 872-7245.

BART

In East Bay, the end of the line is in Fremont, right next to Milpitas, but the Santa Clara County Transportation Agency runs a connector bus to that station. For BART schedules and info, (510) 441-2278.

After years of arguing, agreement appears near to connect BART to downtown San Jose.

One number

Universal number for commute information. New effort to make it simple. (408) 817-1717.

Altamont Commuter Express (ACE)

New service. Proving popular. Because housing prices are so high in Silicon Valley and so low in other places, like Central California, many Silicon Valley workers are buying homes in such places as Tracy and Manteca, and east Alameda County. This commute train starts in Stockton and stops in Manteca, Tracy, Livermore, Pleasanton, Fremont, Santa Clara, San Jose. Phone 800-411-7245.

Tidbits

• Metering lights have been installed on many access ramps to local freeways and expressways, an effort to keep the flow steady. Some freeways have car pool lanes, a reward for people who double up.

Chapter 15

SANTA CLARA COUNTY
Weather

"HE HAD BEEN suddenly jerked from the heart of civilization and flung into the heart of things primordial. No lazy, sun-kissed life was this ...."

Jack London, in "The Call of the Wild," was describing the great dog, Buck, stolen from the Santa Clara Valley and secreted to Alaska to work as a sled dog. Compared to frigid Alaska, Santa Clara was cream cheese, Jack thought, an arguable proposition, but there was no denying he caught the gist of the local weather, "sun-kissed."

One of Life's Joys
Rarely very hot or cold, always finding its way back to balmy tranquillity.

Although appearing somewhat erratic, the weather proceeds logically, responding to broad patterns and local topography. Easily learned, these patterns will make you somewhat of a weather expert, a reliable source on what to wear, when to have a picnic and when to drive slowly.

For starters, it can be safely said that rain will rarely fall between May and September, that Pacific swimming will be warmer in October than in June, that the San Lorenzo Valley to the south and Berkeley to the north will receive more rain or moisture than the Santa Clara Valley.

Five great actors star in the Bay Area weather extravaganza: the sun, the Pacific, the Golden Gate, the Central Valley and the hills.

The Sun
In the spring and summer, the sun moves north bringing a mass of air called the Pacific High. The Pacific High blocks storms from the California Coast and dispatches winds down the coast. In the fall, the sun moves south, taking the Pacific High with it. The winds slough off for a while, then in bluster the storms. Toward spring, the storms abate as the Pacific High settles in.

The Pacific
Speeding across the Pacific, spring and summer winds pick up moisture and, at the coast, strip the warm water from the surface and bring up the frigid.

Cold water exposed to warm, wet air makes a wonderfully thick fog. In

Average Daily Temperature

Location	Ja	Fb	Mr	Ap	My	Ju	Jy	Au	Sp	Oc	No	Dc
Gilroy	47	52	54	58	62	68	71	71	69	63	54	48
Los Gatos	48	52	54	57	61	66	70	69	68	62	54	48
Mt. Hamilton	44	44	43	48	55	64	71	71	65	58	48	44
Palo Alto	48	51	54	57	61	65	66	67	65	60	53	48
San Jose	49	53	55	59	63	67	70	69	68	63	55	49
San Francisco	49	52	53	56	58	62	63	64	65	61	55	49

Source: National Climatic Data Center, Ashville, NC, 1961-1990

summer, San Francisco, Monterey, Half Moon Bay and Pacifica, among others, often look like they are buried in mountains of cotton.

The Golden Gate

This fog would love to scoot inland to the Santa Clara Valley and Bay shore cities such as Palo Alto and Mountain View. But the coastal hills and mountains stop or greatly impede its progress — except where there are openings. Of the half dozen or so major gaps, the biggest is that marvelous work of nature, the Golden Gate.

The fog shoots through the Golden Gate in the spring and summer, visually delighting motorists on the Bay Bridge, bangs into the East Bay hills and eases down toward San Jose, where it takes the edge off temperatures. The Crystal Springs gap, located northwest of Palo Alto, also allows cooling air into the South Bay.

The Central Valley

Also known as the San Joaquin Valley and located about 75 miles inland, the Central Valley is influenced more by continental weather than coastal. In the summer, this means heat. Hot air rises, pulling in cold air like a vacuum. The Central Valley sucks in the coastal air through the Golden Gate and openings in the East Bay hills, until the Valley cools.

Then the Valley says to the coast: no more cool air, thank you.

With the suction gone, the inland pull on the ocean fog drops off, often breaking down the fog-producing apparatus and clearing San Francisco and the coastline. Meanwhile, lacking the cooling air, the Valley heats up again, creating the vacuum that pulls in the fog.

This cha-cha-cha between coast and inland valley gave rise to the Bay Region's boast of "natural air conditioning." In hot weather, nature works to bring in cool air; in cool weather, she works to bring in heat.

In Santa Clara County, this push-pull phenomenon has a diminutive counterpart. At night, fog will occasionally creep over the coastal mountains only to be burned off the following morning by the robust sunlight.

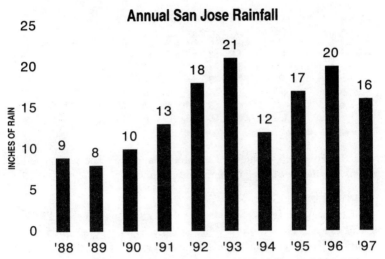

Annual San Jose Rainfall

Source: U.S. Western Regional Climate Center, Reno, NV. Rainfall is calendar-year total.

The Hills

Besides blocking the fog, the hills also greatly decide how much rain falls in a particular location. Many storms travel south to north, so a valley that opens to the south (San Lorenzo) will receive more rain than one that opens to the north (Santa Clara).

When storm clouds rise to pass over a hill, they cool and drop much of their rain. Some towns in the Bay Region will be deluged during a storm, while a few miles away another town will escape with showers. Saratoga reports an average annual rainfall of 29 inches, Cupertino 14 inches.

That basically is how the weather works in the Bay Area. Unfortunately for regularity's sake, the actors often forget their lines or are upstaged by minor stars.

Rainfall at San Jose over 10 years (1975-84) demonstrates the mildly erratic nature of Mother Nature. From 12 inches in 1975, rainfall dropped to 7

San Jose Temperature Patterns

Month	Avg. Max.	Avg. Min.	Record High	Record Low
January	58	41	79	22
April	69	47	93	30
July	81	56	108	43
October	74	51	97	31
Year	70	49	108	20

Source: San Jose Municipal Weather Station.

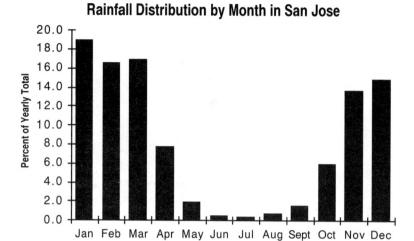

Rainfall Distribution by Month in San Jose

Source: U.S. Western Regional Climate Center, Reno, NV. The chart shows, on average, what percent of the year's total rain falls each month. Rainfall data from the years 1961-1993.

and 9 inches in the drought years of 1976 and 1977 and after bouncing between 16 and 20 over the next five years, zoomed to 33 inches in storm-wracked 1983.

In 1987, a drought began that in subsequent years forced rationing. It ended with the 1992 winter, which soaked all, loaded the Sierra with snow, and filled local reservoirs.

Weather Tidbits: The 'Stick

Candlestick Park, present home of the Giants, lies at the junction of two windstreams that shoot through the Alemany Gap in the hills. The result: eddies and vacuums that do circus tricks with fly balls.

The Alemany Gap also explains why you should always bring a jacket to baseball games at Candlestick. Summer time is fog time and the fog just rolls through the Alemany.

On the plus side, Candlestick basks in balm during the football season. In the winter, the fog departs, the winds abate, and the sun shines. The ocean, in winter, is warmer than the land, and this warmth falls on the coastal towns. San Francisco is cooler than San Jose in the summer and warmer in the winter.

Swimming

September and October are often best months to swim in the Pacific. The upwelling of the cold water has stopped. Often the fog has departed. Sunshine glows upon the water and the coast. Almost every year the summer ends with hot spells in September and October.

Temperatures for Selected Cities
Number of Days Greater than 90 Degrees

City	Ja	Fb	Mr	Ap	My	Ju	Jy	Au	Sp	Oc	No	Dc
Gilroy	0	0	1	2	12	8	20	11	15	4	1	0
Los Gatos	0	0	0	0	4	2	4	9	4	0	0	0
Mount Hamilton	0	0	0	0	0	0	0	2	0	0	0	0
Palo Alto	0	0	0	0	2	2	0	1	5	0	0	0
San Jose	0	0	0	0	4	2	2	4	8	0	0	0

Source: National Climatic Center, Asheville, N.C. 1997.

Temperatures for Selected Cities
Number of Days 32 Degrees or Less

City	Ja	Fb	Mr	Ap	My	Ju	Jy	Au	Sp	Oc	No	Dc
Gilroy	3	1	2	0	0	0	0	0	0	0	0	7
Los Gatos	2	0	0	0	0	0	0	0	0	0	0	4
Mount Hamilton	9	4	0	3	0	0	0	0	0	0	1	12
Palo Alto	3	0	0	0	0	0	0	0	0	0	0	5
San Jose	1	0	0	0	0	0	0	0	0	0	0	2

Source: National Climatic Center, Asheville, N.C. 1997.

Sunshine

Like sunshine? You are in the right place. Records show that during daylight hours the sun shines in New York City 60 percent of the time; in Boston, 57 percent; in Detroit, 53 percent; and in Seattle, 43 percent. San Jose averages 63 percent.

The gloomiest month: January, 42 percent sunshine. The brightest, the summer months, e.g. July, 83 percent.

Humidity

Heat Santa Clara County does experience but rarely muggy weather. When hot spells arrive, the air usually has little moisture — dry heat. When the air is moist (the fog), the temperatures drop.

Fog

Of the Bay Area's two types of fog, one is more dangerous than the other. The coastal fog often forms well above the Pacific and, pushed by the wind, generally moves at a good clip. In thick coastal fog, you will have to slow down but you can see the tail lights of a car 50 to 75 yards ahead.

Valley or tule fog blossoms at shoe level when cold air pulls moisture from the earth. Found mostly in the Central Valley, tule fog hugs the ground and generally stays put. When you read of 50- and 75-car pileups in the Central Valley, tule fog is to blame.

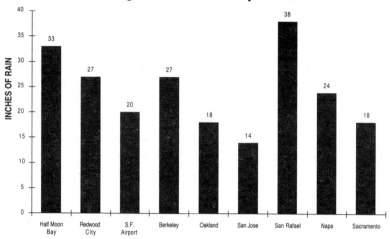

Average Annual Rainfall by Location

Source: National Weather Service.

Occasionally, tule fog is pulled down into the Bay — an effect of the pull of heat on cold air. The ocean being warmer than the land, the Bay Area in winter will occasionally suck in the colder air and fog of the interior — the reverse of the summer pattern.

Before radar and other warning devices, tule fog in the Bay gave captains the jitters. Shipping accidents, including the 1901 sinking of the liner Rio de Janeiro, 130 lives lost, tended to occur during invasions of tule fog.

If you are planning a redwoods excursion to Big Basin in the summer, bring a jacket and an umbrella.

Redwoods are creatures of the fog, need it to thrive. Where you find a good redwood stand, you will, in summer, often find fog, cold thick fog, that will usually burn off by noon.

When fog passes through a redwood grove, the trees strip the moisture right out of the air. In some parts of the Bay Region redwood-fog drip has been measured at 10 inches annually.

Fog is a quirky creature, appearing sometimes in the oddest places. In late 1995, San Francisco International Airport shut down for three hours because a patch of fog had settled over the runways. The control tower had good visibility.

Scorchers

During the summer and fall, the Pacific High will occasionally loop a strong wind down from Washington through the Sierra and the hot valleys, where it loses its moisture, and into the Bay Area.

Extremely dry, these northeasters, which are now called "Diablos," will tighten the skin on your face, cause wood shingle roofs to crackle and turn the countryside into tinder.

The October 1991 fire that destroyed 2,500 homes and apartments in the Berkeley-Oakland hills and killed 25 was caused by a Diablo.

If you buy in the hills, if your home is surrounded with brush and trees, take a look at fire-retardant shingles and fire-prevention tactics.

Storms

Rain is rain, generally welcome all the time in dry California. But some rains are more welcome than others. Storms from the vicinity of Hawaii turn Sierra Nevada slopes to slush and, in the upper elevations, deposit soft snow that sinks under the weight of skis.

Alaskan storms bring snow to the lower mountains and deposit a fine powder, ideal for skiing. Some Alaskan storms occasionally bless the Bay Region with snow on the mountain tops. The air will be crystal clear, with a shiver of cold. Mt. Hamilton and the other mountains, green for the winter, will overnight don a lovely mantle of white.

Allergies

They often kick in during the spring and in October. During the spring, the grasses pop their buds and many trees release pollen.

In the fall, the Diablos dry out the trees and cones and pollen fills the air. Hanky time.

Chapter 16

SANTA CLARA COUNTY

Crime

EVERY neighborhood and city in this country suffers from some crime. Even communities surrounded by gates and patrolled by guards will on occasion see domestic violence or pilfering by visitors.

So the question to ask when shopping for a home or apartment is not: Is this neighborhood safe? But rather, how safe is it compared to other places?

In California, crime often follows demographics: High-income neighborhoods generally have low crime, middle-income places middling crime, and low-income towns and neighborhoods high crime.

For these guides, we label towns with fewer than 50 crimes per 1,000 residents over a year as low in crime. Towns with 50 to 80 crimes per 1,000 residents are placed in the middling category. Towns with over 80 crimes per 1,000 are labeled high in crime or worrisome. The statistics are supplied by the FBI and the California Dept. of Justice.

In many instances, these figures mislead. You can take probably every high-crime city in the country and find within it low-crime neighborhoods. New York City, to look at its statistics, seemingly is overrun with felons but the City includes Staten Island, generally suburban and probably low to middle in crime.

The same for Oakland, San Francisco, San Diego and Los Angeles. These are not crime cities; they are cities with certain neighborhoods high in crime.

Sometimes the statistics give a false picture. Theft is the most common crime. A city with many stores or a regional shopping mall will often have a high number of thefts — and consequently, a higher crime rate. Number of homicides, in some instances, gives a clearer picture of local crime.

The demographic connection also can mislead. Many peaceful, law-abiding people live in the "worst" neighborhoods. But these neighborhoods also contain a disproportionate number of the troubled and criminally inclined.

Why does crime correlate with income and demographics? In many countries, it doesn't. Japan, devastated after World War II, did not sink into

Crime Statistics by City

City	Population	Rate	Homicides
Campbell	39,720	39	0
Cupertino	46,682	29	0
Gilroy	37,455	59	3
Los Altos	28,415	18	0
Los Altos Hills	8,168	9	0
Los Gatos	30,122	30	1
Milpitas	62,588	38	2
Monte Sereno	3,416	11	0
Morgan Hill	30,786	42	1
Mountain View	74,730	38	1
Palo Alto	60,492	46	1
San Jose	893,969	37	43
Santa Clara	101,877	43	1
Saratoga	31,097	16	0
Sunnyvale	131,127	25	0
Santa Clara Co.	1,689,907	36	62

Crime in Other Northern California Cities

City	Population	Rate	Homicides
Concord	113,432	63	0
Danville	39,168	20	0
East Palo Alto	25,429	58	16
Hillsborough	11,543	8	0
Fremont	198,710	40	4
Monterey	33,775	58	0
Oakland	396,310	97	99
Sacramento	392,834	88	41
San Francisco	789,596	66	59
San Ramon	43,509	26	0
Santa Cruz	54,575	67	1
Scotts Valley	10,551	34	0
Stockton	241,058	77	45
Vacaville	87,700	36	3
Vallejo	111,436	79	3
Walnut Creek	63,218	49	0

Source: California Crime Index from State Dept. of Justice, 1997 data, with population estimates from the California Dept. of Finance. Rate is all reported willful homicide, forcible rape, aggravated assault, burglary, motor vehicle theft, larceny-theft and arson per 1,000 residents. Homicides include murders and non-negligent manslaughter.

violence and thievery. Many industrialized nations with lower standards of living than the U.S. have much less crime. In 1990, according to one study, handguns killed 10 people in Australia, 22 in Great Britain and 87 in Japan. The count for the U.S. was 10,567.

Sociologists blame the breakdown of morals and the family in the U.S, the pervasive violence in the media, the easy access to guns, and other forces. Any one of these "causes" could be argued into the next century but if you're

Crime in Other Cities Nationwide

City	Population	Rate	Homicides
Anchorage	255,634	60	23
Atlanta	420,865	139	150
Baltimore	719,587	108	312
Birmingham	275,236	96	108
Boise	156,026	51	4
Boston	555,024	68	43
Chicago	2,765,852	NA	757
Cleveland	496,624	75	77
Dallas	1,077,029	93	209
Denver	525,793	64	69
Des Moines	195,455	86	12
Honolulu	880,272	61	34
Jacksonville	702,545	83	75
Little Rock	183,840	119	34
Milwaukee	628,507	76	122
Miami	391,766	128	103
New York	7,320,477	49	770
New Orleans	488,509	94	267
Oklahoma City	472,046	117	59
Pittsburgh, PA	353,248	58	50
Phoenix	1,172,538	96	175
Portland, OR	473,696	112	46
Reno	166,924	64	13
Salt Lake City	185,553	117	21
Seattle	547,209	104	49
Tucson	485,933	100	50
Washington, D.C.	529,000	98	301

Source: Annual 1998 FBI crime report, which uses 1997 data. Population estimates are based on updated estimates from 1990 census. **Key**: NA (not available).

shopping for a home or an apartment just keep in mind that there is a correlation between demographics and crime.

How do you spot a troubled neighborhood?

Crime is a young person's game, particularly boys and men. In one of its annual studies, the FBI determined that 61 percent of all the people arrested were under age 30. For every female arrested four males were arrested, the same study noted.

Take a look at the academic rankings of the neighborhood school. Very low rankings indicate that many children are failing, that the dropout rate is probably high, that the young people will have difficulty finding jobs — conditions that often breed crime.

In middle-scoring towns, the failures are fewer. In higher scoring towns, fewer still.

Crime In Other California Cities

City	Population	Rate	Homicides
Anaheim	301,176	40	15
Bakersfield	221,689	59	22
Fresno	411,611	94	60
Huntington Beach	192,430	34	5
Riverside	250,799	59	23
Los Angeles	3,722,535	56	576
San Diego	1,224,848	48	67
Santa Ana	311,210	40	27
Santa Barbara	91,223	47	3

Source: California Crime Index from State Dept. of Justice, 1997 data, with population estimates from the California Dept. of Finance (Jan. 1, 1998). Rate is all reported willful homicide, forcible rape, aggravated assault, burglary, motor vehicle theft, larceny-theft and arson per 1,000 residents. Homicides include murders and non-negligent manslaughter.

Drive the neighborhood. The signs of trouble are often easily read: men idling around the liquor store, bars on many windows, security doors in wide use.

Should you avoid unsafe or marginal neighborhoods?

For some people, the answer depends on tradeoffs and personal circumstances. The troubled neighborhoods often carry low prices or rents and are located near job centers. Many towns and sections are in transition; conditions could improve, the investment might be worthwhile. What's intolerable to a parent might be acceptable to a single person.

Tradeoffs also apply when choosing really safe neighborhoods.

If you don't have the bucks, often you can still buy safe but you may have to settle for a smaller house or yard. Or the equivalent of North Dakota. The state is quite safe — 2 homicides in 1995, the FBI reported — but when the temperatures drop to 40 below, the sunny but less-safe places may seem a better choice.

Whatever your neighborhood, don't make it easy for predators. Lock your doors, join the neighborhood watches, school your children in safety, take extra precautions when they are called for.

Subject Index

(See Advertising Index for list of advertisers)

(See Advertising Index for list of advertisers)

—A—
AC Transit, 208
Adult schools, 192-195
Altamont Commuter Express, 175, 209
Alum Rock schools, 24, 26, 47-48, 78, 171
Alum Rock Park, 191
Amtrak, 209
Anderson Lake Park, 191
Apple computer, 144
Association of Bay Area Governments, 179
—B—
Baby Names, 101
Barbie Hall of Fame, 166, 188
BART, 158, 209
Births, 102
Berryessa schools, 26, 48, 78
Board of Supervisors, 18
Busing, 208
—C—
CalTrain, 144, 146, 160-161, 165, 178, 209
Cambrian schools, 26, 48, 78
Campbell, 27, 142
Campbell schools, 27, 49, 78
Campbell Union High schools, 27, 78
Car pools, 208
Catholic schools, 89-81
Children's Discovery Museum, 171, 181-189
Coe State Park, 191
College admissions, 70, 74, 76, 88, 92

Community college transfers, 84
Crime statistics, 218, 219, 220
Cupertino, 144
Cupertino schools, 27-28, 49-50, 78, 144-145, 178, 184
—D—
Day care, Directory of, 106-117
De Anza College, 22, 144, 145, 195
Dial-A-Ride, 208
Dog licenses, 129
Drivers Licenses, 129-130
Dropout rates, 77
—E—
Earthquakes, 12, 131
Earthquakes, Loma Prieta, 17
East Side Union High schools, 28, 30, 51, 78, 79, 171
Education level, 21
Ethnic makeup, 19
Evergreen schools, 30, 32, 51-52, 78, 171, 173
Evergreen Valley College, 22, 173, 195
—F—
Flint Center, 144, 199
Food prices, 132-133
Foothill College, 22, 151, 152, 195
Franklin McKinley schools, 32, 52-53, 78
Fremont Union High schools, 53, 79, 80, 144, 171, 184
—G—
Gavilan College, 22
Gilroy, 11, 20, 146-147
Gilroy schools, 34, 53, 79, 80
Golden Gate University, 194
Grant County Park, 191
Great America, 176, 189

—H—
Health Maintenance Organization, 121, 122-126
Hewlett-Packard Co., 14-15, 19, 169
Hewlett, William, 14-15, 19
High school assessments, 72, 73
Home prices, 150, 151, 161
Hospitals, Directory of, 126-128
Housing, new, 196-206
—I-J-K—
Income, household, 14
Infant care, Directory of, 100-103
Intel Museum, 189
Jobless Rate, 193
—L—
Lakeside schools, 34, 54, 80
Lick Observatory, 175, 189
Light Rail, 143, 163, 178
Loma Prieta schools, 34, 54, 80
Los Altos, 148, 150-151
Los Altos schools, 35, 54, 80, 152
Los Altos Hills, 11, 152
Los Gatos, 154, 156
Los Gatos-Saratoga Joint Union High schools, 35, 80, 156
Los Gatos schools, 54, 80, 154, 156, 159
Luther Burbank schools, 35, 55, 80
—M—
Medi-Cal, 120-121
Medicare, 121
Milpitas, 14, 20, 157-158
Milpitas schools, 35-36, 55, 80, 157
Mission College, 176, 195
Mission Santa Clara, 176, 189

Moffett Field, 20, 145, 163, 168, 184
Monte Sereno, 11, 159
Moreland schools, 36, 55-56, 80, 142
Morgan Hill, 37, 160-162
Morgan Hill schools, 37-38, 56, 79, 80, 160
Mount Copernicus, 12
Mount Hamilton, 189, 216
Mount Madonna Park, 191
Mountain View, 163-165
Mountain View schools, 38, 56-57, 79, 165
Mtn. View-Los Altos High schools, 56, 79, 80, 148
Mount Pleasant schools, 38, 57, 80
—N-O—
National Aeronautics and Space Administration, 145, 184
National Hispanic University, 194-195
Oak Grove schools, 38-39, 57-58, 80, 171
Occupations, 20
Orchard schools, 39, 80
—P-Q—
Packard, David, 14-15, 19
Palo Alto, 11, 166, 168-169
Palo Alto schools, 39-40, 58-59, 79, 80, 169
Park & Ride, 208
Population, 12,
Preferred Provider Organization, 121-122, 123-126
Presidential voting, 22
Private Schools, Directory of, 94-98
—R—
Raging Waters, 189
Rainfall, 212, 213, 215

Reid-Hillview Airport, 163, 173-174
Religion, 16-17
Rents, 138,140
Rose Garden, 189
Rosicrucian Museum, 189-190
—S—
Saint Mary's College, 194
SamTrans, 208
San Jose, 11, 19, 170-175
San Jose Arena, 171
San Jose Center for the Performing Arts, 191
San Jose City College, 175, 195
San Jose Flea Market, 174, 190
San Jose Historical Museum, 190
San Jose Museum of Art, 190
San Jose schools, 40-42, 59-61, 79, 80, 171
San Jose Sharks, 12, 171, 190
San Jose State University, 175-192-193
San Jose Visitors and Convention Bureau, 175, 188
Santa Clara, city of, 11, 176, 178
Santa Clara County Transit District, 144, 179, 208, 209
Santa Clara schools, 24, 42-43, 61-62, 79, 80, 176, 184
Santa Clara University, 176, 193, 194
Saratoga, 179-181
Saratoga schools, 80, 179
SAT scores, 65, 66, 67
School rankings, 23-45, 46-63, 78
School registration, 75

School transfers, 76-77
Shoreline Amphitheater, 165, 191
Silicon Valley, 14-15
Smith, Laurie (Sheriff), 18
Stanford, Leland Jr., 18
Stanford University, 11, 18, 166, 168, 169, 190, 191, 194
Sunnyvale, 182, 184-185
Sunnyvale schools, 43-44, 62-63, 80, 184
—T—
Taxes, 131, 134
Tech Museum of Innovation, 171, 190
Temperatures, 211, 212, 214
Triton Museum, 190
—U—
Union schools, 44, 63, 80, 171
University of California, 193
University of California Extension-UC Santa Cruz, 194
University of San Francisco, 194
Utility prices, 131, 134
—V-W-X-Y-Z—
Vehicle registration, 129
Villa Montalvo, 180, 181, 191
Voter registration, 22, 129
Weather, 12, 210-216
West Valley College, 176, 195
Whisman schools, 44, 63, 80,165
Winchester Mystery House, 191
Year-round schools, 82-83

Advertisers' Index

Developers
The O'Brien Group .... Front Cover, 205
Ponderosa Homes 199
Signature Properties 197
Standard Pacific 201
SummerHill Homes 203

Hospitals
O'Connor Hospital 119

Information Services
DataQuick 4

Major Employers
Hewlett Packard 9

Private Schools
Harker School 96
Presentation High School 97
Rainbow Bridge School 94
Rainbow Montessori 87
Tutor Time 111

Realtors & Relocation Services
Champion Real Estate, Raymond Ong 31
Coldwell Banker, Jim Laufenberg 25
Century 21/Contempo Fine Homes & Estates, Randy Walden 155
Century 21/Contempo Fine Homes & Estates, Simin Malek 37, 181
Coldwell Banker/Cornish & Carey, Sabrina Shewfelt 7
Eichler Homes Realty, Jerry Ditto 167, 183
Executive Brokers, Charlie Stellini 13
Eckert Properties, Paul Eckert .... Inside Front Cover, 149, 153
Fred Sands Realty, Mary Pope-Handy .... Inside Back Cover
Realty Mart Associates, Inc., Georgene Laub 29
Re/Max Associates, Jenny Moore 3

Rental Housing
Bay Rentals 137

BUY 10 OR MORE & SAVE!

If your order adds up to 10 or more, the price drops to $5.95 per book. You also save on shipping. Fill out form and send with check to: McCormack's Guides, P.O. Box 1728, Martinez, CA 94553. Or fax to (925) 228-7223.

Visa and MasterCard accepted on phone orders. **VISA** **MasterCard** **1-800-222-3602**

Next to title, write in number of copies ordered and total below:

No.	McCormack's Guide Title	Single	Bulk
___	Alameda County '99	$13.95	$5.95
___	Contra Costa & Solano '99	$13.95	$5.95
___	Los Angeles County '99	$13.95	$5.95
___	Marin, Napa & Sonoma '99	$13.95	$5.95
___	Orange County '99	$13.95	$5.95
___	Riverside, San Bernardino '99	$13.95	$5.95
___	Sacramento County '99	$13.95	$5.95
___	San Diego County '99	$13.95	$5.95
___	San Francisco & San Mateo '99	$13.95	$5.95
___	Santa Barbara & Ventura '99	$13.95	$5.95
___	Santa Clara County '99	$13.95	$5.95

_____Books @ $_____ (Price) = $_____

CA sales tax (8.25%) _____

Shipping* _____

Total Amount of Order: $_____

* For orders of 10 or more, shipping is 45 cents per book. For orders of fewer than 10, shipping is $4.50 for first book, $1.50 per book thereafter.

Paid by (circle one) Check/MC/Visa or Bill Us

Name _____

Company _____

Address _____

City_____ State____ Zip_____

Phone: (_____)_____ Fax: (_____)_____

☐ **Check here to receive advertising information**

www.mccormacks.com · bookinfo@mccormacks.com